IN SEARCH OF THE

LOST MOUNTAINS
OF NOAH

IN SEARCH OF THE

LOST MOUNTAINS OF NOAH

THE DISCOVERY OF THE REAL MTS. OF ARARAT

ROBERT CORNUKE
AND
DAVID HALBROOK

BROADMAN
& HOLMAN
PUBLISHERS

NASHVILLE, TN

0–8054–2054–1

Published by Broadman & Holman Publishers, Nashville, Tennessee

Dewey Decimal Classification: 221
Subject Heading: BIBLE

Unless otherwise indicated Scripture quotations are from the Holy Bible, New International Version, © copyright 1973, 1978, 1984 by the International Bible Society. Scripture quotations identified NKJV are from the New King James Version, copyright © 1979, 1980, 1982, Thomas Nelson, Inc., Publishers.

Library of Congress Cataloging-in-Publication Data

Cornuke, Robert, 1951–
In search of the lost mountains of Noah : the discovery of the real mts. of Ararat / Robert Cornuke and David Halbrook.
    p. cm.
Includes bibliographical references.
ISBN 0-8054-2054-1
    1. Ararat, Mount (Turkey) 2. Noah's ark. 3. Iran—Antiquities. 4. Bible. O.T. Genesis—Geography. 5. Bible. O.T.—Evidences, authority, etc. I. Halbrook, David. II. Title.

DS51.A66 .C67 2001
221.9'1—dc21
                                                                                2001035215

1 2 3 4 5 6 7 8 9 10 05 04 03 02 01

DEDICATED TO THE MEMORY OF
JAMES B. IRWIN, APOLLO 15
ASTRONAUT, WHO TAUGHT ME TO
FOLLOW GOD'S COMPASS
RATHER THAN MAN'S TRADITIONS.

Contents

Acknowledgments

No endeavor so difficult as the search for the remains of Noah's Ark and the charting of the lost mountains of Noah could even be attempted as a solo enterprise. It requires the help and support of so many—some of whose names appear in the narrative of this book, and many that don't. The list of researchers, teammates, and contributors who helped make this book possible is too great to properly thank here, though I would like to extend a special word of acknowledgment to the following:

Les and Anne Stevens, Daniel and Carol Ayres, Ray and Carole Ardizzone, Mary Irwin, Brian Park, Mary Ramos, Paul and Nancy Cornuke, Ed Holroyd, Darrell Scott, Laura Lisle, Ken Durham, Terry Cornuke, Dan Toth, Dick Bright, Bob Stuplich, Dave Banks, George Kralik, Jim Fitzgerald, Chuck Aaron, Bill Dodder, Rex Geissler, Robin Simmons, Dan Shockey, Ed Davis, Dr. Roy Knuteson, Larry Williams, Mike Barnes, Ron Acton, Ron Hicks, Pete Leininger, John MacIntosh, Bill Crouse, Nahid Noorani, Alireza Farrokhroo, Brad Houston, and Francie Halbrook.

An extra special word of acknowledgment and appreciation goes to Steve Halliday, for his excellent editorial touches, and to David Halbrook, whose monumental effort, skilled literary abilities, and cherished friendship have made the writing of this book both an extreme pleasure and a blessing, which could never be adequately conveyed with mere words.

Introduction

NOAH'S MYSTERY

Has anyone ever seen the remains of Noah's ark?

Certainly many modern explorers have made such a claim. Most of these "sightings" occurred in south-eastern Turkey, on a mountain known as *Ararat*, a seventeen-thousand-foot peak the local Kurds call Agri Dagh—the "Painful Mountain." The ancient Armenians called it Massis, or "Mother of the World."

But did the ark really come to rest here? Is the hull of an ancient, petrified ship entombed in the glaciers of Mount Ararat—or have eyewitnesses been wrong all these years? Hundreds of explorers have spent two centuries searching this mountain yet without a single *confirmed* sighting.

Have they been looking on the wrong mountain?

THE SEARCH FOR THE ARK

With countless newspaper and magazine articles, best-selling books and movies still churning out on the topic, few individuals in the United States can remain unaware of the search for the ark. Fewer still can dispute that its discovery would rock the archaeological world. The late editor of *National Geographic* magazine, Dr. Melville Bell Grosvenor, insisted such a discovery would rank as one of the important events of all time. "If the ark of Noah is discovered," he said, "it will be the greatest archaeological find in human history, the greatest event since the resurrection of Christ, and it would alter all the currents of scientific thought."[1]

In late 1999, the Noah's Ark Alliance offered a million-dollar reward to any person or group who could authenticate the discovery of the ark. This offer targeted a group of explorers—at times a jealously competitive fraternity, at others remarkably cooperative and congenial—who have, with a mixture of humor and stoicism, helped to coin the term *arkaeology* to describe their efforts atop Mount Ararat. These arkaeologists, by and large, believe the peak loosely satisfies the rough geographical requirements of Genesis 8:4 ("and on the seventeenth day of the seventh month the ark came to rest on the mountains of Ararat"). While a more precise reading of Scripture may point elsewhere, the arkaeologists seem drawn to Mount Ararat like moths to a porch light. They remain convinced that, one day, when conditions get just right, the ark will reveal itself.

But will it?

A puzzling Mount Ararat mythology has the ark variously concealed in any number of ice-covered, inaccessible, or forbidden canyons and crevasses. Depending on who one listens to (or which account one reads), the ark survives as an angular, bargelike structure jutting out of a glacier high on the peak or as cypress fragments trapped in an ice core on a northeasterly slope. Some say they've seen the ark peering up at them—a murky, spectral shadow floating beneath the surface of an immense sheet of ice—as they flew over in a passing jet. Others feel certain they've spotted its rounded bow nestled amongst boulders in a sheer canyon wall. Yet with all these sightings—and, more recently, with the aid of modern satellite imagery—there remains no convincing photographic evidence. *Nothing* to confirm that Noah's ark has survived on Mount Ararat . . . or anywhere else.

So what keeps seekers coming back to a mountain responsible for so much anguish and frustration? Why do these stubborn pilgrims persist in risking life and limb to find the ark, when so many before them have tried and failed? Call it a spiritual bent, or an evangelical calling, or simply a bedrock conviction that, as the miracles of Jesus and the acts of the apostles ignited Christianity throughout the pagan world, so, too, the discovery of the ark might fan faith among unbelievers.

With the stakes so high, some ark searchers are agitated to think that certain peoples in the region already *know* where Noah's vessel lies. One legend holds that the ancient Armenians have for centuries acted as self-appointed guardians of the ark, teaching their children that its secret hiding place must be kept in sacred trust. Other reports claim that the people throughout a region formerly known as Urartu widely revere the ark as a holy artifact. And among some isolated villages, one finds a tradition that God has concealed the ark from mortal eyes until the end of time, when it will be revealed to prove the accuracy of both the Bible and the story of the flood.

Even some in the West believe the ark figures prominently in the last days. They cite Matthew 24:37 ("As it was in the days of Noah, so it will be at the coming of the Son of Man") to suggest that the ark will be rediscovered just prior to the return of Christ. If the Second Coming is even remotely tied to the ark, they say, then God himself has had a hand in providentially preserving and concealing it through the centuries.

Dr. John Morris, a research scientist for the Institute of Creation Research, typifies this group. He contends that "most students of the biblical prophecy agree that we are in the last days, and that the world as we know it will soon come to an end. A reasonable assumption confronts us, that God is planning to reveal the ark shortly before Christ returns, issuing a final call to a lost world. A lost world that for the most part does not even realize it is lost; pleading with men and women to accept the present-day Ark of Salvation, Jesus Christ, reminding them of the previous judgment and warning them of the coming judgment. With such overwhelming evidence as this, the ark of Noah, the doubt of many would be removed, calling them to return to Christ."

If Morris is right, the discovery of the ark holds greater promise—and graver consequences—than anyone imagines.

HOW I GOT INVOLVED

I confess I didn't join the fray for such lofty reasons. My involvement had little to do with the Bible and even less with ushering in Armageddon. As always, I started out with nothing more than an insatiable thirst for adventure, aroused one night in the mid-1980s when I turned on the TV. A reporter interviewing Jim Irwin wanted to know about the former astronaut's search for the ark. Irwin founded his High Flight Foundation in Colorado Springs for evangelism, and one of its purposes was to fund explorations for prominent biblical artifacts. Noah's ark topped his list, and he and a team had set off to Turkey to climb Mount Ararat. The station promised regular updates, and I tuned in each night to see what they might have found. An odd introduction, perhaps, but it got me excited. I found myself daydreaming about what such a find might mean.

My passing curiosity soon turned into a full-blown obsession, tugging me around the world to scout the slopes of Ararat and other strategic peaks by foot and by air. That same lust for adventure drove me into the scalding deserts of Saudi Arabia to help find what many believe to be the real Mount Sinai (see my first book, *In Search of the Mountain of God*). Something about the mystery of Noah's ark captured my imagination. From the start, I couldn't resist the allure of making such an earthshaking find.

Time, experience, and some close brushes with death, however, eventually changed my perception of these hallowed artifacts. Although a base appetite for adventure moved me to risk my life in the search for Mount Sinai, I came to see the powerful impact our discovery made on believers and nonbelievers alike. Hard evidence of the sacred mountain and the true route of the great Exodus sparked genuine faith in many, and convinced others of the Bible's truth. The *substance* of our findings made the difference

3
Λ

and caused me to wonder: If Mount Sinai held such power to change hearts, how might hard evidence of Noah's ark stagger modern sensibilities?

Don't get me wrong. I hold no naïve illusions that the ark's discovery would send people scurrying to church. I remember that Jesus himself said, "If they do not listen to Moses and the Prophets, they will not be convinced even if someone rises from the dead" (Luke 16:31). People refuse to believe, even when presented with the facts. Attitudes about spiritual matters have been stirred with the water of doubt and left to set, like concrete, in the sun. The longer concrete sets, the harder it gets. The older a person gets, the more rigid he becomes, and the less likely he'll ever soften to new information or impressions.

Still, I believe a bona fide discovery of the ark would rock skeptical minds, prompting many to take a hard new look at the Bible. *Everybody* knows the ark. More than 180 cultures and civilizations tell a story about an ark and a great flood. It terrified Spanish explorers to learn that New World Indians told their own flood story. The Spaniards finally decided that a Christian doctrine among savages had to be a trick of the devil.[2]

I suspect the discovery of Noah's ark would chisel a few cracks in the cement of our culture's skeptical attitudes (or at least shake and stir the brittle unbelief of the day). I frankly hope that this book creates some stress fractures on the calcified soul of the age.

To that end I have spent fifteen years searching for Noah's ark, scouring the Middle East. I have covered thousands of weary miles by plane, helicopter, horse, jeep, and on foot. I have sat for hour upon hour in Middle Eastern libraries from Ankara to Tehran, poring over maps, ancient manuscripts, and musty old books. I have scaled scores of high mountains in wind, rain, snow, and ice. And I have reexamined what the *Bible* has to say, what history has said, and what legend suggests in my quest for this venerable icon.

Journey with me now across sprawling continents and vast reaches of time, as we try to discover answers to age-old questions. Only then will we rediscover *The Lost Mountains of Noah*.

4

PRELUDE

PAINFUL MOUNTAIN

Sergeant Ed Davis first met Badi in 1943, at the height of World War II, while his unit, the 364th Army Corps of Engineers, worked out of Hamadan, Iran. Davis had been busy building a halfway camp for the Corps, whose mission involved assisting both the British and the Soviet armies in building a supply corridor from the Persian Gulf to Russia. Badi, a young Iranian truck driver assigned to taxi military supplies and personnel about the countryside, hailed from a remote village to the north, where water resources were scarce. As their friendship deepened, Davis helped Badi's village build a permanent water system—an act of generosity that cemented his friendship with Badi and granted Davis honored status with the village. It also made him privy to secrets of village life unknown to outsiders.

One afternoon, as they loaded trucks at a rock quarry near Hamadan, Davis asked Badi where he lived. Badi pointed nonchalantly toward a great range of snowcapped mountains towering in the northern horizon. "That's where I grew up," Badi said. He told Davis the mountains held a sacred, closely guarded secret. Located near the summit of the most imposing peak and locked beneath a year-round glacier, he said, sat the frozen remains of Noah's ark. Davis raised an eyebrow, but Badi remained adamant. "My family has been to the ark," he insisted. "My grandfather has taken me up to see it."

An *intriguing claim*, Davis thought and expressed to Badi mild interest in seeing it one day. He gave the matter no more thought until, weeks later, an elderly Iranian showed up at the base looking for Badi. It turned out to be Badi's father, Abas, who had ventured down from the mountains with urgent news from home. The chisel-faced, brawny Abas eventually found Badi in the company of Davis, and introductions were made. Over the course of several days, Abas confirmed his son's comments about the ark and described in detail artifacts he had found scattered about the ancient relic, some of which he said he had in his possession at home. While these discussions continued to pique Davis's imagination, he remained skeptical, until one day shortly thereafter Abas arrived in camp again, this time to say, "The ice on the big mountain has melted considerably. Part of the ark is showing." Then, after a long pause, Abas added, with a playful grin, "If you like, I can take you there."

It seemed a dubious enterprise at best. Davis didn't know if he even *believed* the story of Noah's ark. Yet he always listened for new travel prospects, and the thought of an adventure in Iran's hinterlands appealed to him. He agreed to accompany his friend to the sacred mountain and secured a short leave of absence. A few days later they bought supplies—three barrels of gas, a case of motor oil, and some coffee—and set out from Hamadan in an army-issue truck. Driving all day and into the night, without a map, Davis noted a number of Russian encampments on the route north and paid casual notice to an otherwise indistinct town Badi pointed out called *Casbeen*.

They arrived at Abas's village—a mud and rock affair that resembled the tan, adobe pueblos Davis knew back home in Albuquerque, New Mexico—in early evening. Abas's family welcomed Davis as a member of the family, and after a dinner of tasty stew, the patriarch eyed Davis and said, "I've got some items out back that might interest you. Please come and take a look."

Davis felt his pulse quicken as Abas led him to a nearby shed and opened the door. Hidden in its shadows and propped against a wall, Abas pulled out an unwieldy object. As Davis's eyes adjusted to the dark, he judged that the object appeared to be a door, about three feet tall and fashioned in the manner of a cage. On closer inspection, Davis recognized it as an incredibly old cage door, with vertical bars woven of twisted branches, hard as a rock. Examining its tightly wound wood grain and hand-carved lock hanging to a side, Davis thought the piece to be petrified. It felt as cold and dense as tempered steel.

Abas then showed Davis other hand-carved latches used to lock pens, cages, and other types of holding compartments, and an array of ancient-looking oil lamps, old clay vats, bowls, jars, and crude tools to go along with a stash of what appeared to be prehistoric farm implements. Abas explained that these and other artifacts had been collected by villagers for generations in the high canyon where the ark lay entombed.

It surprised Davis to learn that no other westerner had ever seen the articles; it startled him even more to hear that, as an honored guest, he must keep all these things to himself. "The ark and its contents have always been considered sacred by our people," Abas explained. "Outsiders would only steal or profane them. For that reason it has been kept hidden from the outside world."

The statement confused Davis. Why should *he* be trusted with such a secret? Without answering his unspoken question, they all retired to the village for the night. Davis slept restlessly, wondering what other surprises this strange countryside held in store.

In the middle of the night, Davis woke to loud shouts and banging outside his door: "Wake up! Wake up! We go! We go!" He rose, tired and stiff, to see Abas, Badi, and seven of his brothers packing supplies in a British lorry. Within minutes the band of adventurers loaded the truck and drove off, traveling through the night.

They arrived in the first light of morning at another primitive-looking village, steeped in the shadows of the great mountain Badi had described. Notwithstanding the magnificent peak, Davis immediately noticed a peculiar vineyard built up around the remote village, like no vineyard he'd ever seen or heard of. It had an ancient, almost arthritic appearance, with vines and trunks so thick and tangled a grown man would have trouble reaching his arms around them. *They look as old as time itself*, Davis recalled thinking. Badi told him the villagers believed the prophet Noah had planted the vines himself. In fact, he said, the village's Iranian name meant, "Where Noah Planted the Vine." Davis's pulse quickened.

After a hearty breakfast of stew, Davis and the Abas family mounted packhorses and began the long, grueling trek up the mountain.

JOURNEY HIGH

A series of hidden caves, spaced strategically to provide shelter and support, marked the arduous route up the peak. By late afternoon they reached the first cave, cloistered in a maze of low ravines deep in the foothills. After a quick meal, they mounted again and rode higher still up a narrow mountain trail, a route named the "Back Door" for the bandits and black marketeers who frequented it. Rounding a steep, blind bend, Davis eyed a pair of decomposing human legs, frozen and half-buried in a snowbank. The brothers barely acknowledged it. "He shouldn't have been up here," they said simply. For the first time Davis felt vulnerable and out of his element.

The route soon turned treacherous. Endless hairpin switchbacks up an increasingly sharp grade made for slippery footing. The awkward gait of the spindly Iranian horses, teetering on the razor edge of sheer cliffs, set Davis's teeth on edge. Still they climbed on, as the rain began to fall, traversing one hair-raising ridge after another. Late in the day the trail ended, wiped out by a huge rock slide. *Are we there?* Davis wondered. His heart sank to see one of Badi's brothers lead the horses away, confirming they would be proceeding on foot. They roped themselves together and strained ever higher into the foggy haze. Just before nightfall they arrived at a larger, second cave and spent the night.

Before setting off the next morning, the party had to wait for a dense mantle of clouds and rain to dissipate. A strong, at times overwhelming, smell of sulfur hung in the air. Davis agonized at how slowly time passed on these heights and felt tremendously relieved when the clouds parted and they continued their journey. By this time the terrain had turned even more severe, and they roped themselves together again to scale an increasingly chaotic tangle of narrow ledges, steep ridges, and high cliffs. At one point the brothers clapped their hands over their mouths and ordered Davis to be still.

"Russian sentries stationed below," Abas whispered, pointing. "They would not be pleased by our presence."

From then on no one said a word. The brothers began communicating by a series of hand gestures, clipped snorts, and whistles. They eventually reached a third cave, where another steaming pot of goulash awaited. Davis wondered who prepared these hearty meals and felt deeply indebted to the phantom chef. Settling in for the night, Davis believed they might have climbed higher but for the Soviet soldiers scattered about the mountain.

Climbing became harder still, and more perilous, on the third day. The group made most of its final dizzying turns tethered together by lengthy ropes, pulling one another up and over sharp ledges. Passing into another dense canopy of cloud, and as the group reached a precariously perched cave, discreetly hidden in the snowy slope, Davis wanted only to collapse. Yet he couldn't help but gaze at the cave walls, beautifully adorned with strange writings and etchings of oddly pigmented lions and other animals. Davis marveled at their look of antiquity. *What was this place*, he wondered, lying back until he fell into motionless sleep.

Next morning found the skies gray and rainy. Storms and lightning kept the party cave-bound until early afternoon, when a short break finally appeared in the clouds. They quickly mustered their gear and made a frantic scramble up the perilous last pitch, up and over a jagged moraine called Doomsday Rock—a great, bulbous outcropping, dropping off on one side into a mile-deep chasm. Abas said it had taken the lives of many a weary climber.

IT'S ENORMOUS!

Edging heel to toe past the terrible drop-off, Davis found himself perched on a ledge overlooking a deep horseshoe-shaped gorge, its belly socked in by a dense cloud bank. They could see almost nothing, which meant more interminable waiting, wondering what lay below. The Abas clan whiled away the hours chattering aimlessly, flapping arms to stay warm. Davis, lost in his thoughts, stood off to the side.

Just before dusk, as the group prepared to abandon the day's mission, a flare of sunlight broke through the clouds, and Davis caught his first glimpse of the shadowy canyon. The Abas brothers quietly began to pray, whispering petitions to Allah. Davis stood to the side, unsure what to do, when Abas walked him over to the ledge and pointed down.

"There it is," he told Davis. "Noah's ark."

For several moments they looked into a horseshoe-shaped crevasse.

"Do you see it?" Abas asked again.

It took Davis's eyes a minute to adjust. He stared hard into the yawning chasm, once, then twice. He saw nothing but heavy, formless shadows—rocks, ice, and mountainside melding as one in the deep gorge, rendering everything inky black. Davis turned in frustration to Abas. After more tense moments staring into the darkness, murky shadow at last yielded to form and depth. An angular object, strangely out of place among ice-polished boulders, emerged like a sleepy leviathan floating up from the abyss. And suddenly there it stood! A huge, rectangular structure lying on its side, like a battleship stuck on a sandbar.

Oh, my God! thought Davis. *It's enormous!*

A few seconds more and he could see its full form and detail. Its bow, partially covered by a talus of snow and ice, appeared blunt and battered, yet suggested a rugged, majestic symmetry. There could be no doubt about it; this had to be a wooden ship, somehow marooned high on an ice-capped mountain.

Davis blinked his eyes, then realized he was looking *into* the craft, its dark, yawning maw easily stretching one hundred feet into the cleft of ice. Twisted, gnarled timbers, splintered up and out where the hull had split apart, framed the hole.

"Look down there," Abas instructed, pointing at another object further down in the gorge. Davis turned to see, about a half-mile from the main section, another massive structure settled in among the boulders, its timbers ripped and protruding at one end, exactly as the first. Both pieces had the same freezer-burned look of antiquity. They had clearly once been connected.

Further down the gorge lay still more pieces of the ship, some sections wedged between rocks, some bathed in a torrent of glacial snowmelt. The rare July heat wave had shaved the ice back just enough to expose what had lain entombed for the better part of the century.

"For ten, twenty years at a time," Abas said, "the ark lies invisible under the ice. Then suddenly it appears."

Davis rubbed his eyes, gazing deeper still into the cross-section cutaway of the main hull. He wondered at the craft's intricate interior design, comprising three distinct floors, stacked one on top of another. Between floors lay a dense gridwork of frail-looking partitions and narrow walkways, some of which seemed to have collapsed. Atop the upper deck sat a sort of raised roof, an elongated ridge running the better part of the ship's length. This contained the crew's living quarters, Abas said—about forty-eight compartments in all. Years earlier, during another unseasonably warm summer, Abas said he and his family had explored the ark and probed its bowels, discovering a mesmerizing array of primitive wooden stalls and cages. Interestingly, he recalled, the wood both within and without exhibited scant decay. In most places it felt hard as rock.

Davis craned his neck over the ledge, willing himself closer to the legendary colossus. His hands shook, partly from the cold but more from a surge of adrenaline pulsing in his fingertips. A freezing rain began to fall, soaking his parka, stinging his nose. Davis remained heedless to all but the overpowering thought of climbing down into the canyon and touching the ark. He wanted so desperately to touch it, as if physical contact would confirm its reality.

A HAUNTING MEMORY

"Come, my friend," Abas spoke softly, reverently. "We must leave. We'll return tomorrow."

But Davis didn't want to leave. He could have stared at the ark forever. It seemed like a dream—strangely familiar yet so large and unnerving it stole his breath. It had taken everything he had to make it this far; how could he just *leave*? Every sensibility told him that what lay below simply could not exist; it must be a hallucination. An enormous ship resting near the summit of a towering peak? Try as he might, Davis couldn't bring himself to believe it really was Noah's ark. Yet there it sat, clear as day.

And almost within reach.

Davis tried to ignore the rain, sleety and cold. Any minute, he knew, the rain would become snow, turning the steep slope into an ice rink. He'd been standing almost motionless for over an hour, staring at the big boat, taking in its every detail, memorizing the scene, when Abas beckoned. The weather refused to wait; they had to leave. Taking Davis by the arm, Abas coaxed his friend away from the ledge. Yet before joining his friend on their careful descent, Davis made Abas promise: "Tomorrow, we must return."

"We'll come back first thing in the morning," Abas assured him. "You can inspect it for yourself firsthand."

They climbed back down the embankment to a cave on the peak's windswept face. The exhausting, precarious hike left them chilled to the bone. A warm fire crackled inside, and a cast-iron stew pot simmered over smoking coals. They hastily devoured a meal and crawled into their bedrolls, their bodies drained from a day in the frigid heights. But Davis couldn't sleep. His stomach churned. Haunting thoughts like, *I might never see the ark again*, kept him awake.

The next two days the weather stayed cold and rainy; the fog-filled gorge allowed them only brief, distant glimpses of the ark. Still Davis remained insistent. He wanted to touch the ark. They decided to stay one more night, but when morning came, Davis's heart sank. A shroud of sleeting rain mixed with snow covered the rock face with a glaze of ice and knee-deep snow, making a return to the gorge unlikely. Wisdom dictated a rapid descent.

But what about the promise? Abas's proud clan tried to find a way to get back up the slope. With hardly a nod to the building storm, they bundled up and bound themselves to a length of rope, marching methodically back up to the canyon through the swelling blizzard. When they arrived on the ledge, the ark, entombed again beneath its icy shroud, had disappeared. In one night the mountain had reclaimed its prize, and Noah's boat had resumed its hibernation among the rocky clefts. Davis felt distraught; he knew he had seen the last of the ark.

"I'm sorry," Abas said. "We must leave. The weather is coming in strong. It's too dangerous."

WHO WOULD BELIEVE IT?

Five days later, through heavy snow and relentless rain, the party arrived, bruised and battered, at Abas's village. Amazed simply to have survived the ordeal, Davis quickly said his good-byes and returned to his unit.

His clothes, filthy and foul, had to be burned outside of camp. Worse, when Davis attempted to describe his exploits, his tale provoked nothing but jeering skepticism. No one, not even his closest friends, took him seriously. Some shrugged politely and turned away; others mocked him and laughed in his face.

"Show us pictures!" they demanded. "Tell us more about your ghosts and phantom boats."

Humiliated, the shy sergeant vowed never to speak of his adventure with strangers. He solemnly wrote in his Bible the date of his discovery and carried it with him the remainder of the war. His note remains to this day.

Soon after, the army transferred Davis to other parts of the Middle East. After a second tour of duty in France (and without ever returning to Iran), he shipped home to Albuquerque, New Mexico. For the next forty years he lived in peaceful obscurity, raising prized Nubian goats. Only seldom did he mention his journey up the painful mountain.

But Ed Davis could never shake the memory of the ark. It haunted his dreams each night for the rest of his life.

* * *

Bible Inscription (written following Davis's return from Iran in 1943):
— Went to Ararat with Abas. We saw a big ship on
a ledge in two pieces. I stayed with him at the big house.
It rained and snowed for ten days. I stopped in Tehran and

got some supplies and got warm and rested up. Also some new clothes. Lt. Burt was glad I got back. He was scared for me. He was afraid I would get killed, I think. I am glad I went. I think it is the ark. Abas has lots of things from there. My legs are almost healed from the horseback ride.

Ed Davis

In order to compile the preceding account of Ed Davis's testimony, a number of sources have been used, including several videotaped interviews conducted by Don Shockey; two transcripts—one by Shockey, the other by Robin Simmons; a cassette recording from the Jim Irwin archives; and supporting documentation from the Rice University Fondren Library. Special thanks goes to Brian Park, a research coordinator with BASE Institute, who reviewed all of the accounts for accuracy and consistency.

Part One

THE EARLY SEARCH

Map of the "Terrestrial Paradise," showing Noah's Ark
on the Summit of "Mont Ararat" (Ararat Mountain) located in present day Iran
Pierre Daniel Huet's conception, from
Calmet's *Dictionnaire historique de la Bible* (1722).

Oɴᴇ

THE WITNESS

I first heard of Ed Davis the winter of 1986 while attending an odd gathering of ark searchers in Farmington, New Mexico. A hundred or so of us watched intently as our hosts introduced Ed as a speaker "with a unique testimony." Up to the lectern he walked, hunched and slow, and began to speak in a voice raspy with years. Standing there, unruffled, and with a trace of dry humor, he led us on the same incredible journey he'd taken fifty years earlier as an army sergeant in Iran.

We sat transfixed as he described the vineyards of Noah, the cave full of artifacts, the petrified cage door, and the arduous climb up the mountain to see . . . the ark? No one knew what to think. Most of us had never heard anyone say he'd actually "seen" the ark. By the time he finished, the electricity in the air made clear we all felt curiously linked to history's most acclaimed artifact.

Ed's talk jarringly climaxed the colorful (and borderline bizarre) gathering, thereafter known as the first (and last) "ark-athon" convention. From around the world they came to Farmington, an amiable group of Noah's ark researchers eager to trade and share theories of the boat's whereabouts. As perhaps the lone neophyte in the crowd, I felt over my head and out of place. I had come only at the request of my good friend, Jim Irwin, who in the coming weeks planned to lead an expedition into Turkey. This would be my maiden trip to Mount Ararat, and Jim figured I could use some grooming in contemporary ark lore. He thought I might learn something useful at a symposium devoted to the ship's recovery.

I had my reservations. Would the participants resemble some fringe zealots I'd encountered, with tinfoil wrapped around their heads, trying to channel Elvis or rambling on about being abducted by aliens?

Hardly!

I found the participants to be a scholarly, generally mild-mannered confederation of businessmen, educators, pastors, and tradesmen, all sharing a singular vision: *to find the ark!* Some had spent years researching the topic and clearly relished the chore of dissecting all the theories, tracking the scholarly record, and then submitting their own hypotheses. Many had climbed huge mountains across the sea and brought back reports of things mysterious and out of place. Others spent their time building detailed scale models or sketching thoughtful portraits of eyewitness "sightings." The mood throughout seemed focused and cooperative, a fact I attributed to its evangelical bent.

Ed Davis didn't fit somehow. His kindly, homespun manner didn't mesh with the event's dogmatic tenor and trappings. Self-deprecating, chuckling easily, this obscure goat farmer from Albuquerque shuffled through the aisles in his cowboy boots, gray cowboy hat, bolo tie, and gaudy, turquoise-encrusted belt buckle. Coupled with the permanent stoop caused by advanced age, he cut a rather eccentric figure.

But once Davis opened his mouth and started talking, he transformed the conference. Here stood a dignified old gent, casually indifferent to the assembled expert opinions and merrily disinclined to match wits with the resident scholars. He didn't even try to hide his occasionally misty memory; frankly he didn't know exactly *where* to find the mountain. Yet he made a pretty convincing case that he'd seen an enormous old boat high on a mountain somewhere. "It *looked* an awful lot like Noah's ark," he said in words so spare and unvarnished that he disarmed even his worst critics. Without the slightest attempt to impress anyone, Davis became the toast of the ark-athon.

Everyone wanted to know: *Who is Ed Davis?* Few knew how utterly happenstance (or, perhaps, oddly predestined) was his appearance at the ark-athon. At the last moment ark-athon sponsor Don Shockey, an Albuquerque optometrist and one of the event's primary organizers, invited Davis to speak. Shockey had heard of Davis quite by accident, one day at work, through a patient. A local man in for an appointment took a shine to, and started asking questions about, a framed photo of Mount Ararat hanging in Shockey's office. He described a special he'd seen on TV about Noah's ark and the great flood, and as he prepared to leave, he turned calmly to say he'd met an elderly gentleman at church recently. "Fellow claims he's *seen* the ark," he said with a shrug.

Shockey did a double take, intrigued but dubious. He quietly tracked down Davis and phoned him a few days later. When Davis answered the phone, Shockey didn't mince words: "Mr. Davis, do you *really* think you saw Noah's ark?" Davis replied directly and without a trace of affectation: "I don't know for sure," he said, almost apologetically. "It didn't have a sign on it. But I don't know what such a big ship was doing so high on a mountain." Smiling to himself, more amused than startled, Shockey asked why Davis hadn't spoken out about his discovery. "Well," Davis said slowly, in words fraught with lingering hurt, "When I mentioned it during the war, they laughed at me." He paused, then added, "No one likes to be laughed at."

Like many, I rolled my eyes when Davis appeared on stage. I took him for an aging publicity hound pining for a whirl in the spotlight, so it startled me to hear him relate a story that sounded so *genuine*. The way he described the journey—describing the native garb and religious customs of his Iranian guides, recalling the texture of the cave walls, the smell of sulphur in the village, the hue and contour of the terrain, even the way the clouds hung and the sun angled in the sky the afternoon he spied the ark—all conveyed the sort of esoteric details one wouldn't *remember*, much less share, if he hadn't actually visited the place.

And something else niggled at me: Ed's shy reticence and calm demeanor belied someone looking to get famous. Davis lacked even an ounce of self-promotion. A man seeking attention just didn't act like this. I checked around and found he'd turned down speaking fees; in fact, he never asked anyone for a dime. Throughout, his motive never varied; he wanted to help *others* find the ark. I quickly decided he was either one of the greatest con artists of all time, or he told the truth.

The ark-athon ended, and I returned home to finish preparations for my first expedition to Turkey. I wouldn't cross Ed Davis's path again for almost two years.

THE BENEFACTOR

Larry Williams, world-renowned stock and commodities speculator, expressed interest—but refused to dismiss his doubt. He certainly possessed the resources to finance our next trip to Turkey, but he made painfully clear that he didn't feel in the mood to throw his money away—*again*.

Two years and two frustrating trips to Turkey had passed since I'd heard Ed Davis in Albuquerque. During that time I had twice conducted pioneering airborne reconnaissances of Mount Ararat, once by plane, once by helicopter—two essentially fruitless trips that left me increasingly apprehensive. On each trip a slew of technical problems, bureaucratic hang-ups, clashes with police, and lousy weather had effectively thwarted our efforts to canvass the peak. In the process I'd caught a fierce case of ark fever and now found myself deep into preparations for a third trip to the mountain.

We needed Williams on board: it would cost upwards of $50,000 to pay for a JetRanger Helicopter and pilot to fly us in low to the peak's hard-to-reach canyons and crevasses—places almost impossible to reach on

17
Λ

foot—and everyone knew Williams could willingly squander money in such a fashion.

As might be expected, money presents the biggest obstacle to mounting *any* major international expedition. Hunting for Noah's ark is no exception. Assembling an experienced team, hiring guides, paying for airfare, ground travel, equipment, supplies—in addition to raising the contingency funds, or *gratuities*, that one must funnel to local officials to get proper clearance—can run into the hundreds of thousands of dollars. And those with the resources to bankroll such ventures typically have little interest in throwing away their money.

While it's always an urgent chore to secure willing benefactors, it's never easy. We had to become ark *thrill* brokers, as it were, hard-selling the adventure while creating modest expectations. Perhaps we'd find an exciting new clue, or make a fresh sighting, or bring back a compelling photo or a piece of ancient wood—*anything* to fuel hope and take the search to the next level. Jim Irwin, and later myself as vice president of High Flight, invested much time and energy massaging relationships with wealthy "adventure" capitalists. Naturally, Irwin—the ex-astronaut and celebrity who had walked on the moon—attracted donations without even trying. But after several trips to Turkey, funded by thousands of dollars in backer's fees, yet without securing hard evidence of the ark, our pool of willing donors began to shrink.

Williams seemed our hottest prospect. But after spending a quarter of a million bucks to search for remnants of Pharaoh's chariots on the floor of the Red Sea—with nothing to show for it—he suffered from a bad case of buyer's remorse.

No wonder Williams felt cool to the idea of turning around and throwing big bucks at another biblical long shot like the ark. Shelling out anywhere from $50,000 to $100,000 to look for a "mythical" boat on a mountain as treacherous as Ararat, without some hard, compelling evidence of its existence, struck Williams as highly suspect. I didn't blame him. At those prices I'd also want some kind of collateral up front to mitigate the risk.

That's where Ed Davis came in.

Williams knew of Ed Davis, at the time regarded by many as the sole living eyewitness to Noah's ark. Williams found Davis's story provocative but questioned its authenticity. For starters most ark researchers assumed that Davis, if indeed he told the truth, had been on Mount Ararat in *Turkey* when he made his sighting. But Davis himself would never, or *could* never, positively confirm it. At times he seemed to capitulate to his questioners' insistence that it lay on Mount Ararat, rather than speak from his own conviction. This troubling aspect of his testimony made Williams nervous. "If I'm going to pay for a helicopter and spend all that money," he said, "I want to find out if this guy is telling the truth." So he asked me to go down to New Mexico and supervise a lie detector test. The prospect didn't excite me; I doubted the old man would gladly cooperate in a probe of his integrity. But Williams insisted, pointing out that his cash, and our lives, were on the line. So I said I'd try. I booked a flight to Albuquerque.

THE TEST

No one beats a polygraph test easily. The day I tried to beat, and *failed*, a polygraph test remains one of the saddest chapters of my early career as a policeman. Some of our worst moments start with a simple lapse in judgment, and this sour episode began innocently enough at the end of a long, stressful shift.

I had made a routine traffic stop, pulling over a woman for speeding in downtown Costa Mesa. Evidently she'd had a hard day, too. As I went through the motions of writing her ticket, she exploded, cursing me like a sailor and calling me a "stinking SOB" for making her miss her appointment. At all of twenty-one years of age, my patience had worn thin. Instead of pressing through, I shot back with my own rude and inappropriate remark—a bad moment, a gross reflex. I knew the instant the words slipped out that I would regret it. It seems that everybody loved to sue a cop.

True to form, the woman made a beeline for the station and lodged a complaint, calling me "verbally abusive." It couldn't have come at a worse time; some recent public relations gaffes had stung our department, prompting a series of special measures to keep us out of the newspapers. Our superiors warned us daily *never*, under *any* circumstances, to sass a civilian. The commander called me in and asked me point-blank: "Did you do it?" It was my word against hers, so in my youth and stupidity, I lied. "No sir," I said without batting an eye. "I didn't."

"Good," he replied, "because you're taking a lie detector test."

It's no secret that the polygraph has a checkered history. Some experts swear by its accuracy; others think it's unreliable—easy to fool and imprecise. To my knowledge, the technology hasn't changed substantially since its invention in the 1920s. Even with computers it still works on the premise that a person's physiological reaction—cardio-rhythms, breathing patterns, and galvanic skin responses (sweat activity)—accurately convey the truthfulness of a response. It detects emotional changes. And my fellow officers knew me as "Cool Hand Luke"—always under control, a wizard at veiling my emotions. Sure, I'd come to trust the polygraph as a law-enforcement tool, but I figured I could fool a machine.

I reported to the department's polygraph unit, and a technician hooked me up. He asked me a few baseline questions to start. The needle didn't move. Then he abruptly asked me if I had lied about my traffic stop. Calmly, with a slow, deliberate breath, I said, "Why no, I *didn't*." The needle jumped off the chart. The examiner said, "You're lying." The machine caught me in the act, humiliated me. I received a one-day suspension and had to write an

19

apology to the lady. It took me a long time before I could look my commander in the eye again—a hard lesson in the foolishness of lying and in the futility of trying to beat a polygraph. It almost seems funny now: the lie detector I failed made me a true believer.

"YOU WON'T BELIEVE HOW BIG IT IS!"

My plane landed in Albuquerque the morning of May 1, 1988. Ed Davis and Don Shockey met me at the airport, and we drove straight to the downtown offices of P.G.P. Polygraph. Once I explained to Ed the nature of Larry Williams's concerns, he graciously agreed to take the test. I felt great relief; Ed didn't seem to mind at all.

Before the examination began, I took a few minutes with the examiner, P. G. Pierangel, a crusty sort, rough and ill-humored, yet well regarded as an authority on the standard Backster Tri-Zone Comparison Specific Examination. I knew the test was only as good as the guy giving it, so it reassured me to find that Pierangel knew his stuff. With a cocky smirk on his face, he assured me, "I've been doing this a long time. If he's lying, I'll break him."

Davis seemed unusually stiff and uncomfortable. Since his performance at the ark-athon, his quiet life had changed. An aggressive new breed of ark searchers, as well as a flock of cynical reporters, called him repeatedly at home, frothing at the mouth to hear his story. Strangers showed up at his farm unannounced, asking Ed to affirm their wacky theories on everything from the great flood to the Second Coming. Others, like myself, wanted to strap him to a lie detector.

I felt guilty. Davis didn't need the attention or aggravation that a bad test score might arouse. He'd lived a good life; he had no use for meddlers questioning his motives or invading his privacy. Still, after nearly half a century, the memory of the ark stuck with Ed like an old war injury—at times evoking his greatest moment, at others feeling like salt in an open sore, but always looming in the background, larger than life. For fifty years it had haunted his dreams, invaded his private thoughts. Watching him remove his coat that day and carefully place his gray felt cowboy hat aside, I sensed he'd wrestled long with the idea of "coming out." He seemed resigned, if not at ease, with his peculiar role in history. "If these youngsters really want to know about the ark," his tired eyes seemed to say, "I guess I'll oblige them."

We'd worked up a comprehensive set of questions. I went over the sequence with the examiner. After brief introductions, Davis and Pierangel sat down in the examination room, a stark, Spartan office with bare, white walls, typical of any police interrogation room you'd find in America. And then the preliminary interview began.

Davis dredged the recesses of his memory to recount the story, shifting his head this way and that as he spoke, turning the scene over in his mind,

20
Λ

moving his legs and torso—consciously reenacting the whole episode. In his mind's eye he saw, *relived*, the appearance and feel of the mountain that day—the exact position of the ark, the falling snow, the rocks, and sky—from his precarious perch on the ledge. It felt eerie to watch. He filled his descriptions with impeccable detail, and as he continued, Davis seemed to gain confidence, drawing energy and taking delight in recalling his story. Fifty years after the fact, his audience still clung to every word.

Once the questioning began, Davis never wavered or waffled, though Pierangel grilled him repeatedly. Pierangel, a no-nonsense guy, seemed interested in only one thing: getting to the truth. His face betrayed the strain and cynicism of years listening to lying thugs and conniving con artists. He came at Davis with a surly, accusing tone: *Are you lying when you state that you were taken to Mt. Ararat by Abas and his seven sons? Are you lying when you state that you climbed Mt. Ararat on horseback and on foot? Are you lying when you state that you saw a large wooden structure high on Mt. Ararat?*

Davis never stumbled. The polygraph needle never spiked. His answers indicated he told the truth when he said he saw Noah's ark. Pierangel seemed shocked and disbelieving, and readministered the test to see if he might get different results.

After an hour the examiner visibly tired. Yet he kept repeating the mantra: "Let's run through this again *one more time*." His expression changed from gritty determination to mild frustration to, finally, utter bewilderment. The test ended, and he slipped from the room, wiping sweat from his forehead and mumbling under his breath. "I don't know if this guy saw Noah's ark or not, but I tell you what I do know—this old man *believes* he saw the ark." I approached, and he looked me hard in the eye. "I don't know *what* he saw," he repeated, "but he definitely *believes* he saw a huge boat on top of a mountain! That's a fact."

Pierangel hustled from the lobby, leaving Davis in the interview room. I waited a few minutes for Davis to collect himself, then I went in and sat down. "Mr. Davis," I said, "could I have a few minutes alone?" He nodded, and I closed the door. We faced one another. His countenance betrayed a man well past his twilight, but his eyes still gleamed, like a child's, full of wonder. The test wore him out, but he seemed relaxed and exhilarated, ready for more. Sharing his story had served as a much-needed emotional release. "I hope they know now I was telling the truth," he said, searching my eyes for a clue of the results. "I hope I proved I'm not a senile old man." When I told him he'd passed the test with flying colors, he grinned proudly. Then I told him I needed to ask him something, man-to-man.

He eyed me curiously, then said, "Go on, young man."

I reminded him that I would be flying to Turkey soon to hunt for the ark, and that, by going, "I'm putting my family at risk." I paused, watching the glint of his eye, then continued. "With all due respect, sir, and in complete confidentiality, I need to know. . . . If you are even a little bit uncertain about what you saw, please tell me. It'll be between us. I won't repeat it or think less of you. If you're trying to save face, that's fine. But I have a wife and kids, and I'm about to put my rear on the line. I need to know the truth."

By using an old police tactic, I gave him an out, a back door with no one looking. It was like telling a shoplifter, "I'll just turn my head if you put the candy bar back." But Ed didn't want an out; his gaze remained firm and sure. He looked me square in the eye, smiled wide, and in typical, unassuming fashion said simply, "You won't believe how *big* it is when you see it!"

A shiver shot down my neck. And I *knew*. Davis saw what he saw; I could take it or leave it. We shook hands, and I thanked him for his patience, then bid him a warm farewell. Watching him shuffle from the room, I felt a twinge of remorse. I wished I had gotten to know him better, on a different level.

As the door closed behind him, the reality hit me. This old man said he saw the ark, and the polygraph said he told the truth—a stunning result. No one, to my knowledge, had ever passed a lie detector test while saying they'd actually seen the ark. It knocked me off balance; how could I have prepared for it?

I walked to a phone and called Larry. When he answered, I didn't even say hello. "Larry," I blurted out, "I don't know if Davis saw the boat, but he definitely *thinks* he saw it. He passed the lie detector test."

Silence on the other end.

"I guess the only thing left to do," I said after a pause, "is to go and try to find it."

22
Λ

Two

MAN ON THE MOON

The plane flight to Istanbul, Turkey, via Frankfurt, takes over eighteen hours—eighteen monotonous hours listening to the high-pitched whine of jet engines droning through the night. On this, my third trip to the Turkish capital, I fought the boredom by reminiscing on all the events that brought me to this unlikely berth in the sky. Rather than sleep, I allowed my mind to wander as the hours ticked by in slow motion.

A sense of calm pervaded. Everything seemed in place. Moved by Ed Davis's polygraph test, Larry Williams coughed up the extra dough needed to lease the JetRanger II, and we had hired master pilot Chuck Aaron—an assertive, self-confident veteran who flew combat missions in Vietnam—to buzz us in close to the peak. With such a potent arsenal at our disposal, the peak would have no choice but to bear its soul to our low-flying chopper.

Three seats away my brother Paul snored like a coffee mill. I had asked him along for fun and companionship; he'd heard enough about my Turkish adventures and wanted to see Mount Ararat for himself. And it might be our last chance. After two trips fraught with more frustration and futility than actual search time, I figured it was now or never. Time was running out. One can't keep searching indefinitely for a boat on a mountain so bent on concealing its secrets.

Still, if the ark were there, we had to make another attempt. A high-performance helicopter and an experienced pilot awaited us in Erzurum. If the weather held and if officials approved all our permits (both big ifs), it seemed our best chance to explore the mountain's most alluring hiding places. One last chance to conquer

Ararat; one last chance to find a phantom ship that had lodged itself in my subconscious. If I were really destined to make history, I wanted Paul with me.

I felt eager and antsy to get started. In neither of my two earlier trips had I felt such urgency to get the mission underway. I couldn't wait to land so we could gather our permits, purchase the helicopter fuel, and rendezvous with our pilot. But something else nagged at me—a pang of sadness I hadn't expected. Amid all the anticipation, I felt strangely subdued, mourning the absence of Jim Irwin. He was the reason I had gotten caught up in this wild-goose chase to begin with, and his absence seemed wrong. He had become both a friend and a mentor, a brother and a father figure. I'd traveled with him all over the world as a personal bodyguard and chief assistant. To me he was the great American hero, a modern-day Christopher Columbus or Marco Polo, surprisingly small in stature, unexpectedly shy, analytical, always humble and soft-spoken, but also bigger than life. He had piloted the Lunar Module for Apollo 15 and had become the eighth man to walk on the moon. He also drove Lunar Rover 1 eighteen miles across the lunar plain. He and fellow astronaut David R. Scott broke records for surface "stay time," spending eighteen hours and thirty-five minutes outside the module, and for the first time charted and explored the Hadley Rille and Apennine Mountains on the southeast fringe of the Sea of Rains. In my eyes Irwin was the consummate pioneer explorer—everything I wanted to be but was not. Without him on board, the trip would surely suffer.

FIRST MEETING

I gazed out my window at the black abyss of the Atlantic thirty-five-thousand feet below. My mind meandered to my first meeting with the famous astronaut, an introduction I'd carefully orchestrated back in February 1985. At the time I was grappling with a strange, midlife crisis of my own. I'd recently suffered a sudden, jarring exit from law enforcement after an almost ten-year career. My snap decision left me badly disoriented, wrestling with withdrawal, yearning for *something* to fill the gap. But what? What could replace the adrenaline, the sense of adventure I'd enjoyed all those years on the beat?

It happened just after I moved from Costa Mesa, California, to accept a job as an assistant police chief in southern Colorado. I thought it would be the last stop of my career—my dream job—in a quiet, beautiful mountain town at the foot of Pike's Peak. I envisioned myself retiring there as police chief and playing out my twilight years camping and fishing.

But bubbles have a way of bursting.

While in those days no one would have considered me an on-fire believer, I viewed myself as a dedicated Christian. And while I didn't make a habit of sharing my views, I didn't hide my faith, either. Unfortunately, the police chief turned out to be a proud and bitter atheist and soon turned a job I loved into a joyless grind. He allowed no room for anyone to express opposing beliefs.

Once, after hours, I expressed some of my views on Christ with a troubled coworker; someone reported us. In a head-spinning sequence the chief ordered me into his office, slammed his hand on his desk, pointed a finger in my face, and angrily warned me "*never* to say the name of Jesus" on the premises again. Shocked and indignant, I reacted on instinct. I tore off my badge, tossed it on his desk, and walked away—a gut reaction that abruptly ended a career I really loved.

Seeking new direction and needing a job, I eased into the booming Colorado real estate market of the mid-1980s as a private developer. Partnering with my brother, Paul (who had lost his job as an air traffic controller when the federal government fired striking air traffic controllers), we chiseled out a successful real estate partnership in Colorado Springs. It got off to a fast start. I built some high-end projects for some influential clients and made some decent investments. But the unfilled void of my past life trailed me like a shadow. I literally felt a hollow place in my chest where my badge had been. Looking for ways to serve, I started working with some local charitable organizations and slowly earned a reputation as a proficient fund-raiser, a handy skill that eventually squired me into Jim Irwin's path.

It came through real estate. Presenting a talk one day to the Colorado Springs Board of Realtors, I met a fellow who said he knew Jim Irwin. I'd heard of Irwin, of course, and knew he lived in the Springs. I'd watched reports of his Turkish expeditions on the local news. But when my colleague mentioned that Irwin was planning another trip to Turkey to look for the ark, my pulse started pounding. Not knowing exactly why, I immediately asked if he'd arrange a meeting. Surprisingly, he agreed. A week later I found myself sitting in a restaurant, having lunch with Jim Irwin.

We hit if off immediately, avoiding any of the stiffness typical of such encounters. He put me at ease, regaling me with stories about space flight and the moon. Engrossed and enchanted, I asked questions like a doting grandchild, hanging on every word. It soon became clear we shared something in common: an insatiable thirst for adventure.

Jim had retired from NASA in 1972 and found himself planning the rest of his life around a cavernous void left by a celebrated career. I understood perfectly, still chafing from my own career trauma. Yet it startled me to learn that a late-in-life spiritual awakening had filled the hole in his life. It came about, wondrously enough, while standing *on the moon*. Jim's eyes grew distant recalling how it happened: "David (Scott) and I were busy taking soil samples," he said, "collecting rocks, doing endless lists of tasks. It was a blistering pace; we were sweating buckets. I stood up for a moment to rest, turned around and . . . there was *earth*, hanging like a dainty droplet of water in the black canopy of space. It looked all misty and moist, framed in bright greens, blues, and whites—like it was *breathing*."

He paused, grinning, eyes fixed on mine. "Here was this little round ball of life protected from deep, subfreezing space by a thin layer of atmosphere, consisting of a perfectly combined mixture of gases. The planet I saw was created by an infinitely wise Creator. It wasn't a cosmic accident. I realized in that instant there was a God . . . and that there was a higher purpose for me."

I tried to lighten the mood, switching topics to Noah's ark. His demeanor softened. "I'm a born-again Christian," he said, and described how his once ravenous thirst for glory and adventure had given way to a serene, indomitable passion to know and serve God. He formed the High Flight Foundation, a nonprofit evangelical organization based in Colorado Springs, and later a vehicle from channeling resources into searching for biblical artifacts from the Genesis period. "It's my calling now to give believers and unbelievers alike solid evidence of the Bible," he said, leaving no doubt as to the source of his obsession with finding Noah's ark.

I admired his conviction, but the appeal of the adventure itself seduced me. Shamelessly I pumped him for more details on his Ararat expeditions, until, without warning, he asked me if I wanted to participate. I felt stunned, flattered, and instantly swept up in grandiose delusions. I fancied myself, ice axe in hand, storming up a high glacier on Ararat. The conceit soon fled, for I soon realized he wasn't asking me to *join* him on the journey but to help him raise the needed funds.

Still I felt honored. The way I saw it, who wouldn't jump at the chance to help Magellan pay for his next worldwide cruise? Any opportunity to get closer to this man—to this *cause*—seemed reason enough. I recruited my brother Paul, and together we came up with an idea to build a house—"The Noah's Ark House," we called it—which we would sell for a profit, then donate the proceeds to High Flight. Paul and I lent the project money up front and used our contacts to get discounts on labor and materials. The house sold quickly, and we turned a tidy profit. The day after it closed, I handed Jim a $15,000 check. It must have impressed him, for the next day he invited me to join him in Turkey.

That's how all *this* got started. God had replaced my wrenching retreat from law enforcement with the promise of raw adventure, springing from a "chance" encounter with a living legend. In the solemn predawn hours before lánding in Istanbul, it cheered me to recall the story.

I glanced at Paul; he hadn't moved in three hours. As the engines of our midnight 747 droned on, I sat there thinking that, in some ways, it felt oddly disquieting to weigh the impact of one life on another. Where would I be on this unforgettable night if I hadn't met Jim? Who knows?

But one thing I could say: As desperately as I wanted to find Noah's ark in the coming days, at that solitary moment over the ocean, I would've traded it all to have a soft-spoken astronaut sharing the silence beside me.

TOO BIG FOR THE GAME

Jim would never take such a trip again. Traveling with him had turned into an *event*, not unlike the media frenzy swirling about major celebrities. It had turned recent trips to Turkey into maddening drills of wonder and wait, beg and bargain.

You simply can't travel large in countries like Turkey, where civil strife and ethnic unrest keep governments on the frazzled edge of paranoia. And looking for an object as controversial as Noah's ark behooves one to keep a low profile—or at least to avoid the critical scrutiny of those who may arbitrarily strip you of the privilege. The search for Noah's ark, always ponderous and unwieldy, requires skillful planning and attention to detail but also great stealth and discretion. With Jim on board, that had become impossible. The media hovered like vultures to get close to the "great American astronaut"; the public hailed him as a god; and government officials eyed us with jealousy and suspicion. Confusion and delays plagued trips with Jim, due mostly to the circus atmosphere shadowing his every move. Such an interesting paradox! While it was Jim who pried open Turkey's doors to renewed Ararat expeditions back in 1982, his presence now invited failure.

Jim's first trip to the mountain marked the end of a decade-long moratorium on such climbs. Turkish officials had banned such exploration after repeated incidents in which ark searchers entered the country under false pretenses and climbed the mountain without permission. The stalemate ended only after Irwin expressed an interest in climbing the peak in 1982; his global visibility and reputation made him an instant hit in Turkey, and the sheer weight of his celebrity compelled the travel ministry to repeal its ban. The landmark decision granting High Flight its rare permit ushered in a new era of Ararat explorations (many of them involving Jim). In subsequent years dozens of teams besieged Turkey with requests to scout the mountain's every ridge and crevasse for a sign of the ark—with very little result, unfortunately, except for some blurred photos, distant sightings of rock formations, and vague shapes in the snow.

Some blame the poor results on the exasperating game of cat and mouse climbers must play with Turkish bureaucrats. Only those who have tried to navigate Turkey's bedeviling state maze can understand the constant trials, miscues, and bureaucratic delays. One must play a game of moving targets and optical illusions that begins in the States, where all American-led expeditions originate. After weeks or months of strained dialogue with the proper Turkish consulates and travel embassies, one can usually obtain, with steely persistence, initial clearance to climb, or fly over, the peak; thus setting in motion the more evasive machinations of securing permits for all phases of the journey. Signed documents and verbal pledges at this stage can bring a false sense of security, convincing a would-be team that everything appears in order, and that, yes, a cost-effective, timely assault can be waged.

27

Sadly, only after all the visas and funding have been secured, flights booked, guides arranged, and the team actually sets down in Turkey, can one see that all has been an illusion. Nothing is as it seems.

To some, simply setting foot in Turkey means starting over. The paper trail vanishes; rules and policies change; messages disappear; paperwork remains undone; personnel have shifted—all pointing to the galling upshot that access to the mountain is denied (or at best, indefinitely postponed). If the necessary permits do, by some windfall, arrive as planned, then the latest political upheaval, tainted election, or terrorist attack will almost certainly stall things out. Time and again valuable days and resources, scrupulously budgeted to be spent searching the peak, waste away in hotels and cafes as the nervous teams await final word. And when official clearance *does* come, it typically bears little resemblance to original agreements: new terms and conditions have been attached; strategic sectors of the peak are restricted or "forbidden"; time frames have been whittled down to nothing.

And if all this isn't enough to dampen the spirits of the most die-hard ark searcher, there yet remains the giant, thundering headache of Mount Ararat itself. Not merely an enormous, sprawling monster of a mountain to climb—inaccessible most of the year due to deep snow and deadly weather—Ararat's very presence brings discord among the region's fractious ethnic groups. The mountain stands like a menacing watchtower along the borders of eastern Turkey, western Russia, and northern Iran—a ticklish proximity that keeps tensions high and raises real and immediate concerns of cross-border spying. A Turkish versus Kurdish war, for example, goes back centuries. On certain of Ararat's slopes (particularly the strategic northwest face), anyone with a strong pair of binoculars or telephoto lens can quietly eavesdrop on sensitive military outposts below. Suspicions run high among Turkish officials and their neighbors that impossible-to-monitor, freelance ark expeditions might be used as fronts for espionage. Such distrust weighs heavily against all expeditions and consistently thwarts the ark search on the mountain's most promising slopes.

By the end it had all become a bit of a bore to Jim. No matter how skillfully he negotiated these roadblocks, one final liability always remained: *him*. He knew, and *they* knew, that by merely setting foot on the mountain he became a walking bull's-eye. History proves that anyone who sets foot on Mount Ararat accepts short odds on being shot or captured by Kurdish terrorists. But here, as always, Jim stood out; officials warned him repeatedly that rebel Kurds would love nothing more than to capture or kill him to draw attention to their guerilla war against the Turks. He amounted to a poor security risk, simple as that. High officials in Ankara and Erzurum wanted neither the responsibility nor the international fallout, should the famous astronaut break his neck or get shot on their mountain. The emerging nation did not need such a black eye.

Jim himself had confided on our last trip, as the permit process reached new heights of lunacy, that the problems could be traced to *him*, not (as some had come to suspect) a sinister Turkish plot to prevent us from finding the ark. He felt at peace with it. He'd taken his best shot, used his influence with integrity. He'd become an unflagging ambassador of good will between nations and had gone that extra mile, almost killing himself one trip in a spectacular fall. Who could fault him for wearying of the hunt?

But that wasn't all. Something else had eroded his resolve, the thing so few of our compatriots seemed willing to see. With so little to show for his trials and labors over the years, Jim now frankly doubted the boat lay there at all.

I suppressed such thoughts. We still had work to do.

ONWARD AND DOWNWARD

29
Λ

The captain's voice broke over the intercom. Flight attendants began scurrying about, preparing for landing.

From my window the lights of Istanbul glittered like a billion stars off a moonlit sea. A flight attendant nudged Paul, who woke with a look of bleary-eyed incoherence, drool glistening from his chin. I tightened my seat belt and closed my eyes for the first time on the flight.

The journey was about to begin.

THREE

ANKARA HOLIDAY

We landed softly at Istanbul International Airport, deplaned, and walked briskly to baggage check. I sensed it immediately: the terminal seemed almost quiet (at least compared to earlier trips). Without Jim no media greeted us, no special envoys from the president bore gifts of welcome, no fanfare whatsoever hailed our arrival. We lugged our backpacks through security unnoticed, anonymous westerners in hiking boots.

Flagging a taxi outside in the street, we saw no sign of the mayhem of previous trips. Back in the spring of 1986, we'd arrived in Turkey to ugly reports of Kurdish terrorist attacks bloodying the streets. In Ankara, for example, shot glass-sized bullet holes riddled airport walls. That had been my first trip abroad, and in my naïvete I expected to be ambushed on the road or picked off by a sniper. The ambush never materialized. But even two years later the terrorist threat remained, albeit to a lesser degree.

No visitor to Turkey can completely ignore the Kurdish problem, and those arriving to climb Mount Ararat see it as a very real threat to life and limb. Kurdish rebels, after all, claim—and often outright occupy—Mount Ararat as their own. The peak widely believed to harbor Noah's ark sits squarely within the ever-shifting borders of Kurdistan, the ill-defined Kurdish empire occupying, at various times and spaces, parts of Turkey, Iran, Iraq, Syria, and Russia. Its fluid borders can obscure the fact that Kurdistan is a real place with its own cities and language, culture and beliefs, woven into the social cloth of its host nations. Today Kurdistan's population exceeds the combined populations of Denmark, Norway, and Sweden.

But to call Kurdistan a "country" stretches the definition. Modernization, the disappearance of traditional cultures, and at times an unkind realignment of national borders have put immense pressure on the Kurdish people. They've been forced to fight for their lives against hostile regimes in countries like Iraq and battle established governments elsewhere to regain control of native lands. Like displaced peoples throughout the world, the Kurds desire a republic to call their own, and, to this end, Mount Ararat remains a coveted prize.

Until recently Kurdish activity reduced the mountain to a hotly contested battle zone and kept the Turkish military on red alert. On a mountain so vast, the terrorist threat can be hard to contain, and ark expeditions seem especially vulnerable to attack. My friend John Macintosh and Bill Crouse, both experienced ark searchers, share a chilling tale of being ambushed by heavily armed Kurdish commandos; they managed to escape kidnap or execution only after seeing their tents ransacked and equipment stolen or burned. Due to dangers like this, Turkish officials have been quick to place the mountain off-limits to foreigners.

RULES OF THE GAME

Kurdish threats aside, while en route to our hotel, I recalled that some things in Istanbul never change. The traffic appeared as lethal as ever, with kamikaze taxi drivers running amok. I'd often joked (only half-jesting), that two types of pedestrians exist in Istanbul: the quick and the dead. Here traffic lanes seem to serve no purpose other than to waste paint, and cars and trucks hurtle toward you, in your own lane, like errant missiles.

We rejoiced at the predictably warm and sunny late-August weather. Any serious ark searcher knows the wisdom of scheduling trips around this well-known, two-week window of Turkish sunshine. One or two weeks on either side of this elusive portal could find the mountain blanketed by high snowdrifts or buffeted by brutal, often fatal, ice storms.

Larry Williams, my friend Bob Stuplich (one of the most experienced Americans to climb Ararat), Bill Dodder, pilot Chuck Aaron, and Dr. Jon Swenson joined Paul and me in Istanbul. The following day we rented a Cessna 421 and flew to Ankara, the Turkish capital, two hundred miles to the east, where all prospective expeditions to Mount Ararat must begin. We boasted a seasoned team, and we all felt optimistic about our prospects for discovery. We had followed all the proper channels back home, culling varying degrees of assurances from the Turkish Embassy that we would be allowed to fly. Still, we knew that, as always, such assurances meant little. Anticipating the worst (one expects delays and complications when dealing with aircraft), Chuck Aaron arrived two weeks early to serve as our advance man, hoping to grease the skids of Turkey's labyrinthine travel ministry. Aaron knew well how to negotiate the perpetual tension between Turkey's military and governmental branches, both of which must sign off on all expeditions. He understood the intricacies of walking permits through these agencies by hand. It requires patience . . . and contacts in strategic places. It means appeasing no fewer than eleven (at last count) national ministries—sports, interior, intelligence, and others—including the military. While no one knows what these seemingly unrelated offices have to do with a mountaineering expedition on the far side of Turkey, gaining their approval can take weeks. Once approved, jurisdiction shifts abruptly—and at times, maddeningly—to the city of Agri.

As the seat of eastern Turkey's provincial government, Agri sits one thousand miles east of Ankara, within eyeshot of Mount Ararat. The governor of Agri ceremonially reviews and (theoretically) rubber-stamps all permits preapproved in Ankara. But it's rarely that simple.

After weeks of deliberating in Ankara, many expeditions stall out in Agri for no apparent reason. The governor there often flatly ignores dictates from Ankara and arbitrarily strikes down licensed permits—a costly and, for most, unacceptable risk. It simply costs too much to plan an expedition, guide it through Ankara's obstacle course, only to watch it die at the foot of Ararat. For that reason we had Aaron run interference for us; he'd learned how to bypass Agri's capricious procedures altogether. He did it by taking all Ankara-certified permits and flying straight to Dogubayazit, south of the mountain. There he'd take his case directly to the elite combat unit charged with guarding the mountain—the *Jandarma*. Barring any current armed conflict with the Kurds, the Jandarma typically waved most expeditions through. And with their blessing Aaron found that he could complete a flyover and evacuate the area before officials in Agri knew what happened. You might call it a cagey approach, but who can guarantee anything in Turkey?

Once we arrived, it took Aaron another week and a half to get our permits, by which time Stuplich and Dodder had already returned to the States, called back on urgent business. That left Paul, Williams, Aaron, Dr. Jon Swenson, and myself to complete the mission.

ERZURUM CONNECTION

When Ankara finally released our permits, the second stage of our journey cranked into high gear. Aaron and Williams flew back to Istanbul to lease the JetRanger B-III helicopter, while Paul and I flew to Erzurum to buy the fuel. We planned to rendezvous from opposite ends of the country in Dogubayazit, twenty miles from Ararat. This would become standard procedure for all airborne missions: one team leases the helicopter in western Turkey (usually Istanbul) and flies it cross-country to the mountain; the other team buys the back-up jet fuel in eastern Turkey (usually Erzurum) and transports it to Mount Ararat by truck or van. The method allowed us to obtain enough fuel to complete the mission, while still having some left to return to Erzurum to fill up for the flight back to Istanbul.

Paul and I felt ecstatic to leave Ankara in the rearview mirror. Erzurum, located approximately 160 miles west of Mount Ararat, is the last airport—and, thus, the final fuel depot—before you get to the mountain. Marco Polo once cited this rustic, timeworn city of ancient mosques and crumbling ruins as a major hub of his northern trade route. The city gained fame for its thirteenth-century Turkish baths, housed in ancient, gray-marbled salons, festooned with high Roman columns and polished stone walls. For fifty cents U.S., Paul and I joined fifty or so towel-wrapped Turkish men in a huge steam room, corseted floor to ceiling by stone gutters filled with scalding water. We sat on short stools as the mineral-infused steam dilated our pores and relaxed our muscles. The soothing experience came to an abrupt end, however, when a small, dark-skinned Turkish masseuse with iron fists and daggers for fingers joined us unannounced. Without a word he sidled up next to our stools, took a stiff wooden brush and, with great spectacle, began scrubbing the skin on our backs and arms until they looked pink and raw. Then he cracked our necks and shoulders with a rapid-fire assortment of therapeutic/wrestling holds devised (I'm guessing) to snap one's body back into proper alignment. While we enjoyed the Turkish baths overall, Paul and I decided on our next visit to decline the massage, which left us both sore and swollen for days.

Erzurum also boasts dozens of weaving institutes, which churn out the prized Turkish and Persian rugs exported throughout the world. We toured one, located deep in the ethnic heart of the city, and beheld a cavernous sweatshop overrun with young women brought in from the countryside to learn the technique; later they return to the villages to teach the craft to their relatives. They all hunched precariously over primitive-looking log-and-wheel looms, hand-spinning the textiles celebrated for their intricate composition and design. Still, it troubled us to see so many of the girls walking about with a permanent stoop, suffering from a chronic curvature of the spine caused by endless days spent bent over their wheels.

After two days sampling Erzurum's old-world charms, we shifted gears and launched the journey's final phase. We bought ten barrels of jet fuel at the local airport, rented a minivan, and made final preparations for a five-hour push across Turkey's eastern outback. We ran into a problem storing the fuel: since we could find no metal drums for sale in Erzurum, we had to buy lightweight, plastic Tupperware-style, 30-gallon drums with flimsy push-top lids. These lightweight, rubberized vats let fuel splash and leak out their ill-fitting tops—a tragedy-in-waiting. It posed a serious problem for the long, bumpy ride that lay before us. But we had no choice; we'd have to make do.

The morning of our departure, we woke at four and loaded the plastic drums into the bed of the van. The van came with a scrawny, toothless driver named Yavuz, dressed in a moth-eaten T-shirt and rubber sandals. We

33

carefully apprised Yavuz of the unstable (and highly flammable) nature of our cargo, then held our breaths as he put the van in gear and steered out of town, accelerating slowly and methodically, trying valiantly (but without much success) to maneuver around endless rocks and potholes. Each bump sent toxic whitecaps of jet fuel splashing across the floor of the van.

Within five miles of Erzurum, fumes overcame Paul and me. The air in the back, thick and caustic, sent vapor trails rippling out the windows. We had become a mobile Molotov Cocktail looking for a target—a fact that mysteriously escaped our driver. Less than twenty miles into the plain, Yavuz popped a cigarette in his mouth and went to strike a match. Partially frozen by horror, partially sedated by fumes, Paul and I lunged forward and screamed, "NOOOOO!" I managed to grab Yavuz's hand before he sent us up in an orange-red mushroom cloud. "Fumes! *FUMES!*" I yelled, pinching my nose and waving a hand at the veil of fumes to make Yavuz understand. With a vacant grin Yavuz nodded blearily and kept driving. He thereafter resisted the urge to smoke.

Four

FAR FROM HOME

Few landscapes dull the senses as hypnotically as that of eastern Turkey. This waterless wasteland of grimy mud huts, dusty, rolling hills, desolate sheep pastures, and rutted roads can induce the woozy traveler into a sleepy trance. We passed field after field of women working in the blazing hot sun, some so poor they didn't even own a sickle to cut the wheat; instead they used their hands to pull shafts of grain from the hard, claylike soil. Little girls in every village mixed sheep dung with straw into round little pies, then stacked them, ten-feet high, next to their homes for use as firewood in winter.

Three hours into our trip, I could just see the summit of Mount Ararat glowering through the distant haze. It still seemed an eternity away. Giddy from the fumes, sedated by the rumbling cadence of the terrain, my mind drifted back to my first encounter with this vast, dreary landscape.

OF SPIES AND GRANOLA

Two years earlier, in late August 1986, our entire search team sat under house arrest, charged with spying. Turkish police surrounded our hotel, searched our rooms, and confiscated all of our film. CNN News sent a team to the scene, flashing bulletins that "Jim Irwin, NASA's Lunar Module pilot, has been arrested for espionage in Turkey." International news wires blared headlines claiming "the eighth man to walk on the moon" had been arrested for spying. Guards at our door prodded us with their rifle muzzles and warned us that "we will beat you and kick you" if we disobeyed their orders.

Earlier that afternoon members of our team had flown a successful mission around Mount Ararat in a Cessna 206. Dick Bright, a pilot for United Airlines, and two Dutch photographers made several passes over the mountain and captured it all on film. That's when the trouble started. When Bright landed at Erzurum's airport, Turkish secret police intercepted our whole team—Jim and Mary Irwin, Bright, Bob Stuplich, Bill Dodder, and myself. Through a typical series of miscues and false assurances from Turkey's Civil Aviation Authority, we thought we had permission to take off, but now, according to the police, it appeared we didn't have authorization to *land*. "That's *absurd*," Bright erupted. "Did they expect us to stay up in the air all night?" To top it off, officials accused us of violating air space over Russia and Iran, an infraction nearly impossible to monitor or prove. The nonsensical allegations earned us a rude escort back to our hotel, where armed guards held us under house arrest.

Worry hounded me. I couldn't get the prison scenes from *Midnight Express* out of my mind. I kept watching Jim, almost indifferently cool. With more than fifty machine-gun-wielding police waiting in the street below, he said simply, "Tell the truth, be respectful. Above all, don't do anything crazy." It seemed prudent counsel, considering we'd been harassed by the Turkish secret police since the moment we arrived. They'd done everything to sabotage our expedition and undermine the "famous American astronaut." Since the day we landed in Ankara, the media had hovered over Jim, making him into a nonstop object of public adoration. It struck the Turkish police as an intolerable affront. Their constant threats and interference let us know they would curb our lingering presence at the first opportunity; now they'd finally found a reason to arrest the American hero.

We knew we had to retrieve our film, since such evidence could be doctored or falsified and used against us. Besides, once police formally charged us and expelled us from the country, we'd never see the film again—a total loss for the trip. We knew several rolls sat in a room down the hall; we had little choice but to try to get them back.

Stuplich, Dodder, and I came up with a plan. We would try to use a diversion to distract the guard watching the room. The film lay among our backpacks and equipment, so one of us had to get in there unnoticed, retrieve the film, and get out without getting caught. Stuplich volunteered, but the chore fell to me. Splashing water on my face to simulate sweat, I grabbed a handful of blueberry granola and stuffed it in my mouth. Then the three of us stepped into the hall and walked slowly toward the guard. Before he could react, Stuplich and Dodder started waving frantically, making a fuss, pointing at me and telling the young guard: "*Our friend is sick. . . . We need help. . . . Please, help us.*" On cue I doubled over and pretended to throw up, spewing half-chewed blueberry granola all over the corridor. Then I fell to the floor, writhing and moaning as if my appendix had burst.

While the guard rushed to my aide, eyes bulging with fright, Stuplich slid into the unlocked room, rifled through the bags, and found the film. He stuffed several rolls in his coat pocket, replacing them with unused canisters, and calmly reappeared, quiet as a cat. The whole transaction took only seconds. I then stood up, shook myself off, and bowed in thanks to the confused guard. We scurried back to our room, leaving the guard rubbing his head in the hall, unsure of what he had just seen. Inside, we erupted into mute cheers, slapping high-fives and celebrating our cunning.

For a novice like me, it felt like exciting stuff—outwitting Turkey's elite secret police. It made me think that I could *do* this explorer gig. Something about the intrigue, the risk, the uncertainty of the hunt, appeased my wanderlust. Although we didn't find the ark on that trip, I left Turkey with an incredible feeling of accomplishment. I couldn't wait to come back and try again.

37

RETURN TO ARARAT

Now here I was, crossing eastern Turkey's infernal countryside for the third time. I had to laugh at myself. I would risk asphyxiation in a reeking, noxious minivan in yet another bid to find Noah's ark and recapture a feeling I knew I couldn't get anywhere else.

The roar of chopper blades piercing the morning calm blasted me from my daydream. The force of artificial wind rocked the van, and for an instant both Paul and I, hats pulled down over our eyes, thought Yavuz had yielded to his nicotine craving and blown us to kingdom come. But when I looked up, I saw the green and white flash of the JetRanger B-III scorching a vapor trail ten feet above our rooftop. Just for the fun of it, Aaron and Williams had decided to strafe our van en route from Istanbul. Yavuz cursed them with a balled fist, but I grinned, imagining them laughing as they careened out of sight toward Mount Ararat.

I turned toward Paul, unsure whether his ghostly pallor resulted from fume-induced toxemia or the goat intestine shish-kabob he'd eaten the night before. "My head's spinning," he said groggily. (Paul loved eating new foods in foreign countries, but dining on goat entrails wrapped around a stick cured him of that habit for the rest of the trip). In my own nauseated, half-coherent state, I counted it a plus to have simply survived the journey. When Yavuz wheeled us into our appointed rendezvous outside Dogubayazit in the morning sun—an unlit cigarette still dangling from his lips—I praised God. Larry ran out to meet us. "The Jandarmas gave us our permits!" he shouted. "Let's get those tanks unloaded!"

At last, good news. I couldn't stand the thought of driving across the armpit of eastern Turkey and *not* getting the go-ahead.

The helicopter sat humming on a makeshift dirt pad, fifty yards away. Staring up at the sky, my heart raced. A perfect, cloudless day—nothing like my first two trips when sudden snow and a dense fog bank disrupted our search. I gazed up at the mountain: the snow had melted back almost to the summit. Conditions looked almost too good to be true.

Aaron emerged from behind the chopper and sauntered over. "Ready to go find the ark?" he asked with his trademark smirk. I've seldom met anyone as arrogant and cocksure as Aaron—and I say that in a good way. Everybody wanted this master pilot to fly their missions in the mid-1980s. He'd made more flights around Mount Ararat than any other American civilian pilot. (Years later Aaron set a chopper down at sixteen thousand feet on Ararat's windswept western plateau, an act of insane daring, and a world record for a high altitude landing). His reputation for these displays of skill and bravura (some might say suicidal) actually put me at ease; it showed me he could make a chopper do the Tango in a pinch. The brash self-confidence, the swashbuckling charisma, came from superior skill and prowess. Sure, Chuck would be the first to claim he was the best; but since I knew he could back it up, I felt completely at ease with him winging us above Ararat's savage heights.

Using a small, hand-cranked pump, it took us an hour to fill the chopper's tanks from our plastic drums. Then Aaron lit up the JetRanger's engines and rechecked his gauges, while Larry and I removed its doors and windows for maximum visibility, and seat-belted ourselves in behind him. Paul stayed behind in the van, well drilled in how to stall for time if the Jandarma or Agri police showed up. We lifted off at nine A.M., a breathtaking blast of cold air slapping me to attention. As far as we knew, ours was the first helicopter expedition over Ararat; we would enjoy the best view of the mountain in recorded history. Within moments we found ourselves streaking across the crystal blue sky. Mount Ararat loomed before us like a granite citadel, as spellbinding as ever. Poised magically between heaven and earth, it looked against the velvet blue backdrop like a diamond-tipped tiara.

As expected, the pristine weather gave us perfect visibility. Rising slowly to fourteen thousand feet, we flew directly to Ararat's west glacier— the famed "western plateau"—where an Italian named Angelo Palego later claimed to have discovered Noah's ark. Experts think the glacier bed sits atop a collapsed volcano cone; some speculate the ark may have come to rest here. Aaron ascended to fifteen thousand feet, letting us look directly into the ice cap, some two-hundred-feet thick in places. During years of heavy melt back like this, the ice forms a small lake in whose mirror-clear waters some have seen a shadowy, arklike structure. Rolling deftly with the currents, Aaron feathered us down to within one hundred feet of the surface, giving us a straight-on view of its crystalline depths. We saw nothing—no shadow beneath the ice, no fuzzy image in the clear waters. For the first time that day, we shared a tug of disappointment.

In a flash Aaron took us up to the Cehennem Dere ice rim, then swooped down across to the northeast ice cap, popularly known as the

38

Abich II Glacier. Propped between Ararat's two peaks, Abich II forms a broad, saddle perch that yields infrequent sightings of a large, boxlike structure tucked beneath ice and snow. Some think the ark lies here, but once again, from our unimpeded vantage, we saw nothing.

We circled to the northwest side, surveying a feature known as the "Ark Rock," an outcropping conspicuously avoided by local Kurds, who believe it to be the ark itself. As such, they recoil from the presence of heavenly spirits. But Ark Rock is just that—a rock sitting near the fourteen-thousand-foot Cehennem Dere. We then skimmed over the Parrot Glacier, made famous in the 1950s, when a Frenchman named Fernand Navarra claimed to have found hand-hewn wood, which he and his son chopped from the glacier. Carbon-14 dating later indicated the wood to be no more than two thousand years old—not nearly old enough to be the ark—but we gave the glacier a thorough inspection nonetheless. It turned up nothing.

I became concerned, then agitated. None of the promising landmarks had yielded anything. Eyewitnesses swore they'd made compelling sightings here; did they lie? Did they see optical illusions? We couldn't have asked for a better day; no one could recall clearer visibility. We skimmed across the windswept peaks, yet the mountain—dry, brown, stripped of snow except for its eternal glaciers—lacked anything remotely resembling a boat or wood. Still we held out hope.

One prominent feature yet awaited inspection: Davis Canyon, sitting deep within the famous, yawning maw of the Ahora Gorge. It sat below a familiar feature known to ark searchers: the heart-shaped glacier, suspended under the lip of the Cehennem Dere. More than other parts of the mountain, Davis Canyon seemed a rough fit of the geological profile given by Ed Davis in repeated interviews. And at fourteen thousand feet, the upper Ahora Gorge boasts a rich legacy of ark sightings in its own right, featuring all manner of uncanny boat-shaped objects or sharp, angular shards jutting illogically from the sides of cliffs or tilting up from the canyon floor. Aaron slanted the chopper sideways, like a scalpel plunging us into the belly of the gorge. Within seconds we were skimming its lower depths, noting the flinty, basaltic cliff walls and jagged formations.

At one point the narrow gorge prevented Aaron from maneuvering into a good viewing position, so he asked me to hang out the side to take a look at an interesting fissure directly below. With a leery glance at Larry, who saluted me with a look that said, "Better you than me," I extended the seat belt as far as it would go, then wrapped the metal tongue with electrical tape to make sure it wouldn't accidentally release. Then, with my heart hammering in my ears, I stepped out on the skids, fighting the icy gusts and trying to keep my balance under the tremendous force of the rotors. Craning my neck as far as I could, I gripped the door housing with frozen knuckles and peered straight into the gut of Davis Canyon. Empty. No ark, no shattered hull, no pieces of boat floating down the ravine.

Don't get me wrong—I could see how, from much greater distances, others might have mistaken the huge, cleaved fragments we saw for the chiseled hull of a ship or petrified striations of wood.[1] But we inspected each cliff face closely, charted every notch and ravine and eliminated every possibility. Ararat revealed itself to be a dry well. But knowing it might be our last chance, we kept searching the Ahora Gorge, revisiting every crag and crevasse, hoping we might make a sighting. I wanted, *needed*, to see something. But the sad fact remained: aside from provocative shapes in stone, the canyon looked bare.

We exited the gorge and canvassed the entire mountain for as long as our fuel held out, cataloging questionable landmarks, eyeing each ice cap and formation from different heights and angles. We determined to leave no slope, rock pattern, or crevasse unexplored. In a single afternoon we inspected every viable geologic anomaly cited by dozens of eyewitnesses. But we saw no ark; no boat; no wood. *Nothing.*

I felt deflated. I kept thinking that at any moment the ark would miraculously materialize, perhaps in a brilliant shaft of sunlight around the next ledge, like in the movies. But with each unfruitful pass I resigned myself more and more to the inevitable. Low fuel meant we had to end our search and return to Dogubayazit. Aaron noticed a red blinking light on the console, and suddenly his calm, cocky demeanor disappeared. "That's not good," he said vaguely. "I'm going to have to land this thing."

The party had ended, dashing my hopes. I'd returned three times to Ararat, each time fully expecting to find the ark. I'd invested three years in the search and still had come up empty. Like everyone else who'd risked life and limb on the mountain, I had assumed it lay there . . . *somewhere.* How could I now calmly accept that it didn't? We'd done everything right, scoured the peak from low elevation, probed sites others didn't know existed, and still hadn't found it. Aaron did a masterful flying job, poking and probing clefts and contours like a dentist cleans teeth. And yet . . . *nothing.* We had to face facts. I turned to Larry, his face drawn and dejected, and said simply, "It's not here."

For the first time I felt the full, heartbreaking force of those words.

Aaron curled the chopper around and dropped us out of the sky. We set down a mile or so into the plain, beside a dusty Kurdish village, where ten or twelve wide-eyed kids stood by, squinting bravely into the stinging dust of our copter blades. Only a few shacks and mud huts stood around, but by the time we stepped from the cockpit, more than 200 villagers had appeared from nowhere to surround us in a warm welcome. When I removed my headphones, they gawked at me like I'd landed from Pluto, then started clapping and cheering as if we were some kind of Aryan gods.

After exchanging a few handshakes and hellos, I noticed, far back in the crowd, a beautiful little girl on her father's shoulders, dressed in peasant clothes. When I turned away, they vanished into a mud hut near the village edge. *Had we scared them off?* A few moments later, when they returned, I understood. The father proudly led his daughter—now in a pretty white dress—by the hand. She wore the dress for special occasions, adorned with pretty frills and white piping. Any father could empathize. He didn't want his little girl to be seen in rags by the village's honored guests. I walked toward them and knelt down. The papa grinned proudly as I led his daughter back to the helicopter. Aaron lifted her into the cockpit and let her play with the controls while the rest of the villagers stared in disbelief.

Aaron finished his inspection. I led the child back to her father. At least we'd accomplished *something* that day, making her queen of the village. Our van driver, Yavuz, saw us land and picked us up in the village. We piled our stuff in and took off toward Dogubayazit, waving good-bye to the villagers. I turned to see the father and his daughter standing off to the side. With the sun's last rays, her smile radiated, setting her apart from the crowd. I turned and saw Ararat, its summit disappearing behind a mantle of afternoon clouds. I knew I'd never return. Still the vision of the girl's pretty smile lingered. I figured I could live with that as my parting memory of Mount Ararat.

41

Part Two

LOOKING FOR SHINAR

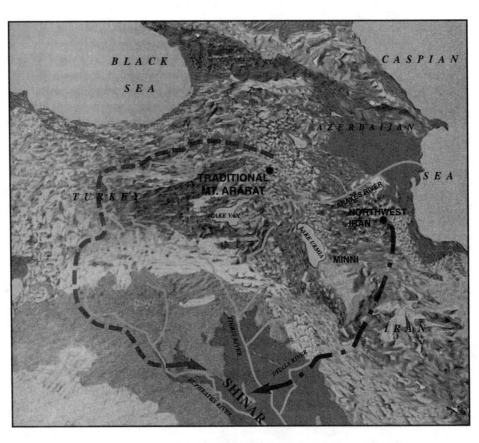

BLACK

SEA

CASPIAN

AZERBAIJAN

SEA

TRADITIONAL
MT. ARARAT

ARAXES RIVER

NORTHWEST
IRAN

TURKEY

LAKE VAN

LAKE URMIA

MINNI

IRAN

TIGRIS RIVER

DIYALA RIVER

EUPHRATES RIVER

SHINAR

▬▬▬ ■ ▬▬▬ PROPOSED MIGRATION ROUTE FROM NORTHWEST IRAN
COMING FROM THE EAST DOWN THE DIYALA RIVER

▬ ▬ ▬ ▬ PROPOSED MIGRATION ROUTE FROM ARARAT IN THE
NORTH DOWN THE EUPHRATES RIVER

FIVE

THE MOUNTAINS OF ARARAT

Ten years passed before I gave the search for Noah's ark another serious thought. Other adventures beckoned, especially a clandestine trip into Saudi Arabia to search for the real Mount Sinai.

When we returned from Jabal al Lawz (what I consider to be the real Mount Sinai), I began recounting our adventure to eager audiences—whose wild enthusiasm shocked me. By 1992, I'd formed Biblical Archaeology Search and Exploration Institute (BASE), dedicated to finding and validating biblical artifacts to authenticate Scripture. In 1998, I quit my job with Family Research Council to devote full time to BASE Institute and to a speaking outreach that has grown beyond my expectations. Through it all the search for Noah's ark got misplaced in some distant corner of my mind. I hadn't expected it ever to surface again when I caught wind of a Bible verse that jarred me from my indifference.

PHONE CALL OF FATE

One fall night in 1998, the phone rang at my downstairs office in Colorado Springs; an elderly gentleman named Phil Burman wanted to talk about Noah's ark. After a brief introduction this retired engineer with time on his hands related a unique story on the ark's possible whereabouts. "You're all looking for Noah's ark in the wrong place!" he declared bluntly. "It *can't* be on Mount Ararat in Turkey."

His manner struck me sour, reminding me of countless calls I'd fielded from an assortment of quacks and conspiracy theorists. I tried gently to extract myself from the phone call, politely reminding him that others had proposed such a possibility and softly explaining that I had moved on to other things. But he refused to quit. He bulled ahead, saying he had read about my Mount Sinai adventure in a magazine and admired the way I'd trusted the Bible to lead us through the desert. I thanked him and prepared to hang up, but he resisted, ordering me point blank to open my Bible. "Read Genesis 11:1," he barked. I hesitated but grudgingly obliged, curious how he might try to bend Scripture to serve his cause. I'd skimmed the verse a hundred times; it detailed the years after the flood when Noah's ancestors migrated into neighboring lands to repopulate the earth. "Read it out loud," he continued, so I recited the passage, hoping to humor him: "Now the whole earth had one language and one speech. And it came to pass, as they [the clans of Noah's sons] journeyed from the east, that they found a plain in the land of Shinar, and they dwelt there" (NKJV). Before I could continue, Burman interrupted. "*There!* Now back up and tell me what that phrase means: 'journeyed *from* the east to find a plain in the land of Shinar.'"

I didn't catch his drift. "Don't you *see?*" he persisted. "The verse proves the ark couldn't be on Mount Ararat. Or *anywhere* in Turkey, for that matter."

"Why?" I asked, still scratching my head. Burman explained that the passage offered a rare fixed point from which to determine the ark's approximate landing site. After the flood Noah's descendants branched out, moving *eastward* into the land of Shinar. And where is Shinar? Experts widely identify it as latter day Babylonia, planted in the heartland of the Mesopotamia Valley. Babylon, of course, stood near present-day Baghdad—*in Iraq.*

"Look at any map," he insisted. "Mount Ararat lies due north of Iraq—not east." And of course he was right. The Bible itself did seem to say that the ark couldn't have landed in Turkey, which lies clearly north of Iraq.

"Case closed!" Burman snapped. "If you believe the Bible, then the passage eliminates the possibility that either the ark or Noah's family could've landed in Turkey."

He now had my full attention. The implications intrigued me. Scripture declared that Noah's descendants lived somewhere *east* of Shinar—in other words, east of modern day Iraq. That could only mean they'd lived in Iran, or somewhere beyond, like Afghanistan or India. They came somewhere from the east and migrated west into Shinar (or Iraq) (see map, pg. 44). Such a solid, plausible clue sheds light on why no one had ever conclusively found the ark on Mount Ararat. That mountain lies indisputably *north* of Shinar, not east. On the weight of Burman's words, I could see the temptation to eliminate Turkey altogether as the happy hunting ground for the ark. But if the ark can't be found in Turkey, I asked, "Where is it?"

"That's not my problem," he replied. "I simply called to alert you to what the Bible says. Now it's up to you, or someone *else* who believes the Bible, to do your homework and *find* it."

He meant it as a non-too-subtle dare. I took it as such and thanked him for the call, assuring him I'd look into the matter. But as I put the phone down, a torrent of doubt rushed in. "What a crock!" I whispered to myself. "Everyone knows the ark landed on Mount Ararat, and Mount Ararat is in *Turkey*."

As the days passed, I couldn't get the conversation out of my mind. I inspected some old maps and writings and verified Burman's claim about Shinar: it *did* lie in the area of ancient Babylon. Modern scholars decisively identify Shinar as the region of modern-day Iraq; the *New Bible Dictionary* defines Shinar as "the land in which were situated the great cities of Babylon," or "the country around Baghdad." The Bible itself tells us that the first cities of the kingdom of Nimrod (Noah's great-grandson) included "*Babylon*, Erech, Akkad and Calneh, in *Shinar*" (Gen. 10:10). So Noah's descendants really did migrate from the east into a region now known as Iraq.

47

I almost felt the Bible whispering to me, as it had in Egypt and Saudi Arabia on the trail of Moses. But what, specifically, did the Bible mean when it said the clans of Noah traveled *from the east*? That's a huge area. Iran certainly lies *east* of Shinar, but so do other lands. The phrase could include any spot from Afghanistan to the high mountains of Tibet.

Still it was a clue and a solid one. Amazingly it had waited there all along. How had we—Jim Irwin, Bob Stuplich, Chuck Aaron, all the dozens of men who'd explored Mount Ararat from top to bottom—missed it? A short, ten-minute phone call from Burman accomplished what nothing else had in ten years: he'd sparked a flash of wonder, breathed new fire into my complacent heart, and restoked my hunger for an answer. Almost as reflex I began revisiting the question that had nagged me since my last unfruitful trip to Turkey: *Why have we been looking for Noah's ark on Mount Ararat?*

THE POWER OF TRADITION

In days to come I phoned some friends, most of whom had invested much time and resources in Turkey searching for the ark. When I casually asked, "Now, remind me . . . why are we looking for the ark in Turkey?" the unanimous response came back, "Because that's where *Mount Ararat* is."

Then I mentioned Genesis 11:1 and noted the pertinent compass headings for Shinar and Babylon. They responded with empty silence. No one wanted to explore this detour. I quietly received their admonitions on chasing pipe dreams and listening to crackpots armed with Bible verses; I listened patiently as they peppered me with accounts of the eyewitnesses "who've *seen* the ark on Ararat." Then I let it go.

I'd asked a fair question but got answers that said, in essence, "Don't confuse me with the facts." This stubborn reluctance even to address the question clarified something I'd long suspected but rarely voiced: all of us had bought into someone's tradition and renamed it a fact.

A quick check told me, for instance, that nowhere does the Bible even mention *Mount* Ararat. Yet everyone camps out on Genesis 8:4, which says the ark came to rest "on the *mountains* [plural] of Ararat." Somewhere in recorded history, someone made a broad leap and interpreted the verse to mean *Mount* (singular) Ararat. Naturally, the only mountain by that name lies in eastern Turkey, so of course that's where the ark must be. It embarrassed me to think we'd all been reading the verse with selective vision, twisting "mountains" into "Mount" and leaning on eyewitness reports to make our case. Where, I wondered, had this leap first occurred? How did it happen?

No one knows for sure. It's a murky task, at best, to track a stream of reputable scholarship dating back far enough to make a clear connection. The vague historic record leaves us with such a spotty chronology that we're left to reconstruct a puzzle without many critical pieces. Suffice it to say that the basis of any tradition linking the ark to Mount Ararat leans heavily on alleged sightings. Paired with gross generalizations of Genesis 8:4, the reports seem to fit and assume a life of their own. Generations of explorers drew similar conclusions based on similar assumptions. Now I wondered: Had we all wanted to believe one thing so badly, that, with the best of intentions, we'd massaged the facts to fit a lie?

Others had asked similar questions before me, but now I needed to answer them for myself. I knew staunch Christians, those who fully trust in the biblical flood account, who harbored grave doubts about Mount Ararat as the holy sepulcher of the ark. They didn't allow the books to sway them or the TV specials on the mysteries of Noah's ark that do more to distort than inform.

Yet where to go for answers? While the topic generates much popular interest, biblical scholars have almost totally ignored the ark's true location as a viable topic of inquiry. As an unfortunate result, we lack almost completely the sound resources that could give us a calm, balanced view of contrasting theories. Three fruitless excursions to Mount Ararat had convinced me that either the ark was not there, or it no longer existed. Now I'd begun to suspect that layers of inbred bias and misinformation had sullied the entire premise underlying the modern search for Noah's ark. A fundamental question burned in my mind: how had *this* mountain been christened ground zero of the modern search for the ark?

I knew that centuries prior the Turks had called it Agri Dagh, and the ancient Armenians, Masis. Who had first called it Mount Ararat? And what of Genesis 8:4, which speaks unambiguously of the *"mountains of Ararat"*?

I'd seen it before, in my research into the whereabouts of the real Mount Sinai: a scholarly herd mentality weaving full-blown traditions out of speculations and shallow research. Through time, repetition, and reputation, myth and legend become canonized as fact. That explains why tourists flock to St. Catherine's Monastery in the Sinai Peninsula, eager to genuflect at the foot of a peak barren of any evidence to commend it as the sprawling campsite of a million-plus Jews. They've bought into a tradition that came to life, not through sound research, but when a third-century prophetess said she saw the mountain in a dream. By contrast our guiding clue to Mount Sinai's location in Saudi Arabia came from a simple Bible verse, Galatians 4:25: "Now Hagar stands for Mount Sinai in *Arabia*." Eight short words from the Bible told us that Queen Helena, and scholarly tradition, got it wrong.

I asked myself: *Was history repeating itself with Noah's ark?* If not, then why, when the Bible says "mountains," had the modern search for the ark focused on a single, volcanic peak in the vast, mountainless Anatolian Plain of eastern Turkey? James Bryce in his 1877 meditation on Mount Ararat, *Transcaucasia and Ararat*, observed: "There can be but few other places in the world where so lofty a peak (17,000 feet) soars so suddenly from a plain so low, 200 to 3000 feet above the sea, and consequently few views equally grand. . . . Here in Armenia the mountain raised itself, solitary and solemn, out of a wide, sea-like plain."[1] To be sure something strange and puzzling continues about the significance of Mount Ararat. But its veil of mystery, I began to realize, is due almost entirely to its legacy of supposed ark sightings.

FROM EYEWITNESSES TO TRADITION

Multitudes of eyewitness reports tied to the mountain have spawned a near cultlike mythology among ark searchers. One mysterious report leads to another, then another, until everyone accepts on faith that the ark sits there, waiting to be found. Ark scholar Lee Spencer says, "The story of Noah and the ark is so well entrenched in Western thought that any mountain found to contain the ark is going to be called 'Mount Ararat' by definition."

But without its catalog of alleged sightings, it boasts little to attract serious attention. So should we take the sightings seriously? The prickly fact is that, almost without exception, the recorded sightings generate far more fanfare and excitement than hard evidence can justify. As Bill Crouse— longtime ark searcher, founder of Christian Information Ministries, and author of the well-regarded *Ararat Report*—observes: "If it were not for these (alleged eyewitnesses), it is doubtful that a search would ever have taken place on the mountain the Turks call Agri Dagh and the Armenians call Masis."[2] Crouse has plenty of company in rejecting the sum of the accounts as grossly contradictory or of suspect origin. He charitably allows that most sightings (and the amateurish photos supporting them) may be explained by the peak's high composition of large, angular blocks of basalt, which can, under the right conditions, create an optical illusion, appearing as "huge, ark-like barges." I came to the same conclusion after a close viewing of the Ahora Gorge. Its flinty, angular boulders, sculpted by wind and ice, transform themselves into shapes mimicking the prow of a ship.

49

What once seemed so enigmatic now seemed quite logical: No one had found the ark because they looked for it in the wrong place. Not surprisingly, many who had most to gain from a sincere reading of the great flood account had either misread or carelessly ignored the Bible's subtle clues. I knew from tracking Mount Sinai across Egypt and Saudi Arabia that we can trust the Bible's accuracy; yet I'd seen respected scholars treat Scripture like cheap fiction, and great men of learning trust in tradition and innuendo to interpret history. Not me; no longer. Phil Burman caught my attention when he called to say the ark couldn't be in Turkey, then backed up his claim with Scripture.

Today when I read the Bible and it says the ark landed in the "mountains of Ararat," I believe it. It landed in *mountains!* Twin volcanic cones standing alone in a vast plain do not qualify. From the summit of Mount Ararat, one can indeed see small foothills, but no signature peaks or anything suggesting a bona fide mountain *range*. So the *mountains* of Ararat must refer to a mountainous *region* or range somewhere else. On this point alone we can reasonably reject the entire Araxes Valley in eastern Turkey as the land from which Noah and his family hailed. A single word of Scripture provides a defensible argument for rejecting Mount Ararat as the ark's final port.

But prejudices die hard. By their nature most people prefer having others confirm their opinions than in testing new theories. Though I initially doubted Burman's observation, he opened my eyes to a new paradigm, one that blew open the floodgates of new research possibilities. His call drove me to the library, where I picked through old scholarly Hebrew texts and esoteric writings on Iran and Iraq.

I quickly learned that only in relatively recent times—certainly many centuries after Moses penned Genesis—did someone link the term *Ararat* to the Turkish mountain. Moses wrote Genesis around 1450 B.C., at a time when *Ararat* simply denoted a broad, remote *region* north of Assyria (or the upper Mesopotamia Valley).

With the rise of kingdoms and the tumult of wars, Ararat's borders fluctuated. Yet ancient records show that, even as it consistently hovered near present-day Lake Van in eastern Turkey (near Mount Ararat), Ararat's borders extended well into the territories of modern-day northern Iraq, northwestern Iran, and southern Soviet Georgia—a fairly broad region from which to mine clues of the ark's fate. With very little effort I'd stumbled upon preliminary leads pointing me in directions not many had considered. A juicy detective story had plopped in my lap. And nothing excited me more than solving a good mystery.

With each new tidbit of fact, the specter of the ark loomed bigger and sturdier, more real than ever. I soon found myself in the grip of a new cause, walking the ancient trail of discovery into the land of Ararat, one that veered far afield of the famous mountain in eastern Turkey.

SIX

WHERE *WAS* ED DAVIS?

Despite my eagerness to explore new possibilities, I faced a major problem: how to decipher Ed Davis's claims, ten years removed from our last meeting, that he'd seen the ark on Mount Ararat?

Davis died in 1998, ending any further hopes of extracting important details. I revisited my files and read the transcripts of his lie detector test, reminding myself why he had so won my respect. True, he'd given an uncanny performance. Everyone left believing he was telling the truth, and to my knowledge no one has ever seriously questioned his integrity. Still his story hadn't moved any of us closer to the ark. Ed Davis knew only one thing for certain: he saw an ark on top of a mountain he *thought* was Mount Ararat. After so long that thesis had worn thin.

How to proceed? Should I disregard his testimony and start afresh, solely because it didn't fit my new paradigm? Or better yet, how could his testimony now be used to promote the search effort? I didn't want to abandon his testimony, but neither could I accept it whole cloth as before. I needed to go back, once more, and review the facts. I had to resolve whether any valid reason existed to keep open to the possibility of finding the ark on Mount Ararat. A review of the facts told me this: the Bible fails even once to mention "Mount Ararat," citing instead the *"mountains* of Ararat"; Mount Ararat lies due *north* of the ancient land of Shinar (or Iraq), rather than due east, where it should be according to Genesis 11:2; no one even called the peak Mount Ararat until several centuries after Moses wrote Genesis; and every alleged ark sighting to date remains conspicuously unconfirmed.

The fact is, literally dozens of expeditions combed the mountain in the twentieth century alone. In their breadth and focus, the search efforts covered everything, including ground, helicopter, and plane expeditions to the summit; aerial mapping photos taken at low elevations; and high resolution satellite imagery enhancements of its face. The mountain has been examined under the lens of ground penetrating radar (GPR) and stripped bare by every other high-tech detection device known to man.

And still the ark remains at large.

I once shared a limousine ride to a fund-raising event in San Clemente with Dan Quayle, former vice president of the United States, and my close friends Tom and Kim Bengard. During the one-hour drive through traffic, Tom turned to Dan and said, "Mr. Vice President, you might be interested to know that Bob has been on Mount Ararat looking for Noah's ark."

I thought the vice president would think me crazy, but his eyes lit up. "Hey, the president and I have looked for the ark, too," he said and proceeded to tell me how he and George Bush once procured U2 reconnaissance photographs of Mount Ararat and knelt on the floor of the Oval Office looking them over with a magnifying glass.

They found nothing.

How could this be? Everyone, from the president of the most powerful nation on earth down to local Kurdish shepherds, has looked for the ark on Mount Ararat. Still no one has been able to present physical evidence of its presence. If it still exists, given its estimated size—longer than a football field and three stories high—it seems incredible that no one has found it by now. Why have so many supposed eyewitnesses failed to bring back a shred of conclusive evidence? And after so many years, and so many attempts, *why*, if the ark indeed lies hidden on Mount Ararat, hasn't someone managed a single irrefutable photo of it?

Some would interpret these as clear signs that investigators ought to train their sights elsewhere. Yet despite the seemingly unending stream of questions, there remain in many minds solid reasons to target this peak. Its size and raw dimensions, for one, seem to make it a compelling candidate. At seventeen thousand feet, Mount Ararat towers over every other peak in the region. And it sports a permanent ice cap, thick and dense enough to conceal an ark. Many point to the mountain's glacial features to explain why the ark hasn't yet been found. For if the ship lay packed in deep ice these thousands of years, they argue, it might appear from its hibernation only rarely (as past sightings seem to suggest) during unusually warm years of heavy melt back. This also explains why so many entertain such high hopes of its being found intact. An icebound ark, after all, might never decay (or only very slowly), and might still be discovered as it peeks out from the edge of the ice, like a frozen mammoth.

The mountain's commanding height provides yet another cause for optimism. Once the rains of the great flood stopped, Noah must have watched patiently from a very high perch for land to reappear gradually.

Genesis 8:5 tells us that it took almost three months for the flood waters to recede before the tops of nearby mountains began to break the surface. Scripture specifically tell us that "on the first day of the tenth month the tops of the mountains became visible," indicating that the mountain cradling the ark had to be the tallest for some distance. Since Mount Ararat looms higher than any peak in a region extending into the Caucasus Mountains to the north, the Taurus Mountains to the west, the Zagros Mountains to the south, and the ancient Elburz range to the southeast, it rightly becomes a prime candidate.

Yet closer inspection reveals that neither Ararat's dense ice cap nor its imposing height supports the theories they seem to defend. As we've established, the peak stands alone in a vast plain, neither within nor nearby a legitimate mountain range. From its summit Noah and his family could hardly have observed *any* other peaks rising from the deep. Moreover, the mountain's estimated age and composition run counter to the profile of a peak once submerged. The *Ararat Report's* Bill Crouse observes that "for a mountain that supposedly rose from the depths of the Great Flood, there seems to be an almost complete lack of evidence that the mountain was ever underwater."[1] He notes missing fossil records and deficient layers of sedimentation, both of which should exist if the peak sat for even a brief time beneath the waves. The mountain's inadequacies point instead to its truer status as an extinct volcano. Crouse believes Ararat's geologic DNA indicates it probably formed during an enormous eruption some centuries *after* the great flood.

Which brings us back to the mystery of Mount Ararat's ice cap. Any who views its icy crown as a sort of protective shroud, within which the ark rests secure and whole, fails to understand the true nature of glacial ice. Glaciers *move;* they flow downward. And glacial ice flows faster near the surface than near the bottom, which means that anything caught within would get sheared into pieces, not preserved. Ararat's grinding, slow-descending glacial plates would long ago have torn the boat to shreds and reduced it to sawdust.

Taken together, these extenuating circumstances make it "difficult to be optimistic that remains of the Ark of Noah might someday be found on Mount Ararat."[2] I reached the same conclusion ten years earlier, after inspecting every nook and cranny of the peak in a high-performance helicopter. But until Phil Burman's phone call, I gave up hope that the ark might still exist. Either the elements had consumed it, or survivors had dismantled it over time for firewood or building materials. Now other possibilities began to suggest themselves. I tended to agree with Crouse's assertion that "from the perspective of history, there seems to be compelling ancient sources which argue for another site as the final berth of Noah's Ark."[3]

I had a lot of questions but few answers. My premature intuitions needed to be developed. I'd tracked some faint footprints through the sand and stumbled on a couple of enticing nuggets: new, unmistakable clues pointing

53

to mountains other than Ararat. Yet Ed Davis's recollections left me perplexed. If he hadn't seen the ark on Mount Ararat, where *had* he seen it?

REVISITING THE DAVIS ACCOUNT

The story itself, and not merely the lie detector test, drew me back. I vividly recalled how the examiner tried to expose Davis as a fraud. He put the old man through his paces yet exited the booth both humbled and befuddled by Davis's steely consistency. The test proved one thing: Davis's testimony could be trusted. He'd seen *something*. But chunks of the puzzle remained missing. In truth I felt less impressed by the polygraph results than in the manner in which Davis told his story. His recollections, uncommonly rich in detail, belied someone trying to propagate a hoax.

I'd watched con men spin their yarns: they always skimped on the details, cutting quickly to the heart of the deception, as in, *"I saw the ark! It was on a big mountain; it looked like a barge."* Whatever details followed usually seemed tacked on for effect. My experience interviewing criminal suspects taught me a typical pattern: a liar's guise *always* starts with the lie itself, then threads outward like a spider's web.

Davis didn't fit the pattern. He led us on a casual guided tour of the countryside before even *mentioning* the ark, its size, or its appearance. He delicately embroidered his descriptions with countless details and lavish background information, chatting on about his friendship with Badi and his work for the Army Corp of Engineers. He summarized in painstaking detail the diversity of the terrain and surrounding lowlands, noting subtle shifts in the weather, recalling odd geologic formations along the trail, the peculiar gait of the horses, the sharp angle of the sun, all the endless, distinctive sights and sounds of his trek to the summit. Then he debated the thermal properties of the clothes they wore, commented on the peculiar customs of the villagers at Noah's vineyards, and even critiqued the respective pots of stew hanging in the hidden enclaves along the way.

Frankly, Davis's cheery insistence on sharing every little tidbit wearied us; we wanted to hear only about the ark. We wanted him to cut to the chase, give us the big scoop. But in hindsight, this irksome tendency did more to sell me on his story than anything else. His stockpiles of minutia would've been impossible to fabricate unless he'd seen it for himself. His propensity to embellish a scene spoke to its authenticity.

All of which, in the end, got us nowhere.

Without knowing where Davis was when he saw it all, the most fascinating details did us no good. Here I must say Davis always expressed lukewarm convictions about the ark's specific whereabouts. I never believed he knew for sure where he'd seen the ark—only that he'd *seen* it.

In three trips to Turkey, I'd continually struggled to line up his account with the actual Mount Ararat. Prominent features we observed flying in close in Aaron's chopper—ridges, rocks, canyons—never jibed with Davis's descriptions. On the one hand he confidently described sizable rivers rushing down the mountain in wide, roaring channels; but as anyone who has ever climbed Mount Ararat knows, it lacks even a single river. Even in years of heavy snowmelt, its volcanic substrata drinks up excess runoff, leaving only a few meager streamlets trickling into the lower valleys.

On the other hand Davis failed completely to notice Mount Ararat's massive ice fields. "Nope, didn't see those," he said indifferently. And distinctive rock formations and trail routes he described (and later meticulously recreated in a hand-drawn topographical map) seemed to belong to another peak altogether. Davis's recitations clashed badly with other so-called eyewitnesses on such fine points as the angle of the ark to the peak and its relationship to the surrounding terrain. I found it astonishing, in fact, that others seemed to be able to read into Davis's accounts enough similarities to keep them interested in Mount Ararat. From my vantage his testimony stood alone.

Privately, I think I always knew Davis's mountain didn't conform to the Turkish Agri Dagh. Yet I rationalized it away, nodding along with those who blamed his advanced age and spotty memory for the discrepancies. Who was I to challenge the Ararat experts who'd made multiple trips to the mountain and knew its secret recesses by heart? Still, hard as I tried, I could never line up Davis's story with the mountain I saw unfold below me from Aaron's helicopter.

It brought me to a crisis of belief. To break the stalemate and sate my curiosity, I dug up the old Ed Davis videotapes stored in my supply closet. Had I missed something in those early interviews? Did his marathon monologues contain hidden clues that might yet shed some light? I popped a tape in the VCR, and within minutes it had validated my suspicions. Important clues whispered to me from the spaces between his words, guiding me forward, like tiny bread crumbs on a faint mountain trail.

On the first tape Davis seemed restfully at ease, sitting at home in his big easy chair. He started off by telling how he'd been stationed in Hamadan, Iran, building roads with the Army Corps of Engineers. He reminisced about his Iranian driver, Badi, who first alerted him to the existence of the ark. While loading rocks on a truck at a Hamadan rock quarry, he said, Badi casually pointed toward a huge mountain range towering far in the distance and said, "That's where my grandfather found the ark."

I tried to listen and watch as one who had never heard Davis (or anyone else) mention Mount Ararat. The technique enlightened me. I saw the strained logic of his observations change dramatically, as when he recounted the road trip he and Badi took to find the ark. Davis said they drove from Hamadan through *Casbeen*, and arrived at his father Abas's village (situated near the base of the mountain) within eight to twelve hours. That would be more than five hundred miles to Mount Ararat on primitive, rutted roads— accomplished in a 1940s Army truck, in slightly more than an average work

55

day. Even on today's modern interstates, riding in a new car, such a schedule would be hard to maintain. But back then, on rugged roads, trundling
five hundred miles through the mountains in that time span? It strikes one
as insane. I pulled out a map of the region and noted a handful of mountains
(some of them of requisite size and elevation) situated within striking distance of Hamadan. All lay well within Iran's borders.

Then, in one of Davis's last interviews, the topic of Badi's ethnicity
came up. The guide's roots had a direct relation to the location of his village, and thus the identity of the mountain. Davis said Badi was a tribal
leader of some sort but couldn't seem to remember if he was a "Kurd" or a
"Lourd." (Properly spelled Lors, or Lurs, as they are sometimes known in
English. Thought to be part Persian, part Arab in origin, they inhabit the
province of Lorestan, as well as a wider, mountainous region of western
Iran.[4]) If Badi were a Kurd, it seemed reasonable that his village sat near the
base of Mount Ararat; Kurdish tribes have for centuries migrated and settled throughout eastern Turkey, northeast Iraq, some states in the former
USSR, and even into western Iran. But if Badi were indeed a "Lourd," or
Lur (as Davis later confirmed), then it seemed far more plausible they'd
climbed a mountain in Iran. The Lurs, simply put, live in Iran. How preposterous to think Badi would have held a leadership post in a village in
eastern Turkey, at the heart of a Kurdish population center!

The sum of the evidence didn't add up. The obvious travel distances
and social demographics made it almost impossible to imagine that Davis
saw the ark on Mount Ararat.

But something else bothered me. I couldn't help noticing the consis-
tent and exasperating manner in which the interviewers kept *leading* Davis
through the interviews. They coached him, interrupted him whenever he
mentioned the mountain or the ark, forever interjecting, "That's Mount
Ararat, *right* Ed?" or trying to mold his observations to fit a handy map of
the Turkish peak. It irritated Davis, too. He'd hem and haw and shrug as if
to say, "I'm not sure," then finally mutter a reluctant, "Well, I guess so."
Other times Davis would recall the angle of the slope on a particular ridge,
or envision the layout of the canyon floor from a certain ledge, and find
himself halted in mid-sentence: "You're referring now to the Ahora Gorge!"
Or, "Now you're describing the Cehennem Dere! *Right*, Ed?" In each
instance Davis's facial expression and body language shouted, "*I don't know.
It could've been Mount Ararat, or it could have been some other mountain altogether.*" Yet his words invariably acceded to the carefully guided questions.

It pained me to watch. By the last tape a disturbing transformation had
taken place. Ed had bent to the pressure and now seemed quite agreeable to
the suggestion that he had, in fact, climbed Mount Ararat. Though his
descriptions rarely, if ever, reconciled with Mount Ararat's true physical
profile, he clearly wanted "to help." I understood. This old man had come
to enjoy the attention he received from men who seemed genuinely
entranced by his story. A transition had indeed occurred. Where I once saw

a man wholly at ease in his stubborn self-confidence, I now saw someone who simply wanted to please. Subconsciously he had capitulated, worn down by the constant editorial input of men with a proprietary interest in Mount Ararat. The search for the truth got lost, along with any objectivity.

It looked a lot like the story of Mount Sinai, except this time with a boat. Everything I had assumed now appeared to be based on myth, legend, and scarcely veiled prejudice. Mount Ararat in Turkey had become a very poor candidate for the resting place of the ark. Yet as my good friend, professor Ken Durham, said, "Once a holy site, always a holy site." It's almost impossible to break the stranglehold tradition exerts over history's anointed landmarks.

My observations sent me scurrying back to the library, searching through old tomes on the ancient lands of Assyria, studying maps on the Mesopotamian Valley, grabbing anything I could find on the long-lost kingdoms of Armenia. Cross-referencing these texts with early Bible translations, I stumbled upon what may be the earliest literary reference to Noah's ark landing on the mountain we know today as Mount Ararat, written in the thirteenth century A.D., by a fellow named William of Rubruck. Rubruck's travelogue, *The Journey of William Rubruck to the Eastern Parts of the World; 1253-1255*, chronicled an old Armenian folk tradition that Noah's ark had settled atop Mt. Masis (the Armenian term of Agri Dagh), or Mount Ararat.

I found far more interesting, though, an even earlier account written by Faustus of Byzantium in the fourth century A.D. Nine hundred years prior to Rubruck, Faustus coined the term "Mount Ararat" in reference to a specific mountain—versus a *region*—for the landing place of the ark. Remarkably, their stories sounded almost identical, each relating the tale of a monk who tried to scale "Mount Ararat" in search for Noah's ark. The monk fell short, but not until an angel of the Lord brought him a piece of the ark as a consolation prize.

What's strange about these nearly identical accounts, written nearly a millennia apart, is that, in his fourth-century essay, Faustus indeed placed the incident on Mount Ararat—but *not* in Turkey. His Mount Ararat lay hundreds of miles south in the Gordyaen Mountains, along Iraq's northern border. Rubruck's latter version had somehow made a drastic leap, either by mistake or as a result of endless repetition, and had transported the monk, ark, and angel to *Turkey's* Mount Ararat. From my studies on Mount Sinai, I recognized it as the kind of leap that occurs more frequently than one would expect.

Snippets of clues emerged, each dragging me farther from Turkey. Reviewing the Ed Davis tapes, I sensed more urgently than ever that he'd seen the ark, or at least, what he thought was the ark.

Only not where everyone was *telling* him he'd seen it.

Now I had to dig in my heels, trying to piece together a fractured, arcane picture. If Noah's ark were ever to be found, I determined, I'd first have to set my sights *east* of Shinar.

SEVEΠ

THE MOUNTAINS OF NOAH

By faith Noah, when warned about things not yet seen, in holy fear built an ark to save his family. By his faith he condemned the world and became heir of the righteousness that comes by faith (Heb. 11:7).

The writers of the New Testament clearly revered Noah as a man of faith. They employed imagery of both the flood and the ark as warnings of coming judgment and the promise of salvation. Peter, for instance, uses the waters of the flood to symbolize a type of saving baptism—"not the removal of dirt from the body but the pledge of a good conscience toward God. It saves you by the resurrection of Jesus Christ, who has gone into heaven and is at God's right hand" (1 Pet. 3:21–22).

Yet they didn't show much interest in nailing down the actual location of the ark. Aside from the Genesis passages, the Bible mentions Noah's ark in only four other instances: Matthew 24:38; Luke 17:27; Hebrews 11:7; and 1 Peter 3:20—and never in reference to where it might be found. Contrast this with the generous offering of ark speculations contained in ancient literature. Authors in antiquity graced countless books with explicit references to Noah, the ark, and its prospective landing sites.

In fact, ancient fascination with the topic contrasts sharply with the general indifference of more recent times. Only in the last two centuries—as the Bible came under increasing fire from secular groups—have archaeologists and Bible believers begun hunting these historic artifacts in earnest. To that end Noah's ark occupies a position of rare prominence.

In searching for Mount Sinai, I realized that, though the Bible seldom spells out exact locations for its famous landmarks, it rarely fails to yield potent, subtle clues pointing toward the right direction. That same principle held in my early ark research. As we've seen, Genesis 11:2 says that after the flood waters receded, Noah's descendants journeyed "from the east"[1] to settle in the land of Shinar. Today we understand Shinar as the broad Iraqi valley surrounding modern-day Baghdad. So one verse serves two functions: it gives us the strongest possible clue that the ark came to rest somewhere in the direction of modern-day Iran; and it tells us the ark couldn't have landed on Turkey's Mount Ararat.

Yet we needn't rest our case on a single verse. The same block of text offers other hints. Earlier in Genesis we read of the travels and conquests of Nimrod, Noah's great-grandson. Nimrod was "a mighty warrior on the earth . . . a mighty hunter before the LORD" (Gen. 10:8–9), and his early conquests included the cities of "Babylon, Erech, Akkad and Calneh," all in Shinar. After settling the land of Shinar, however, Scripture says Nimrod traveled "to Assyria, where he built *Nineveh*" (Gen. 10:10–11).

Here the Bible provides more rich food for thought. This passage strongly suggests that Noah's descendants wouldn't have migrated to Shinar from the region of Mount Ararat in Turkey. Nimrod first settled in Shinar, then journeyed north to conquer Nineveh in northern Iraq. Why would a conqueror have journeyed north to Nineveh if he'd just come south through that region from Turkey? Chances are he wouldn't have. Not only do almost impassable mountain ranges form a veritable wall between Turkey and the Mesopotamia Valley, but a military man like Nimrod wouldn't have backtracked to subdue a city in a region he'd just visited. Rather, as Genesis 11:1 plainly states, Noah's descendants journeyed from the *east* to settle Shinar, *then* Nimrod cut a path north to conquer Nineveh.

While the Bible refuses to tell us exactly where the ark may be, it provides plenty of clues telling us where the ark clearly is *not*. As the clues add up, it appears more logical to pursue a landing site in Iran, or points farther east (see map, pg. 44).

OF FLOODS AND ARKS

The potent combination of human curiosity and long tradition has fueled a vast archive of colliding assumptions. In the twentieth century this pair has spawned a tendency to gather every ancient report and alleged sighting of the ark pertaining to "Mount Ararat" and automatically interpret it to mean Agri Dagh in Turkey. While expedient, such a trap clashes first with Scripture, then with the dozens of ark landing sites proposed through the millennia. Some bear the name Mount Ararat; most, however, claim no relation whatever to the majestic mountain in eastern Turkey.

Hidden within the pages of antiquities' obscure texts lies a veritable treasure trove of early sources on both the great flood *and* the boat that bore our ancestors to safety.

Consider the crumbled shards of baked clay discovered in the 1850s by a British archaeologist in ancient Nineveh. These old clay tablets, called cuniform inscriptions, related (in a strange language) the story of an ancient, catastrophic deluge that covered the earth. The tablets came to be known as the Gilgamesh epic, but in their time they served as a swift kick to an archaeological establishment that had mocked the story of Noah as little more than a cartoon parable. Its unmistakable narrative of a family and animals entering a boat, of a fierce storm that raged for many days, and of the release of a dove, proved that commentary on the flood extended well beyond the pages of the Bible.[2]

The Gilgamesh epic is but one of several ancient sources whispering to us of the flood. An obscure Sumerian text, thirty-six hundred years old (written centuries before the birth of Moses), also recounts a great flood and humanity's survival on a boat. Or consider the Atrakhasis epic, penned some thirty-six hundred years ago, about a great flood and of animals herded into a great boat as a mighty storm rages.[3] From another time and place come the forty-five-hundred-year-old writings of Naram-Sin, a famous king of ancient Akkad. He relates an account of a massive deluge of water occurring early in humankind's history.

All relate strikingly similar versions of an event largely dismissed by modern science. From vastly distant realms, and in languages unrelated, we find a common record of a catastrophic flood that occurred at the dawn of recorded history. Most make at least passing reference to a great boat.

Untold volumes contain cryptic references to a mountain, or mountains, upon which a big ship alighted. If these present a less unified record of events, they seem no less compelling. The more one reads these candid accounts, the more it seems that numerous villages and provinces in the Near East boast their own ark tradition, each commemorating its own landing site.

Included in this ancient lexicon of ark-ana we find a tradition centered around the fifty-six-hundred-foot peak Jabal Judi, cited in the Muslim Koran and located in present-day north-central Saudi Arabia. While obviously far removed from the famed Turkish mountain, it nonetheless had its champion in the second century: Bishop Theophilus of Antioch confidently reported, "The remains of the ark are to be seen in the Arabian mountains to this day." The Muslim tradition seems to establish a new location for the ark and includes the odd belief that the ark sailed seven times around the Kaaba in Mecca before traveling to its final resting place.[4]

Not so, says Nicholas of Damascus.[5] He's the only historian who specifically names a peak where the ark came to rest. In 30 B.C., Nicholas wrote that the ark landed on a summit called Mount Baris, perched "above the Minyas in Armenia." Nicholas further noted that upon Mount Baris, "many refugees found safety at the time of the flood, and one man, transported on an ark, grounded on the summit, and relics of the timbers were long preserved; this might well be the same man of whom Moses, the Jewish legislator, wrote."[6] Not surprisingly, Nicholas neglected to spell out clearly the actual location of Mount Baris.

Lloyd R. Bailey, associate professor of Old Testament at Duke Divinity School and author of *Where Is Noah's Ark?*, suggests it might be a high butte at the northern boundary of what scholars believe to be ancient Armenia. Yet Bailey says, "There is no real reason to identify it with Mount Ararat (Agri Dagh)."[7] Yet according to Nicholas, we need to find a mountain that lies north of the Minyas. Dr. John Warwick Montgomery, author of *The Quest for Noah's Ark*, suggests that "Minyas" relates to the Minni tribes,[8] who hailed from the region south and east of Lake Urmia in northwest Iran. The tallest mountain in this region is Mount Sabalon, at nearly sixteen thousand feet.

From here the ancient record bobs and weaves around a muddle of far-reaching speculations. I found most of them impossible to trace. The Samaritan Pentateuch, for example (a manuscript containing highly edited versions of the first five books in the Old Testament) declared in the fifth century B.C. that Noah's ark had settled in the Kurdish mountains north of Assyria.[9] That's like saying the ark landed somewhere in a region the size of New Zealand, a huge territory encompassing any number of mountain ranges and thousands of square miles of terrain. Large blocks of "Kurdish mountains" can be found straddling the borders of Iraq, Iran, Turkey, and the former Soviet Union.

Other sources place the ark somewhere in the Qardu mountains, also known as the Gordian, or Gordyene mountains. According to the Targums, the ancient Aramaic tomes written for the Jews returning from Babylon, the Qardu lie some distance south and southeast of the traditional Mount Ararat, between the Tigris and Upper Zab rivers.[10] Such broad generalities do little to pinpoint the mountain of Noah.

Elsewhere we find Josephus, the historian of the Jews for the Roman Empire and a contemporary of the apostle Paul, speculating on the ark's whereabouts. Three times in his *Antiquities of the Jews*, he quoted the Chaldean priest, Berossus, in placing the ark squarely in the "Cordyaean" mountains (likely derived from "Gordian"). Berossus claimed that "a portion of the vessel still survives in Armenia on the mountain of the Cordyaeans, and that persons carry off pieces of the bitumen, which they use as talismans."[11]

Some believe the peak spoken of by Berossus to be Cudi Dagh, so named by the Turks, and sitting about two hundred miles south of Mount Ararat near the Turkish-Iraqi border. It not only contains many archaeological ruins pertaining to the ark but was also believed by the ancient Nestorians (Syriac-speaking Christians) to have sheltered the boat. They contended the giant boat settled somewhere on Cudi Dagh's sixty-eight-hundred-foot summit, towering just north of the Tigris River at the edge of the Cordyene/Qardu range. They built several monasteries on the mountain to commemorate it; the one called the "Cloister of the Ark" is said to have been destroyed by lightning in 766 A.D.[12]

Then comes a tradition hailing from the seventh century A.D., which seems to contradict itself. Found in a brief passage in the Koran, we read that, "The ark came to rest upon Al-Judi," or (as translated by the *Modern Muslim Encyclopedia*) "Jebel Judi." This passage argues that the mountain lies deep in the "Judi" mountains of Saudi Arabia—a theory sorely at odds with the ninth century A.D. conviction of Bishop Eutychius of Alexandria, who observed that the ark rested on a *different* Mount Judi: "The ark rested on the mountains of Ararat, that is Jabal Judi near Mosul." This site lies nowhere near Saudi Arabia; Mosul was an ancient city near Nineveh, some 80 miles south of Cudi Dagh and a far cry from the Arabian mountain cited in the Koran.[13]

Adding to this rich, disorienting tapestry—but doing little to narrow the search—are the words of Benjamin of Tudela. Writing in the twelfth century A.D., Benjamin reported traveling "two days to Jesireh Ben Omar, an island in the Tigris on the foot of Mount Ararat . . . on which the ark of Noah rested. Omar Ben al-Khatab removed the ark from the summit of the two mountains and made a mosque of it." Of which Mount Ararat does he speak? It is impossible to know for sure.

Or consider the memo of Vincent of Beauvais, whose thirteenth century A.D. treatise recalls a noble city in Armenia called Ani, which sits near "Mount Ararat, where Noah's Ark rests, and at the foot of that mountain is the first city which Noah built, called Laudume." Whether these reports conflict or agree, I cannot say.[14]

Last, we hear from none other than Marco Polo. Jotting in his fourteenth-century A.D. journal, he said, "In the heart of Greater Armenia is a very high mountain, shaped like a cube, on which Noah's ark is said to have rested, whence it is called the Mountain of Noah's Ark. It is so broad and long that it takes more than two days to go round it."[15]

These reports (and others not mentioned) make obvious that the story of the ark and the flood pervades Christendom and the Muslim world. Certainly some of these accounts intersect and agree, using terms peculiar to their age. Yet examined together, they present a widely diverse and deeply divided catalog, suggesting the ark landed anywhere from the ramparts of north-central Saudi Arabia to southern Soviet Georgia, from northwestern Iran to somewhere along the border of northern Iraq, and as far west as Celaenae in ancient Phygria (western Turkey) to the traditional Mount Ararat in eastern Turkey.

I cannot begin to guess the reasons for this vast difference in ark history. All reports appear rooted in eyewitness testimony. Yet given the wide disparities, all likewise seem to have been molded prejudicially to fit a region's religious customs or culture.

In the end I kept my own analysis simple and focused. Wading through reams of mixed accounts, wrestling to make sense of it all, a single question floated above the tumult. A still, small voice kept whispering: Where are the *real* mountains of Ararat?

I came back repeatedly to the simplest reference point: Genesis 11:2. No matter what Josephus or Nicholas of Damascus or the Nestorians said, Scripture anchored me—the mountains of Ararat lie *east* of Shinar. The mountains of Ararat lie *east* of Iraq. My investigative instincts nudged me to the realization of the most likely site for the mountains of Ararat: *Iran!* This soft refrain became a symphony ringing in my ears: *The remains of the ark, if they still exist, lie in Iran!*

Iran!—sitting bold, unabashed, unavoidably due east of ancient Babylon—suddenly loomed large. After months of speculation and research, Iran alone seemed to withstand the biblical litmus test.

But whittling it down to a manageable framework was another matter!

Finding the ark in such a vast expanse would be like locating a ruined WWII blimp hangar in a state the size of Alaska. No ark searcher had investigated that region before. While I'm a determined man, the scope of the task alarmed me. Here again I deferred to Jim Irwin. He once told me: "Faced with an impossible situation—persist, press on, and persevere."

The time had come to test the theory.

Eight

EAST OF SHINAR

"Why don't you just go for it?"

"*What?*"

I didn't expect to hear those words from Terry, my wife. So I asked again.

"Did you *hear* me? I said I'm thinking of going to Iran to do research on Noah's ark."

"I heard you, Bob," she said softly, her eyes reflecting quiet resignation. "You know I'm not keen on your going to Iran, but if you definitely feel God is guiding you, I support you." She paused, then added: "Think of it, Bob. If you ever found that old boat, it would change the way people look at the Bible, evolution, everything. If you think the ark is there, go for it!"

Terry is my best friend. She's been my biggest supporter since the day I formed BASE Institute and embarked on this wild career. She demonstrated a saintly patience and cheerful heart while I traveled all over the world searching for biblical artifacts. She'd been my confidante, sounding board, and a calm, listening ear. More than that, she provided a steadying voice of reason in moments of doubt; she never hesitated to provide stern words of caution in the face of my crazy schemes. I trusted her instincts and more than once backed off a dangerous project when she expressed grave concerns.

So when she said, "Go for it!"—into *Iran!*—I thought I must be hearing things. Didn't she know? Iran regards the United States as the "Great Satan." U.S. citizens simply don't travel there. A travel advisory, in effect for more than two decades, warns Americans against even the thought of visiting the Islamic Republic of Iran. And for good reason. It seemed like only yesterday that I sat gripped by a TV set pulsing with news of the Iran hostage crisis.

The shah of Iran, as I recalled, had been admitted into the United States for medical treatment when Iranian militants seized the U.S. Embassy in Tehran. They took sixty-six Americans hostage, promising their release if the United States returned the shah, under a death sentence, to stand trial in Iran. President Carter refused and struck back with economic sanctions. When the militants finally released their prisoners in January 1981—444 days later—it marked the start of a long, ugly season of self-defeating relations between these two countries.

In the hearts and minds of many Iranians, we committed the unforgivable sin of supporting the late shah and his hated Pahlavi regime, blamed for perhaps the worst cycle of poverty, joblessness, and repression in Iran's history. While the shah and his inner circle enriched themselves on a flood of petro-dollars, the masses suffered from runaway inflation and the abuse of the shah's Savak security force, which killed thousands of demonstrators in the streets of Tehran.

America added insult to injury by supporting Iraq in the bloody Iran-Iraq War of 1980–88, in which Iraq used poison gas to invade Iran's oil-rich Khuzestan Province. Things worsened when the U.S. shot down an unarmed Iranian jetliner over the Persian Gulf in 1988.

The domestic chaos created by Ayatollah Khomeini's regime prompted Iran to turn increasingly inward and hostile toward outsiders. Following the Ayatollah's death in 1989, a shaky economy crippled the country, while the Persian Gulf War further exacerbated anti-Western animosities. Today Iran finds itself ostracized by the international community for its complicity with violent terrorist groups like the Hezbollah and the Iranian Revolutionary Guard—each responsible for a series of bloody bombings and kidnappings around the globe.

Given this sordid past, I doubted I could have picked a more threatening environment in which to commence my search for the ark. Two decades after the hostage crisis, Iran remained one of the most fearsome places on earth for a traveling American. Yet as I saw it, I had no choice. I felt I had to take a risk.

I made a quick mental note of the pros and cons of blitzing Iran. On the pro side, it's cheap to travel there. If I could swing a visa, it meant taking one week of my life to have a fun adventure, see some exotic new sights, and maybe even catch a drift of the ark. In the best-case scenario, everything goes smoothly, and I make the discovery of the ages. At worst, I could get arrested, thrown in jail, or (gulp) . . . I didn't finish the thought.

I calculated five to three in favor of going.

Wait a minute!

I caught myself in this farfetched daydream. Was I *crazy?* This was *Iran.* I turned to Terry.

"Are you trying to get rid of me?" I asked. "They *hate* Americans in Iran! They regard us as *heathens*. They despise our culture as a modern-day Sodom and Gomorrah."

My good wife just smiled and put her hand on my shoulder.

"Don't worry about it, Bob," she said. "I'll get the life insurance agent on speed dial and hope for the best. I knew when I married you I wasn't getting a normal husband." We both laughed. "Besides," she added, "I couldn't stop you if I tried."

She closed the door behind her. She knew me too well. I pulled out a phone book and started flipping pages to see about getting a visa into Iran.

IRAN OR BUST

Initial reports brought no encouragement. I kept slamming my head into the same brick wall of bureaucratic double speak I'd encountered trying to enter Saudi Arabia. The more foreign consulates and travel consultants I spoke with, the less likely it appeared I'd get a visa.

Iran has no industry to speak of, which might provide a prospective "investor" a good excuse to visit; and tourism there is all but extinct. Even a subtle softening of relations between the countries (prompted by Iran's desire to boost domestic tourism), had yet to trickle down to the travel bureaus. Its new leadership announced its readiness to open its doors to foreign tourists, but Iran being Iran, the authorities failed to inform its consulates of the new policy. "Americans are not traveling in Iran!" they all agreed, as if reading from identical press releases.

Next I checked off a very short list of contacts who might have the clout or connections to pull a few strings. I called upon a Jewish attorney I knew in New York City. He'd sought me out on the Mount Sinai discovery and once mentioned some friends who might be willing and able to assist me—clients of his, strategically employed at five travel agencies in the Big Apple. None proved much help; each expressed incredulity that I wanted to visit Iran, and each recited the standard, brusque refrain: "Americans are not traveling in Iran."

Now I began to worry. I needed a breakthrough while I still had the nerve to "go for it." It didn't take long to realize I would have to pull the strings myself. I asked the attorney to fax me the New York City Yellow Pages and quickly noticed several listings for Iranian travel agencies. I called them all, but none wanted to help a non-Iranian from Colorado travel to a country where he might get shot. Finally, I saw a listing for an agency called Unique Travel. I called, and a woman named Nahid answered the phone. I asked her about a visa. "Yes, I can do that!" she replied without hesitation. It happened that her Jewish relatives still lived in Iran, part of a shrinking but still sizable Jewish population active in the bazaar and jewelry trade in the cities of Tehran, Hamadan, Shiraz, and Esfahan. "We're all descendants of the Jerusalem Jews," Nahid said. When I didn't make the connection, she clarified: "You know! The Jews taken captive in Jerusalem by Nebuchadnezzar, and sent to live as exiles in Persia during the time of Esther and Mordecai" (Esth. 2:5–7).

Descendants of Esther and Mordecai . . . in *Iran?* I hadn't considered that, but it pleased me to be reminded of the eminent role Persia played in the Old Testament. Nahid turned out to be a godsend. She lined up my visa in no time. A few faxes sent back and forth to her Jewish cousins did the trick; then she hooked me up with a guide, a fellow familiar with the terrain and friendly to my cause. My spirits soared; it looked like a done deal. I set a date of departure, reserved my plane tickets, and set about planning my itinerary.

THE ZAGROS MOUNTAINS

I narrowed my search to the Zagros Mountains, a rugged range straddling the Iraqi/Iranian border. Scripture clearly instructed me to set my sights *east of Shinar*. The Zagros sat due east of modern-day Baghdad, running southeast to northwest from the Persian Gulf to southeastern Turkey. It seemed a logical place to start.

Phil Burman disagreed. He believed the mountains of Ararat lay much farther east, perhaps into Afghanistan, or even the high mountains of Tibet. But those sites never made sense to me, primarily because the flood's survivors would somehow have had to cross Iran's Dasht-E Kavir Desert. That central Iranian plateau remains one of the most inhospitable places on earth, an arid, salty wasteland so vast and hot that ancient populations avoided it like death. Even today travelers consider it almost impassable; I couldn't see how even a stubborn warrior like Nimrod would willingly cross it to reach Shinar, a land he'd never seen.

No, the real mountains of Ararat lay "east of Shinar," indeed—but not east of the Dasht-E Kavir. I put my money on the Zagros Mountains, rising like a great granite curtain dividing Iran from Iraq. Even Cyrus the Great in the sixth century B.C., leading his great army west from Persia to attack Babylon, had to zigzag through the Zagros along the Diyala River to reach his adversary.[1] Perhaps Noah's descendants blazed a similar trail as they migrated west into the Mesopotamia Valley.

COINCIDENCE OR SOMETHING ELSE?

By now I'd begun to feel a sharper sense of mission. I retraced the bizarre twists and turns that landed me in the middle of this ominous undertaking; reexamining, for instance, my friendship with Jim Irwin. If he hadn't taken me under his wing all those years ago, I never would have given Noah's ark a passing nod. And what of Ed Davis? His raspy words—*"You won't believe how big it is!"*—echoed in my head ten years after our last meeting. Or Phil Burman? He pointed me east of Shinar, while everyone else remained glued to Mount Ararat.

Could mere *coincidence* explain all this? Or was something else, something larger, at work? Was that God tapping me on the shoulder? Could he be tagging me to take the search in another direction, perhaps even one day to *find* the ark? It sounded crazy, but these same gray impressions, these same unspoken impulses and soft whisperings, once put me on the scent of Mount Sinai. The same sense of calling I felt a decade earlier had emboldened me to infiltrate Saudi Arabia—a land no more friendly to Americans than Iran—to launch a do-or-die search for the mountain of God.

So I wondered: could I use the same tactics in Iran that worked so well in Saudi Arabia? To find Mount Sinai I simply followed the trail sketched in the Bible and then asked the locals, "Where is Jabal Musa?" I quickly discovered the Bedouins confirmed what Scripture hinted. The locals knew all about it: the prophet Musa (Moses) had camped in their towns; the Hebrews had refreshed themselves at their springs. The signposts of the great Exodus lay everywhere, hidden within the Saudi landscape. Would the same blunt, unvarnished strategy work in Iran? I didn't have a clue, but it couldn't hurt to try.

I settled the matter in my mind. What harm could come from flying into Tehran, hiring a guide, driving to the southeast rim of the Zagros mountains, and poking around? I'd simply ask the locals if anyone had heard of Noah's ark. Maybe I could look in museums and check out the local libraries—perhaps I'd get lucky and find a clue. If local traditions of the ark existed, it shouldn't take long to ferret them out. Perhaps some old Lourdish shepherds might step up and take me straight to the ark, just as they had Ed Davis.

DARK FOREBODINGS

From the beginning I planned to take two cameramen to film the journey. I suspected the trip might yield some interesting sights and possibly supply valuable footage for a future video. I'd learned the hard way to plan ahead: I didn't want to get over there, see something exciting, then have no way of documenting it. It matters little how electrifying one's sighting or discovery might be; if you don't catch it on film, you have no story. So I contacted a pair of topflight videographers and debriefed them on the trip. They seemed intrigued and enticed by the mission and appeared eager to get underway. We worked up an agreement and nailed down our strategy. Everything seemed to be falling into place.

Enter the truly bizarre.

Less than two weeks before our departure date, both cameramen called me. The breathless edge in their voices betrayed their cold feet. As they began asking questions, they realized dangerous territory lay ahead. At first they gave me a whole string of excuses, saying this and that had come up, that it didn't seem a good time to go. But when pressed, the truth came out. Each confessed to paralyzing fears about entering Iran. One said he'd endured a series of bad dreams about the trip and took them as a sign to stay home. The other said a friend had described an equally chilling dream, prophesying that if he went, he wouldn't return. I didn't know what to say. Both apologized profusely, but I couldn't, and wouldn't, talk either out of backing out. So mere days before leaving, I found myself alone.

The incident reminded me how deeply the specter of Iran still shakes the American psyche. That country remains a thorn in our national consciousness; the old hostage footage still plays in our minds, haunting us and framing Iran and its people as dark and forbidding—a place where you might get kidnapped or killed.

A film crew would've eased my burden and provided needed companionship and support if something went wrong, but now I planned to head into the lion's den by myself, jumping headlong into the unknown. No one I knew had ever traveled in Iran as a tourist; the only Americans I could ask included former hostages or Iranian immigrants. Bad scenarios ran through my mind. Fear welled up, and I started questioning my motives: *Am I even supposed to go? Am I walking into a trap?*

Terry saw my distress and asked, "What are you going to do?" I shrugged. I didn't seem to have a choice. I knew in my heart I *had* to go, or rather I felt *called*. I saw myself on a strange collision course with Iran. I needed to find out if that region harbored any legends, traditions, or historical references to Noah's ark.

I shook off my anxiety and drew an imaginary line in the sand to prevent me from turning back. I visited the camera shop and bought a small, expensive digital video camera; then I bought a battery charger and lots of film. Finally, I took out a good life insurance policy and started packing my bags. On November 17, with a tourist visa in my vest and a lump in my throat, I hopped a plane for Tehran.

Part Three

IRAN, ROUND ONE

Map of Armenia showing Ararat Mons (Mountains in Region of Northwest Iran) from *Petras Plantius 1552—1622* Amsterdam.

Πiπe

INTO PERSIA

In addition to subtle clues contained in Scripture, other fascinating (and seemingly unrelated) facts support the idea that Noah and his family settled in Persia following the great flood and from there fanned out into surrounding Asia to rebuild the human race.

An inquisitive mind might, for instance, be interested to learn that the oldest known written language, Proto-Elamite,[1] originated in Iran. ("Elamite" got its name from Elam, Noah's grandson, a man some believe founded the Elamite Empire in southwestern Iran.) Or that the world's oldest known pottery, unearthed in the dusty plains west of the Dasht-E Kavir desert, also came from central Iran. A veritable paradise for wildlife, Iran boasts 129 species of mammals—a haven nearly equal to the whole of Europe, which is four times larger and much more varied ecologically.[2] Iran contains some of the most abundant species of birds (450) and lizards (some 250) on the planet[3] and likely spawned some of the world's first cultivated grains and domesticated animals. All these enticing bits of trivia contribute to the rich testimony of the land's ancient roots. Weighed together, they tempt one to conclude that, just perhaps, Iran became the cradle of life for modern civilization following a devastating global flood.

While it's interesting to speculate on such things, to the newcomer landing in teeming, sooty Tehran, such thoughts quickly fade. Circling Tehran's international airport, Iran looks just like scores of densely populated, heavily polluted societies around the globe. Upon landing, passengers funnel into a great, gray, cinder-block structure devoid of charm or warmth, its corridors crawling with more armed guards than anywhere I'd visited. I deplaned in late afternoon, took a deep breath, and promptly found myself neck deep in a gauntlet of security checkpoints.

Since my exploits in Saudi Arabia, I'd learned to regard this compulsory rite of travel in the Middle East with particular dread; and right on cue, as I approached the first checkpoint, an Iranian security guard eyed me with surly disdain. *What's he looking at?* I wondered, my imagination taking quick flight.

Handing the customs officer my visas and passport, I braced myself for the worst, knowing the nightmarish ordeal of having one's documents pored over and one's bags searched in countries hostile to the U.S. In Iran, as in Saudi Arabia, enduring the scrutiny of young, clench-jawed officers trained in the art of making you sweat becomes an aggressive, invasive rite. They search passenger's eyes for the least sign of strain, then tap their computer keyboards with such speed and urgency that one might easily imagine his smallest childhood indiscretions popping up on the monitor. Five minutes of this prepares one to run for the nearest exit. I'd been in Iran less than fifteen minutes, and the veins in my temples already pounded.

Oh No! I thought, *what are they finding?* I imagined them looking at a ten-year-old arrest warrant from Saudi Arabia, marking me as an enemy of the kingdom, a blasphemer of Mohammed, a trespasser suspected of defiling forbidden archaeological grounds. *What a fool!*, I thought. To think I could waltz into Iran, collect my luggage, and be on my way. With concern turning fast to panic, I feared Muslim countries must be linked by a common database, helping them keep a sharp lookout for one another's heathen fugitives. At that moment I envisioned the guard staring at my profile on a digital wanted poster labeled: *"Arrest on sight!"*

Then, as abruptly as it all began, it ended.

The young officer stopped typing, looked up, and calmly handed me back my visa, then motioned me on to baggage claim. "Yes," I stammered, "Thank you." Fighting for composure, I grabbed my paperwork, claimed my bags, and breezed through the final security gates. *Hallelujah!* I wanted to shout. I'd made it into Iran and done it legally.

Once outside the terminal, I searched for my guide, picturing a stocky, bearded Iranian with one tooth and a patch over his eye, probably named Ali. Nahid said he'd meet me in the waiting area, but a huge crowd milled about, dozens calling out, waving signs with people's names. I finally saw my name bobbing up and down on a dainty placard toward the back, in the hand of a *woman* in full Iranian raiment.

I looked her over for a moment. Young and petite, arrayed in customary dark head-scarf, she wore the traditional black chador, the loose, flowing, one-piece cloak that covers Iranian women from head to ankle. I raised a hand and she approached: "Mr. Bob . . . hello, my name is Fatima. Welcome to Tehran. I am your guide."

Expecting a man, I blurted out something idiotic like, "Oh—you're a woman." A clumsy start, I knew I offended her. She replied graciously. "I'm sorry you are disappointed. But I am your appointed guide. If you have all your bags, we shall go! You will rest tonight, and tomorrow we will tour Tehran. The next day we will leave for Ahfaz."

Though touring Iran with a woman didn't seem such a good idea, I soon warmed to it. Her English struck me as flawless. About thirty years old, with dark, olive skin, Fatima seemed friendly enough, and under her scarf I saw kind, pleasant eyes. I reached out to shake her hand, offering an apology for my clumsy greeting, but she pulled back. "No, I'm sorry," she said, "it is not allowed."

It reminded me that I had a world of things to learn about Iranian etiquette, a problem greatly complicated by the fact I'd been assigned a female guide. I knew, for instance, that men cannot even *sit* next to a woman in Iran unless specifically invited to do so. Yet here stood Fatima, the lovely, smiling face of Iran to the outside world: a pure-blooded Iranian, devout Muslim, highly educated—holder of two masters degrees, one in engineering. On the surface, anyway, she seemed a public relations dream. I understood why Iran's travel bureau paired her with an American tourist. Fatima hailed a taxi, and we sped through Tehran's swarming streets to the stately Grand Azadi Hotel.

STREETS OF TEHRAN

I'd read that Iran sat near the bottom of the list of the world's loveliest capitals, and the rumors proved true. Tehran's thick pollution, chronic overcrowding, and seeming lack of responsible civic planning made it a city even a travel agent would have trouble praising. At first blush it seemed anything but the exotic Persian crossroads steeped in Oriental splendor I'd envisioned.

Viewed from the backseat of our taxi, Tehran seemed to have been built with a complete lack of architectural vision or sense of aesthetics. Rather than remind one of the romance and beauty of Persia's renowned spiritual center, its buildings and general character conjured up the stark austerity of East Berlin. Worse, the entire city seemed to be choking under a shroud of smog. Nahid said the cloud gets so dense in summertime that multitudes flee to the mountains or to the beaches of the Caspian Sea and that those with weak hearts must lock themselves indoors.

Still I reminded myself that Tehran represents the uncontested spiritual and economic center of every field of Iranian life. It's not only the capital of Iran and the country's largest city, but its citizenry, now approaching fourteen million, makes it one of the most populous cities on earth. The Iranian Islamic Revolution—the first of its kind in the world—sprang from the streets of Tehran, and in ways I couldn't begin to fathom, this dingy sprawl of concrete and smokestacks remained a revolutionary city at heart. I didn't deceive myself that I would soon understand the inner workings of the

Iranian government, or how it interfaces with this society's age-old religious mores. In my Iranian guidebook under "Government," it states simply, "Iranian politics are a complete mystery."

Wending our way through oppressive traffic, Fatima defended Tehran, noting that despite its culturally adrift appearance, the city boasts excellent museums, wonderful restaurants, and, if you know where to look within its labyrinthine maze of streets, a diverse offering of shops, bazaars, and boutiques. Prepared, even eager, to find evidence to reverse my dismal first impression, I agreed to sample them all.

MOSQUES AND MUSEUMS

Unfortunately, Tehran today looms so vast and groans under a traffic gridlock problem so appalling, that it would take weeks for an ambitious tourist to cover its most rudimentary highlights. Nonetheless, after a good night's sleep, I set out with Fatima on a frenetic, whirlwind tour of the sprawling city.

With rested eyes I realized that much of Tehran's initial blandness comes from its unexpected modernity. Clearly blessed with good infrastructure, wide, modern streets, a renowned water system (Tehranis claim they have some of the purest tap water in the world, bubbling straight from springs in the nearby Elborz Mountains), Tehran struck me as a mostly clean, well-maintained metropolis. On closer inspection I saw that the government hadn't crudely or thoughtlessly paved over its past.

Blended discreetly amongst white block buildings peeked the lovely Muslim mosques and minarets I'd anticipated: some overlooked elegantly shaded courtyards, while others looked royally appointed with swirling, gilded tiled spires. It also pleased me to see, interrupting Tehran's sterile skyline, an assortment of breathtaking, platinum-plated domes, arched shrines, and colossal monuments to bygone war heroes.

Deeper into the heart of the city, I saw, glazed into the sides of buildings, beautiful Persian frescoes, massive tiled mosaics, and slashing calligraphies (often forming the single word *Allah*, repeated hundreds of times in a heavy-handed script) any trusting tourist might expect. Thriving within the city's military/industrial layout, I spied countless old world touches: sweeping Oriental vaults and arcades, shaded porticoes and eivan walk-outs of classic Persian architecture. Though harder to find than expected, mythic, exotic Persia still survives in sterile Tehran.

After an interminable crosstown drive, we stopped at the famous Muze-ye Abgnine, the "Glass and Ceramics Museum of Iran." Housed in the former Egyptian embassy and framed by a beautiful, walled garden, the Abgnine showcases Iran's complete history of glassware and ceramics. The museum features an amazing array of ancient glass artworks and Persian vases, some dating back ten thousand years, and a stunning collection of glass beads, amulets, inlays, colored vessels, ceramic bowls and urns from the second millennium B.C. Among the delicate glassblowing specimens can be found a uniquely Iranian innovation, hailing from the first century B.C.: "crying bottles," which Fatima was eager to show me. Once used by Iranian women to gather their tears when the men left on caravans, the long-necked bottles, gracefully fitted with a funneled eyepiece, allowed women to gather their tears as a show of affection. "When the men returned," Fatima explained brightly, "the women would show them how full are their bottles of tears. The fuller the bottle, the deeper their love."

THE RESTAURANT

Lunch brought us to an airy, albeit smoke-filled, lair called Nadir, where men in robes and turbans sat on pillows lying on raised platforms draped with luxurious Persian carpets. With men sitting cross-legged on the floor, sock-footed, smoking their ornate, hand-painted water pipes (and the women sitting separately in their hot, black robes), it seemed a throwback to the days of imperial sultans and Arabian knights. Yet not so. It's simply business as usual in workaday Iran, Fatima assured me, offering to "do Mr. Bob the honor of ordering an authentic Iranian meal." I gratefully consented, and within minutes plates of exotic-looking food surrounded us, some of it green, some brown—some green and brown—most composed of ingredients I could not identify. At first I recognized nothing.

Off in a corner sat a whirling dervish—his large, white plume of hair rising like a water spout—wailing a mournful Farsi poem at the top of his lungs. A young male attendant in an ornate Persian vest served a gelatinous appetizer made of warm goat's milk and seasoned meat laced with yogurt and pepper. It tasted, and felt to my tongue, like nothing of my world.

Just then a "feeling" came upon me. The shrill music and surreal surroundings left me unsettled, disoriented. The smoke and food and music combined for a mildly narcotic effect, and a sudden wave of paranoia swept over me. Noting the curious glances from other patrons, I momentarily imagined *everyone* staring at me: a hated American, attaché of the "Great Satan," emissary of everything Iranians despise.

Fatima sensed my unease and passed me a bowl of rice. "You know," she said, as if reading my thoughts, "I have heard many fascinating things about your country. Many Iranians admire Americans and would like to visit there one day." Her words calmed me, and, as the anxiety passed, I settled back on my pillow to enjoy a delightful meal built around big, steaming bowls of rice sprinkled with saffron, and spicy lamb, chicken, and vegetable kebabs. The rice, big-kerneled and nutty in texture, came in vast helpings. I'm told it's prepared in stages over twenty-four hours. I found it delectable compared with the standard American strains; indeed, it seemed almost transcendently fluffy and tender. Cultivated in the rainy plains of

Mazandaran near the Caspian Sea, Iranian rice is considered perhaps the best in the world, with its distinctive, wheaty taste. Ours arrived cooked with yogurt and egg, forming a crunchy golden crust, which we broke and ate as a topping. The bread, too—served hot from the oven, crisp and salty, with a glazed and finely latticed crust—tantalized my taste buds.

I'd begun to relax. Pleasant and welcoming to a fault, the Iranian people attended, almost embarrassingly so, to my every imagined need or desire. It was a reception like nothing I'd imagined and nothing like I'd feared.

Even so, one can't help but notice the troubling idiosyncrasies of a radically conservative, clergy-dominated country founded on some militantly backward ideas. Some I never got used to, such as the sight of women relegated to the back of every bus, or *never* appearing in public without their heads covered. Until recently, Fatima explained with some consternation, police rode around on motorcycles, spraying paint on the bare arms of any man rash enough to wear a short-sleeved shirt in public.

And something else: unlike other Middle Eastern countries, Iran flaunted utterly no signs of *anything* American: no Western appliances, no Nike shoes or T-shirts, no ads for American movies or movie stars. Even neckties were officially banned as an unwelcome and un-Islamic symbol of western cultural imperialism (though jeans seem quite acceptable). Ironically, while Iran seems to have effectively banned all products and images borne of the United States—deeming them the unclean, contaminating filth of infidels—a quick look around the streets of Tehran reveals an abundance of cheap, cheesy imitations of outdated Western fashions (most, of course, worn by men).

In both mood and appearance Tehran looked to be making a concerted effort to catch up to the late twentieth century. Beyond isolated bouts of paranoia, I never felt overt anti-American scorn, nor did I fear for my safety.

RUG SHOP

For our last stop I longed to see an authentic Persian rug shop. I wanted to see the thousand-year-old craft of Persian carpet making in its raw element.

Fatima took me to a shop that sat directly across the street from the old U.S. Embassy, where guards with machine guns patrolled the perimeter and razor wire ringed the outer walls. A shiver shot down my spine to think I sat in front of the very building where the American hostages were held. Anti-American slogans and graffiti were splashed all over the walls of the compound, long ago converted into a military institute for teens. On one wall beneath a guard tower, a huge mural of Ayatollah peered down; a few panels across towered a sick caricature of the Statue of Liberty, painted as a skeleton with blood dripping from her robes.

Stepping from the taxi, Fatima stopped me: "I must warn you," she said. "Do not even *look* in the direction of the American Embassy. It is still a very sore wound for our country. The military authorities here are quite suspicious of outsiders."

We ducked quickly into the shop, a small space filled from floor to ceiling with stack upon stack of beautiful carpets. From the ceiling on countless racks hung scores of lavish tapestries and ornate silk runners. The proprietor, a large, oily-looking fellow with a huge, rolling belly spilling over his belt, stood off to the side, rubbing the top of his bald head with his hand as if he were polishing a bowling ball. I found it an odd mannerism, and one from which he never refrained. Fatima introduced me in Farsi as, "My American friend," and the shopkeeper replied in his best broken English, "Please come in. I am at your service."

As an amateur Persian carpet enthusiast, I'd collected a few rugs and knew something of the ancient art. Yet it floored me when Fatima told me it still takes a woman an entire year to hand-weave a single rug. The tighter the weave, the better the rug, and some of these gold-braided wonders boasted hundreds of knots per square inch: the less expensive ones made of common wool, the expensive samples of finest silk. These felt like liquid velvet to the touch.

The shopkeeper stood at the back of the shop with his two sons, each a study of Persian chic with their black, slicked-back hair, five-day-old growth beard, and baggy, pleated pants. Wherever I strolled in the small shop, I could feel their eyes watching me. I heard their whispers across the room as I moved off to inspect the finery. Mesmerized at the age of some of the carpets, I knew the best designs last hundreds, even thousands, of years.

Even surrounded by this Oriental splendor, I found myself tense and distracted. A morbid fascination, both oddly coincidental and eerie, swept over me to be so near the U.S. Embassy. For whatever reason it inspired the same strange sense of wonder I felt staring at Mount Rushmore or the Great Pyramids. I made my way slowly toward the front window, easing my way toward a rack of rugs suspended vertically in the front of the window, careful to keep my eyes fixed on the carpets. As I pretended to admire the goods, I stole quick glances through the rug-rows at the embassy directly across the street.

The whitewashed embassy had always struck me as something of a cultural icon, but seeing it up close brought the memories flooding back. It felt like November 4, 1979, all over again, watching the drama unfold on TV from my Costa Mesa living room. There the hostages, blindfolded and beaten, marched single file through the spitting, screaming crowds. Not ten feet away from where I stood, the streets swarmed with tens of thousands of enraged Iranian students, venting their hatred for the shah on the American diplomats. It conjured up the same sick, sinking feeling I had as a youth.

Today the young guards strutted about with shiny machine guns in front of the embassy—too young even to have a passing memory of the crisis. I stood there between rows of rugs, staring at that long-abandoned symbol of pain and animosity between our countries. Suddenly I sensed someone behind me, swung around, and bumped into the massive belly of the shopkeeper. He and his two sons stood watching me, blocking my path to the door.

I grinned sheepishly, when the shopkeeper blurted, *"Kill him!"* I stood motionless.

"Kill him!" the sons repeated, watching my every move. They'd caught me inspecting the embassy, probably believed me to be a spy. A bolt of panic shot through my chest.

"Fatima," I called out, "Please come here!"

She strolled casually over. "Yes, Mr. Bob, have you found something you like?"

"Fatima," I said, trying to stay calm. "There appears to be some confusion here. I'm led to understand that these gentlemen want to kill me!"

"What?" Fatima frowned. She turned to the shopkeeper, muttered something in Farsi, then turned back around just as the shopkeeper reached out toward me, as if to grab my neck. I stumbled back; he stepped forward, and, with one hand raised to strike, softly tugged on the corner of carpet hanging next to me. *"Kilim,"* he said, holding a corner of the rug for my inspection.

"Kilim," the smiling sons repeated. Fatima grinned, too, softly explaining: "I'm afraid you misunderstand. They were telling you the *style* of the carpet—it's called *kilim*. You know, the *weave* of the rug."

The shopkeeper started laughing, first softly, then harder, then so hard his belly shook like thunder. Fatima eyed me sympathetically, but I couldn't contain my own laughter. "Kilim," I said with an exaggerated shrug. "Oh, I get it. The jokes on me." I turned to Fatima and whispered, "Let's get out of here."

We left the shop to the sounds of side-splitting laughter, but before stepping into the taxi, I stole one last peak at the dreary embassy. It remains frozen in time, a sad, shabby reminder of a terrible rift yet to be healed.

Arriving back at the hotel, I thanked Fatima for a full, satisfying day.

"Please," she implored me, "get a restful night's sleep. We have long, challenging days ahead. Tomorrow we fly to Ahvaz."

I nodded. The time had come to get on with business. The time had come to look for the ark.

†ᴇ π

THE ZAGROS MOUNTAINS

"Lotfan," said a voice from behind. I turned to see the fully scarfed, black-robed Iranian flight attendant glaring down at me. "Please, sir," she continued in halting English, "dat," she pointed at my video camera, "iz note permitted."

I'd taken the opportunity presented by our flight, and my window seat, to videotape a stretch of the Zagros Mountains thirty thousand feet below. "Oh, beba . . . khshid." I stammered, trying to summon an appropriate Persian phrase but quickly resorted back to English: "Oh *this*," I said, lifting up the small camcorder. "Forgive me. I didn't know."

The stewardess smiled weakly and continued her rounds. I put the camera back in its case and leaned back in my seat.

"What's the big deal?" I whispered to Fatima. "Is it a national secret that Iran has *mountains?*"

Fatima had turned quiet. I could see by her knitted brow I was making her nervous. Since the rug shop incident, her game demeanor had soured. She couldn't disguise a growing dismay with her unpredictable American guest.

Our Iran Air commuter flight took us south toward Ahvaz, a sprawling industrial city located eighty miles due north of the Persian Gulf. Its berth on the southwestern flank of the central Zagros Mountains made it the ideal starting point; for the purposes of my trip. I regarded the Zagros as nothing less than the "mountains of Ararat," towering due east of ancient Babylon. Not quite the imposing peaks of the Colorado Rockies, they looked impressive from the air, easily the Middle East's dominant mountain range. From my window they appeared as they do on a map, forming an impenetrable curtain between Iran and Iraq. They define the western portion of Iran.

Descending into Ahvaz, the Zagros slowly shrank and ultimately flattened into a vast plain descending into hundreds of miles of marshy lowlands, sand dunes, and salt lakes dipping south toward the gulf. The great Karun River cut though the landscape like a knife, bisecting plain and mountain and slicing the Zagros like a serpentine scimitar en route to the sea. For thousands of years the Karun has served as a narrow gateway to Iran's interior, carving a meandering pass through the mountains and bridging the Persian Gulf to the southern mainland.

The plane tilted into landing position. Fatima leaned over and, with her finger on the window, traced a triangle from Ahvaz, south, to the Persian Gulf, then west to the Irano-Iraqi frontier. "See the triangle?" she asked. "That's where southwestern Iran meets the great Mesopotamia valley, just east of where the Tigris and Euphrates rivers meet."

Ah, I thought, *the land of Shinar.*

Landing at Ahvaz's unremarkable Kheyaun-e Zeitun airport, we found our driver, a real-life Ali, waiting for us at the gate. Though not nearly as jolly as I'd pictured, his appearance fit perfectly the stereotype I'd imagined of a toothless, bearded guide. And if Ali seemed rather humorless and gruff, his punctuality more than made up for it. He appeared to be someone we could depend on.

Heeling to Fatima's orders, Ali packed us into his forest-green Peugeot and chauffeured us in the direction of downtown Ahvaz. The road into town, bounded on all sides by vast tracts of rhythmically pumping oil wells, greasy oil storage facilities, and immense, smoke-belching refineries, looked like those I'd traveled in central Texas. We'd landed in the fertile crescent of Iran's inestimable petro-industry, and a quick surveillance told me why, a mere decade earlier, Ahvaz stood on the front line of the Iran-Iraq War.

Saddam Hussein, the Iraqi premier, knew what he wanted in 1980 when he made his land grab in southern Iran, attacking on the feeble grounds that the oil-rich Khuzestan Province was once part of Iraq. Looking around at all the refineries, I could see his motive amounted to pure greed. He wanted oil, nothing more.

While the war exacted an incalculable toll on both sides, costing hundreds of thousands of lives, Iran fought with a vengeance. Badly outgunned and a clear underdog, Iranian troops seemed possessed of a fierce religious fervor, seizing on a golden opportunity to spread the Islamic revolution by force of arms. When a cease-fire finally came in mid-1988, neither side had achieved its objectives. But as the smoke cleared, the world witnessed, for the first time since WWI, the grisly effects of poison gas and trench warfare.

AHVAZ

To my surprise Ahvaz boasted a rich biblical history, its origins dating back to the reign of King Darius in the sixth century B.C. Much of the Old Testament unfolds nearby, though unremitting Iraqi bombardments and a history of military conquest and subjection have reduced most of its historic past to rubble.

The city itself resembles a giant war memorial, its prominent thoroughfares bedecked with solemn murals and oversized statues of martyred soldiers. Throughout Ahvaz, strategically placed walls and buildings sport plaques eulogizing the town's faceless "Brave Ones." The scars of war even desecrate the city's impressive network of modern suspension bridges, still pitted and cracked from the heavy artillery fire. I took a moment to orient myself geographically: mere miles to the south lay Kuwait; due west sat Basra, the base of Iraq's invasion forces. I had unwittingly wandered into the epicenter of some of the deadliest, most destructive, cross-border combat of the past century. Despite the government's valiant campaign to rebuild Ahvaz, the enduring violence of war cannot be concealed.

Observing these battle scars, still fresh even more than a decade after the last SCUD missile fell, unnerved me. I'd never paid much attention to the occasional headlines or video clips about the conflict. News of bombs exploding in remote parts of the world never left much of an impression and certainly never conveyed the reality of lives being torn apart or the sad legacy of mass destruction. But now it surrounded me; I stood spellbound, a stunned eyewitness to a regional disaster. The immediacy struck like a blow to the chest. From that moment on I knew I'd never watch reports on disasters in Somalia or the Balkans without genuine heartache.

We arrived at our hotel at dusk. The Fajr Grand Hotel, on the east bank of the Karun River, sat across the street from an old, rundown amusement park whose Persian-motif carnival rides squeaked and wobbled in comic disrepair. Lightbulbs dangled from cords, signs tilted on their hinges, and everything had the general look of being plucked straight from the junkyard. Unpacking in my room upstairs, I could see the rickety Ferris wheel, missing several seats and revolving on its rusty axis like a flat tire.

Off to the north of the city, however, I could see the surreal, radioactive-orange glow of dozens of refinery towers, blazing like an artificial sunset. Flames from their spouts leapt hundreds of yards into the air, lighting up the night sky for miles, causing me to marvel at the sheer volume of excess oil and gas needed to emit such a brilliant glow.

After a late dinner Fatima and I took a walk into downtown Ahvaz, which, with little else to offer, remains one of a handful of Iranian cities that doesn't close down after dark. The amusement park now teemed with twilight revelers, beleaguered Ahvasis who never thought of it as a grimy old facility but rather as a Persian Disneyland offering welcome distraction from life's cruel travails. Strolling the midway, now swarming with flies and reeking of diesel fumes, I sensed a glint of weariness in people's eyes—perhaps a sad, enduring fatigue with the wretched memory of war.

Wherever we walked, I pressed Fatima into interrogating the locals about Noah's ark: Had anyone heard legends of its whereabouts or perhaps seen it in the mountains to the east? She proved a willing foil, bravely approaching complete strangers with the question: "Have you, by chance, heard anything of Noah's ark in the area?" The looks we got in return I considered priceless. We canvassed downtown Ahvaz, asking everyone we met—porters at the hotel, taxi drivers in the street, waiters at the restaurant, folks standing in line at the amusement park, street vendors selling water, old men in restaurants smoking their water pipes—if they'd heard rumors of the ark. Most thought we were spinning a hoax; others let us know by their startled looks that we'd struck a shrill note in their twilight reverie.

Person after person either shook their heads, annoyed, or blurted, "Na!" to Fatima's query. And for a time I could see she seemed to relish the assignment. Interpreting for the zany American explorer seemed fun and a fresh experience. But as the evening wore on, the rude looks and curt responses tarnished the novelty, and Fatima became less exhilarated by the drill. By night's end we'd queried nearly fifty Ahvazi residents, whose consistently rude, one-word brush-offs began to feel like poison darts to the personable, chatty Fatima. She returned to the hotel, shoulders stooped, and her face red and flustered.

I thanked her for her persistence and said good night but retired to my own room concerned. I needed Fatima, my sole means of interfacing with the locals, to keep a stiff upper lip. Our adventure had just begun, and we had a long way to go.

SUSA

We left Ahvaz early in the morning and drove north toward the southern Zagros. I told Ali to stop at every little roadside village or market, and at each stop Fatima dutifully got out and asked those assembled: "Have you ever heard anything of Noah's ark in the area?" After a few terse "Na's!" Fatima invariably returned to the car humbled and crestfallen. "I'm sorry, Mr. Bob," she would say, "but *they* haven't heard of your ark, either."

By late afternoon we reached Susa, still some distance into the Mesopotamia plain but within easy driving distance of the Zagros foothills. Any studious Bible reader recognizes "Susa," or *Shush* in Iranian, as one of the great cities of ancient Persia. Its prehistoric roots extend back four thousand years before the birth of Christ, and, if not the oldest city in the world, it could be counted among them.

In the third millennium B.C., Susa reigned as the crown jewel of Elam. Many believe the city was named after Noah's grandson. Perhaps Elam himself helped build these once illustrious ramparts. Susa's ruins, inscriptions, tombs, even the dust of its streets, served as a living link to Scripture's earliest events, perhaps even back to the great flood or to Noah and his descendants. Seeing it with my own eyes illuminated a distant past I'd been wrestling to understand.

Hundreds, even thousands, of old artifacts, pottery, and bronzes from those ancient empires can be found littered among Susa's burial mounds. Most sit scattered above ground, lying naked in plain view. The mounds, highly prized in archaeological circles, leave most Iranians indifferent. Susa's extremely rare bounty of Parthian-era "painted ware"—whose geometric designs of water birds, hunting dogs, ears of corn, horse heads, and palm leaves lay strewn among the half-buried remnants—provide a clear glimpse into the aesthetic tastes of the Elamite culture. I leaned down and casually plucked a four-thousand-year-old shard from the dirt. Turning it over, I saw, fired into its glaze, four distinct fingerprints, no doubt belonging to the goblet's potter. My heart leapt to think I might have touched the work of an artisan commissioned by Darius's court.

Strolling the grounds set me to daydreaming, and I imagined the entire region covered by the waters of the flood, all drowned but Noah and his family. As the waters receded and the mountains rose, I saw men and their descendants migrating down into these ancient plains, building cities, fashioning a culture. I kicked at the dust beneath my feet, surmising it gave birth to that first civilization.

Cited repeatedly in Scripture, Susa appears first in the Book of Ezra as the home of the Elamites (Ezra 4:9). Later the prophet Nehemiah wrote of carrying on his affairs "in the citadel of Susa," during the time that the Lord inspired him to rebuild Jerusalem (Neh. 1:1). Later still, Esther, Mordecai, and the rest of the exiled Jews called Susa home when their lives became embroiled in the intrigues of King Xerxes's court. Finally, the prophet Daniel was cloistered in Susa when he fell under a trance: "In my vision I saw myself in the citadel of Susa in the province of Elam" (Dan. 8:2).

Sadly, from those grand years Susa's splendor faded. Destroyed in 331 B.C. by Alexander the Great, it exists today as little more than a dusty village, its storied past nowhere in evidence. Gone are the lavish palaces of kings such as Untash Gal or Darius I, the latter a successor to the gloried potentate Nebuchadnezzar, who threw Daniel's friends into the fiery furnace (Dan. 3:19–21). Eventually its ruins disappeared completely beneath the dusty landscape, resurfacing again only in the mid-1800s, when a British archaeologist stumbled upon the site and began to excavate its wonders.

Entering the city, Fatima remarked, "Mr. Bob, did you know that the prophet Daniel's tomb remains in Susa? Perhaps you would like to see it?"

"Yes, of course I would," I replied, surprised—awestruck really—to learn the tomb of one of God's greatest prophets could still be seen *here* . . . on the far side of the world. I hadn't until now fully appreciated the antiquity and historical richness of this dusty plain.

I arrived at Daniel's tomb, housed in a large, white building with a classic domed, sugarloaf tower, in the heat of the afternoon. The rectangular courtyard was filled to capacity with praying, kneeling Muslims gathered from across Iran. The throng of pilgrims, mostly men, approached the ornately carved, gold-plated crypt with stoic reverence, almost as if the prophet still lived.

"Daniel's bones lay inside still," noted Fatima, as we watched the crowd circle the tomb, lost in their meditations. Each in turn rubbed it affectionately with their hands and, in some instances, kissed it or pressed their foreheads against it, then rubbed themselves all over as if anointing themselves with some invisible benedictory oil. The closer and more intimate one got to the prophet's tomb, it appeared, the more potent the blessing. It called to mind other great men of God—Abraham, Moses—revered in the Christian tradition but also honored as prophets of *Islam*. Seeing this commotion over Daniel's tomb dialed up the bedrock genealogy shared among Christians and Muslims.

While I reflected on the proceedings, Fatima's torment continued unabated. As per our agreement, she shuffled glumly about, approaching one pilgrim after another with the baffling question: have you heard or seen anything of Noah's ark? Here, as elsewhere, came a flock of blank stares and cold shoulders; here, as elsewhere, Fatima emerged from her chore oppressed and humiliated, clearly wanting nothing more to do with Noah and his blasted boat.

CHOGHA ZAMBIL

From Daniel's tomb Ali drove us up a dusty, rutted road, forty-five miles east, to an obscure wonder of the Middle East: the towering ziggurat of Chogha Zambil, an ancient, pyramid-shaped, desert skyscraper. Standing over twenty-five meters high, though badly eroded at the top, the colossus had been lost to the world for more than twenty-five hundred years when petroleum geologists for an Anglo-Iranian oil company accidentally spotted it from the air in 1935. Archaeologists believe it once served as the vortex of Persia's religious activities, a mountain-sized monument to a culture that attached great spiritual significance to mountains.

High up one wall sat a broad, brick platform, probably once used as an altar, and everywhere its huge, hand-carved tiles told stories of a mysterious people, their gods, and animals. Standing slack-jawed before this thirteenth-century-B.C. monolith, a wild thought struck me. Maybe Chogha Zambil had been erected as a high place from which to escape a *flood*.

Milling about the ruins, I bumped into an old, fully robed Iranian, seated on a folding metal chair beneath a scrawny palm. He called himself Karim, Chogha Zambil's official tour guide, and spoke enough English to give me the dollar tour. Karim led me first into the plain, to an old, dried riverbed where workers once made mud bricks for the pyramid, then out to the original walls that surrounded the town of *Dur Untash*, dominated by the ziggurat. We strolled in and around various temples and palaces dedicated to assorted Elamite gods and goddesses, Karim expounding on the fantastic peculiarities of a bustling, highly advanced society. Under the reign of King Untash Gal, Chogha Zambil became the chief pilgrimage site of the Elamite empire—Susa, farther west, serving as Elam's royal seat and political center.

Finally, Karim said, "Now I shall show you the king's treasure vault," and led me to the eastern edge of the town. There he lit a kerosene torch and walked me down a dreadfully dark tunnel to a vaulted chamber where, he said, lay the collapsed remains of the King Gal's palace. Years earlier, archaeologists dug up the king's crypt along with his royal treasure, traditionally buried with the ruler for use in the afterlife. The musty, claustrophobic space, once filled with treasure, now reeked of trash and urine. Karim demonstrated how the king's attendants wedged giant timbers into fortified sockets on either side of the entryway, in order to seal the vault's huge doors airtight from the *inside*. I watched, pondering the arrangement, then asked Karim, "If the vault was sealed from the *inside*, how did the servants get *out?*"

"Unfortunately," Karim said, "they *didn't*. The archaeologists found their bones inside when they opened the vault." A shiver ran down my back, and the room seemed suddenly cold and eerie.

With me close on his heels, Karim walked back up the narrow, mud-brick hallway. *How awful,* I thought, *to be buried alive down here in this dungeon.* I wondered, *How did those poor souls cope once the doors closed and the last shaft of light disappeared? Did they see themselves as heroes, giving it all for the king, or did they, with their last gasps, mourn their fate? Sitting there in total darkness, with the air running out, did they panic or start pounding on the door for someone to let them out? Or maybe echo a final, doleful complaint like,* "Maybe we should have gotten into another line of work"*?*

Emerging into the blinding sunlight, I breathed deep and shuddered at the cheapness of life out here on the Zagros. Looking around for Fatima, I found her dawdling back at the car with Ali, both in unusually good spirits, almost giddy.

"Did you enjoy your tour, Mr. Bob?" she chirped, as we hopped in the car and drove east toward the foothills.

It was then I diagnosed the cause of her sudden mood change. Chogha Zambil, nearly deserted throughout our stay, gave poor Fatima a brief reprieve from having to ask anyone about the ark.

That would soon change.

Eleven

THE OLD MAN AND AN ARK

From Chogha Zambil, Ali chauffeured us on a bone-jarring ascent into the high Zagros. Navigating its terrible folds and crags, I understood why Cyrus and other invaders found this knobby cordillera such an imposing range. Back home in Colorado, modern interstate highways tamed the Rockies; yet no such feats of engineering had yet humbled the Zagros. Up here, narrow craggy passes and difficult, rutted cart paths ruled.

By mid-afternoon we'd reached an obscure little town known as Khorromabad, at the bottom of a yawning gorge. An impoverished, third-world village, Khorromabad boasts few modern amenities to soothe the road-weary traveler. Mangy beasts roam the streets, and the town's only hotel features rooms without windows—mine had only a square hole in the wall—no air-conditioning and smelly, Spartan bathrooms. Outside my "window" a blacksmith grounded metal against a sparking, screaming stone wheel, thus settling my opinion of Khorromabad as a noisy, hot, inhospitable little hamlet. I counted it a lackluster honor when the hotel manager told me no other American had set foot in this town before me.

We quickly stowed our bags and ventured out to mingle with the natives. We had yet to secure a single clue of the ark's whereabouts, and my time in Iran neared its end. This crude village represented perhaps my last chance to leave the country with an arguable defense for my theory. Needing to get Fatima pumped up for another round of inquiries, I asked, "Are you ready?" Then added, "Time's short, and we have to stay focused."

She didn't bite but rather, openly rebelled. "*Please*, Mr. Bob," she pleaded, "don't make me ask again. It is no good now. They will just think I'm crazy."

I felt her pain. Of the close to two hundred people we'd surveyed, not one had even smiled at us, much less given us a solid lead. For a dainty flower like Fatima, this lengthy record of reproach smelled of disgrace.

We walked to the town square, an outdoor market smelling of pungent, exotic meats and overripe vegetable matter combined in a moldering potpourri drawing clouds of flies. Scanning the colorful crowd of shoppers and vendors, I hoped, for Fatima's sake, to single out a friendly face. Wending our way through the gallery, my eyes glanced about, regarding the indifferent stares of many but finally settling on those of an old man with a woolly, white beard. He stood across the square, leaning casually against a stone arch, striking the pose of the resident sage (or at least one of the oldest guys in town). If someone knew anything of the local legends, I guessed, *he* might. "Fatima," I said gently, "see that old man? Go ask *him*." Like a scolded child, she exhaled a long, pitiful groan, hunched her shoulders, and shuffled off across the square. I trailed close behind.

As we approached, the old gent flashed a grin, eyeing me intently. I thought it a cheery omen, but Fatima had long since run out of smiles. She walked right up and asked him bluntly if he had seen or heard of Noah's ark. The old man's eyes grew large, and he smiled to show us a mouthful of rotten teeth before reeling off a rapid-fire string of sentences. I had no idea what he said, but it ranked as the first time we hadn't been either rudely mocked or ignored. He jabbered some more and for a moment I saw Fatima's face go slack. She glanced back at me with eyes round and pensive, then turned and irritably grilled the poor man with a new round of questions, leaning in close to hear his response. He kept grinning and prattling and pointing, and when Fatima finally swung back around, it appeared as if she'd seen Daniel's ghost.

"Mr. Bob," she said, breathless, "this gentleman says he knows of Noah's ark."

"You're kidding!" I said, unsure how to react. "*Where?*"

"He says it lies between Nehavand and Hamadan, and . . ." halting in mid-sentence, she added warily, "he says it can still be seen *today*."

Blood rushed to my face; my mouth went dry. "Between Hamadan and Nehavand?" I sputtered. I'd heard of Hamadan, where Ed Davis had been stationed, but—"Where is *Nehavand*?"

Fatima's droopy countenance lifted, her gloom replaced by a glint of excitement. In a matter of seconds, she'd been drawn into the heady rush of adventure. The old man kept up his breathless commentary, as if he'd been waiting years for just such a moment.

Fatima translated, slow and careful: "He says that after the flood, the ark of Noah came to rest in the mountains of Nehavand," she explained. "Nehavand means 'Noah's land.' He says that between Nehavand and

Hamadan lies a tall mountain called Sarkashti. This mountain . . . he says we will find the ark there."

GETTING THERE

Standing in the teeming market as if alone, we winnowed from the old man a complete list of details and instructions, including a rough map and the name of a driver with a four-wheel-drive vehicle who could take us high into the upper Zagros, to Mount Sarkashti. We learned Sarkashti meant the "head," or "top portion of a ship," evidently named for the ark.

Had we really struck pay dirt? I wondered. There was only one way to find out. We'd drive back down the mountains to Kermanshah, some three hours west of Khorramabad, and find our driver; then we'd spend the night at Kermanshah, rise early and take the back roads to a secluded town known as Oshtorinan, situated between Hamadan and Nehavand. In between would flash by lots of towns and villages whose names I couldn't pronounce or remember—I would leave the details to Fatima—but we'd find Mount Sarkashti in the heights above Oshtorinan, the old fellow insisted. And on its summit we'd find the ark.

I shook with excitement but suddenly found myself leery. It all seemed too simple. Here we were, staking our hopes on the story of a complete stranger, who, quite possibly, made the whole thing up. But then again, in my line of work, one couldn't avoid such risks. I recalled the local Bedouin in Saudi Arabia who helped us get our truck out of the sand and ultimately pointed us to Mount Sinai. These "happenstance" meetings had *always* been my strategy. I'd been praying for just such a moment since arriving in Tehran. With that settled I thanked the old man warmly, then turned to Fatima.

"What's this about a driver with a Land Rover?" I asked. "Where do we find him?"

"The old man says to follow his direction and take the main road to Kermanshah," she said, matter-of-factly. "The driver will find *us*."

Captive now to events beyond my control, I realized I had neither the time nor energy to sweat the details, no matter how eccentric they seemed. We retrieved our bags, hopped in Ali's Peugeot and rumbled back down the hogbacks toward Kermanshah. I felt exhausted.

In four days I'd traveled more than a thousand miles across Iran— roughly the distance from Colorado to California—and had nothing to show for it but a chip of Elamite pottery. Entering the plain of Kermanshah, thoughts of home filled my mind, and, after long hours of driving, it startled me to see an older model, olive-gray Land Rover draw alongside us on the gravel road. The driver motioned for us to pull over.

"This is our driver," Fatima said nonchalantly.

What? I thought. *How did he recognize us? Had someone called ahead?* It still seemed quite strange, but this late in a grueling journey I lacked the energy to protest.

I got out of the car and found myself instantly engaged in an awkward haggling session with the owner of the Land Rover. As always, Fatima translated, informing him of our objective and asking his price. A handsome, sturdy youth with jet black hair and a chiseled jaw, he began carping and quibbling, fussing and flapping his arms, before even mentioning a price. His plan appeared to be to make the very idea of a trip to Oshtorinan seem a fearsome nuisance. He finally motioned that he would simply wash his hands of the whole mess and barked out a Farsi expression meaning, *"You can't afford me!"*

I quietly inquired of Fatima, "How much is he asking?"

"He wants $25 in American currency," she replied.

I almost laughed, reaching for my wallet, but Fatima, embarrassed and insulted by the man's poor manners, pulled me aside.

"This man is a Lor," she whispered disdainfully. "They are a people who prize themselves on stealing you blind. He will consider it an honor to rob you of as much money as possible."

I looked him over. He owned a Land Rover, which in Iran meant he was either a gifted businessman or a skillful swindler. I handed him two twenty-dollar bills with instructions to "keep the change." Forty bucks didn't seem too much for asking him to abuse his beautifully maintained SUV. The Lor pocketed the cash, no doubt thinking he'd pulled the biggest heist of his week, and trailed us into Kermanshah.

That night, lying in my hotel bed, I couldn't sleep. To this point the trip had been a pleasant, mostly calculated tour of some ancient towns and ruins. Now it seemed to be tilting out of my control. I'd bought into an old man's story about Noah's ark and had put my life in the hands of a Lorish con man, trusting him to navigate us through a land I'd never understand in a hundred years—and he might just slit my throat to boot. *What,* I wondered, tossing and turning through the night, *had I gotten myself into?*

MOUNT SARKASHTI

We rose next morning before sunrise, threw our things into the Land Rover, and began a circuitous, marathon drive into the rugged Zagros highlands. For hours we climbed into an increasingly austere, scrub-brush-covered mountain range, higher and higher—eight thousand feet, nine thousand feet—bouncing in the back of the SUV and churning up roads that turned increasingly narrow.

This harsh country boasted some of the most intimidating clusters of high peaks I'd ever seen; numerous angry streams roared past us, spilling west into the lowlands and giving rise in the east to a majestic, contrasting land of enormous domes and peaks, dizzying gorges and some surprisingly mild, grass-carpeted valleys. Off to the north stood a series of imposing volcanic cones perched nobly on vast plateaus, well above timberline. Still we proceeded on a relentless, neck-popping ascent, past a few tiny villages and odd collections of old mud huts, by an infrequent goat farmer or two, until, at midday, we reached the high mountain pass of Mount Sarkashti.

The mountain sat in a washboard-ribbed basin, surrounded by high, saddleback ridges ringed in clouds. When our Lorish guide said, "*Sarkashti,*" I took it on faith he told the truth. I still didn't fully trust him, and the endless climb into increasingly remote mountains gave me ample time for paranoia. For all I knew, he'd lured us to his mountain lair to set his gang of Lorish bandits on us. I knew that to disappear in these canyons would be the last anyone would ever hear of me.

"Do you think any other American has ever been through these passes?" I asked Fatima, uneasily.

"No, Mr. Bob," she said, warily inspecting the premises, "you must be the first."

We stopped at the top of a windblown pass next to a roadside stand— a makeshift mud hut, actually—tended by a middle-aged Iranian with an AK-47 slung over his shoulder, selling bottles of Fanta soda chilling in a small brook beside the road. Children appeared and started an impromptu game of tag about the car. Fatima approached the man with the rifle.

"Is this Mount Sarkashti?" she asked. When he nodded affirmation, she proceeded: "Can you tell us where we might find Noah's ark?"

It seemed a silly introductory question, but suddenly another man appeared and shouted gleefully, "*Bale', bale'!*"—Farsi for "*Yes!*"—then pointed skyward to a near vertical ridge angling away from the town.

I stared up at the steep knoll. "If this is Mount Sarkashti," I said, "then ask him what the ark looks like."

After a quick exchange Fatima translated the man's vague description. "He calls it big, and square, and . . ." she paused, uncertain of the local slang, "He says it's the color of *soil.*"

I had no idea what that meant, but I began to bounce on my toes, eager to sprint up the mountainside. Trying to remain calm, I asked, "Can he take us there?" After so many years and so many false leads, I could now scarcely wait to see what lay over that ridge.

"Yes," Fatima answered. "He says he will take us to it."

THE "COLOR OF SOIL"

Hardly a majestic mountain, Mount Sarkashti stood no more than eleven thousand feet. It struck me as a particularly dreary, desolate butte in a range already poorly vegetated. We set off with the rifleman in the lead, hiking and, in places, scrambling up the ridge on a slender, hand-hewn trail.

In little over an hour we reached a broad, downward-sloping plateau with a splendid view of the nearby tablelands. Adrenaline rose in my throat as we crested the last stony crag.

"Where to from here?" I asked, my eyes darting about. Something told me we had a ridge or two yet to climb, as we remained several hundred feet below the summit. But then Fatima said something that shocked me.

"It's *here!*" she said, pointing to the man with the rifle. "This fellow says it's *here.*"

Here?

I looked around and saw nothing of interest but knew by the look on Fatima's face that something felt wrong. She pointed to a spot on the ground, forty yards off, and said, "He says it's over *there!*"

I scanned the hillside. I could see no ark. My heart sank. The trickle of adrenaline turned bitter in my throat. Silently, I walked over, searching the ground for old pieces of wood, or something—*anything*—to hint of a primitive boat or wooden structure. I found nothing but a massive, sloping indentation in the ground, a sunken hollow, of sorts, looking to be a shallow crater. I turned to Fatima: "What's *this?*" She turned to our host, lifting her arms, bewildered.

The man completely ignored me as he addressed Fatima, her face turning hot shades of red. She finally turned and said blankly, "Mr. Bob, he says this . . . this . . . *hole* . . . is where the ark used to *sit.*"

Ah . . . the *color of soil.* Now it made sense. Staring at the ground, I felt my blood pressure rising. I stared at the concave depression, trying to visualize a large boat nesting in the cavity. But then I came to my senses. *Where's the ark?* I wanted to know.

Fatima looked flustered, trying to extract information from our now tight-lipped escort. In bits and pieces she managed to learn that, according to local lore, "the ark has been broken apart through the years, and has been carted off by the villagers for firewood and to build their homes."

My temples throbbed. As I paced the plateau, searching for a happy ending to this bad dream, I noticed the cliff side fifty yards away. It seemed to drop off into a steep valley or canyon, so I walked over to take a look. Maybe a piece of the ark had fallen over the edge. But just as I craned my neck to peer over the edge, two loud shots rang out, and I heard the whistle of two AK-47 slugs scream past my right ear. I stood paralyzed in my tracks. *Here it comes,* I thought. *He's going to rob and kill us. Dummy! You played right into their hands.*

I turned slowly around. Our host stood forty yards off, aiming his AK-47 in my direction. Fatima ran over, holding the hems of her robe in her hands, trying to shield me from his sights. Very calmly, very quietly, she said, "He's very angry and says to go no farther. He says we *must* go back down the mountain *now!*"

"Why?" I whispered. "What's the problem? What's down there?"

"He won't say."

She spoke slowly, calmly, but her eyes showed fright. "He says you must not look into the canyon. We must go back now."

Hardly the glorious ending I'd imagined. Her words left me speechless. I kept staring at our guide in disbelief, but he wouldn't return my gaze. The man with the gun had spoken. What else could be said?

We turned as a group and walked silently down the mountain, an awful tension in the air. Nothing more was said of the ark. To do so, I feared, would invite disaster. At least the much-anticipated robbery never happened. Of that I was thankful, but it seemed a small consolation.

Questions hung in the air like a foul odor. *Had there ever been a boat on Mount Sarkashti? What of that ark-shaped crater? Had we been duped? Did the old man in Khorramabad lie to us? Had we misread his instructions?* I'd probably never know.

We reached bottom. I paid the Fanta salesman a couple of bucks. We returned to the Land Rover and rumbled down the mountain, not bothering to look back.

I felt crushing disappointment. My time in Iran had come to an end. In two days I'd be back in the States, saddled with this failure. I felt helpless.

Fatima, too, seemed disconsolate. She'd hitched a ride on my emotional roller coaster and, in the end, had probably hoped for more than *this*. I wanted, in that instant, to leave, to be home with my family. But I couldn't shake the thought: *Where did this leave me?*

Much as I hated to admit it, it meant I'd returned to square one.

On the long drive back to Kermanshah, the whole notion of finding the ark in Iran began to chafe and grate at me. Had I been a fool to go off by myself and test this new theory? Why did I have to be the lone ranger? Serious doubts crept in: Had this star-crossed venture simply been a product of my overactive imagination?

OTHER TRADITIONS

Following our misadventures atop Mount Sarkashti, we headed north toward Hamadan, meeting others en route who shared hazy stories and distant legends of Noah's ark. The murky collection featured the tale of one old man in Hamadan who said he knew of the ark's whereabouts. He agreed to take us there after some haggling and led us to a nearby mountain the locals consider holy. In reverence of the prophet Noah, he said, Muslims still sacrifice sheep near its summit, which still holds traces of the ark. But when we climbed to the top, we saw nothing but dozens of hikers and picnicking families competing for space on the main trail.

What made these people regale us with tales of arks that did not exist? I don't know, but as we continued our northern arc toward Tehran, we encountered little nibbles here and there of regional traditions pointing to its existence. As in other parts of the Middle East, it soon became apparent that anecdotes and legends of the ark, the flood, and Noah abound through-out the central Zagros Mountains. My disappointment on Mount Sarkashti typified a chance encounter with one of them. With more time, perhaps, I might've met others whose proud oral traditions assumed sole stewardship of Noah's famous boat.

Yet with each mention of the ark, my mind hearkened back to Ed Davis: Could *this* be the mountain he climbed? Did Ed drive these roads? Had these rugged Lors been of the same tribe that took Ed under their wing? I kept hearing his words—*"You'll never believe how big it is!"*—and envi-sioned the ark appearing over every other ridge. But it didn't happen, not on this trip, at least.

I departed Iran with the warmest feelings of gratitude toward Fatima and Ali, promising them that, if I ever returned, I'd look them up. The trip's results cheered me less, but I resolved to stay the course. It remained, after all, only my virgin foray into Persia. I kept coming back to the central the-sis: the Zagros Mountains—*Iran!*—lay due east of Shinar. That much I knew. It would be my sole consolation for the time being.

✝ WELVE

THE MOUNTAINS OF ARMENIA

It felt good to get back to Colorado Springs. I needed to regroup, take a few weeks off, rethink my game plan. I figured I'd start piecing the puzzle back together when the spirit moved, not realizing until I got home how completely the whirlwind junket had exhausted me.

After a wonderful reunion with my family and a few days of rest, the rhythms of life returned to normal. I settled into my routine with BASE, attended a backlog of speaking engagements, and slowly, after a passage of weeks, began to feel a familiar stirring. I took an hour here or there from my busy days to revisit the mystery of the ark.

That meant going back to the source, back to Scripture, to that famously vague reference—"the mountains of Ararat"—which now struck me as more of a tease than a reference point. Seen through the lens of time, the verse seemed almost a sly diversion from the truth rather than a reliable compass heading. One thing remained clear in my mind: the passage *did not* mean Mount Ararat in Turkey. Did it therefore mean Iran? On that I kept an open mind. Either way it would require a subtle rethinking of basic premises.

Where, for instance, could Ararat have been (besides east of Shinar), when Moses penned Genesis around 1450 B.C.? What did the world look like at the time? How did it square with Bible commentaries describing Ararat as a broad, remote region north of Assyria, somewhere above the upper Mesopotamia Valley?

THE MYSTERY OF ARARAT

As easily as "Ararat" rolls off the tongue, the word itself appears only sparingly in Scripture. The word can be found only four times in the Bible. Genesis 8:4, of course, cites the "mountains of *Ararat*" on which the ark landed; 2 Kings 19:37 speaks of the assassination of Assyrian king Sennacherib by his own sons, Adrammelech and Sharezer, who then "escaped to the land of *Ararat.*" Isaiah 37:38 replays Sennacherib's assassination nearly word for word; and, finally, Jeremiah 51:27 brings us this cryptic battle cry: "Lift up a banner in the land! Blow the trumpet among the nations! Prepare the nations for battle against her; summon against her these kingdoms: *Ararat*, Minni and Ashkenaz."

The latter, a prophetic utterance by Jeremiah from around 630 B.C., rallied Ararat, Minni, and Ashkenaz to battle. And while the war itself actually came to pass one hundred years later, in 539 B.C., when Cyrus the Great of Persia attacked Babylon, the verse portended more than a future mustering of troops; it spoke clearly to the close, widely recognized alliance (both geographically and politically) of the kingdoms of Ararat, Minni, and Ashkenaz—a simple if telling clue to the true region of Ararat. Through its neighbors the region of Ararat can be traced back to its origin as a political kingdom in a mountainous area north of Mesopotamia. I suspected the relationship of these three kingdoms might whisper faint truths about the ark's final port.

Ancient geographers tell us that the kingdom of Minni (also pronounced Minyas, Minnai, or Mana) arose from the loose unification of several small city-states sitting just south and east of present-day Lake Urmia in northwest Iran[1]—in other words, a mountainous region north of Mesopotamia.

Then, in the next breath, these same scribes report that the "Mannaean society" grew up immediately southeast of *Armenia*, the latter term understood as a more modern version of Ararat. It's no secret that, in the ancient lexicon, the two words—Ararat and Armenia—were regarded as synonymous. At different times in history, Armenia and Ararat occupied roughly the same territory north of Assyria.

This widely circulated viewpoint gains strong support in the *International Standard Bible Encyclopedia*, which states: "The ark is said to have rested upon the mountains of Ararat, or, in the mountainous region of Armenia." (Interestingly, the same passage notes that eastern Turkey's Mount Ararat "lies outside the general region.") (see map, pg. 72)

We find the proximity of Minni to Armenia (or Ararat) confirmed by Nicholas of Damascus, who in his ninety-sixth book asserts that the ark landed above the Minyas on a great mountain in Armenia: "There is above the country of Minyas in Armenia a great mountain called Baris, where, as the story goes, many refugees found safety at the time of the flood, and one man, transported upon an Ark, grounded upon the summit, and relics of the

97

timber were for long preserved; this might well be the same man of whom Moses, the Jewish legislator, wrote."[2]

The Ashkenas, likewise, also known as the Scythians, can be found prominently displayed on most maps of the ancient Near East as a kingdom that once occupied the Mukan steppe of Soviet Azerbaijan.

THEY FLED TO ARARAT . . . IN NORTHWEST IRAN

Several clues from the Bible strongly argue that Noah's lost mountains rest in the northern region of present-day Iran. In 2 Kings 19:37, for example, we see a clear reference to Ararat in an account of the assassination of the Assyrian king Sennacherib in 681 B.C. by his two sons: "Now it came to pass, as he was worshiping in the temple of Nisroch his god, that his sons Adrammelech and Sharezer struck him down with the sword; and they escaped into the land of Ararat. Then Esarhaddon his son reigned in his place" (NKJV).

Scripture clearly states that, after they killed their father, the pair "escaped into the land of Ararat." What do we know of the location of this safe haven, where the assassins knew they would receive asylum? A key clue is found in the *Jewish Encyclopedia* of 1902 telling us that the nations of Ashkenaz and the Minni—both of which sprang from the region of Lake Urmia in northwestern Iran—had revolted about the same time as Sennacherib's assassination. If so, it seems logical that to escape punishment the assassins would have fled to the allies who helped in the revolt: an area near Lake Urmia in northwestern Iran.

Jeremiah 51:27 closely identifies Minni and Ashkenaz with Ararat during the reign of King Cyrus, who conquered Babylon in 539 B.C.: "Set up a banner in the land, Blow the trumpet among the nations! Prepare the nations against her, Call the kingdoms together against her: Ararat, Minni, and Ashkenaz." In the next verse Scripture states that the kingdoms of Ararat, Minni, and Ashkenaz served among the kingdoms of the Medes: "Prepare against her the nations, with the kings of the Medes, Its governors and all its rulers, All the land of his dominion." Where do historians place the Medes? *The New Bible Dictionary* states that "Media was the ancient name for northwest Iran, west of the Caspian Sea."

Professor Ken Durham, associate professor of biblical studies at Colorado Christian University in Denver, postulates two possible understandings of the connection between biblical Minni and Ashkenaz, and historical Armenia, or Ararat. "One view holds that the name *Armenia* originally meant 'region of the Minni,'" he says, "while the other view contends that the ethnic term *Minni* was derived or contracted from 'Armenia.' While the first view gains more favor because of the greater antiquity of the word *Minni*, both theories recognize an unmistakable coidentity of Minni with Armenia. Each term refers to essentially the same ethnic and geographic region."

Likewise, in the *Zondervan Pictorial Encyclopedia of the Bible* (Zondervan, 1975), Merrill C. Tenney writes, "Probably Ashkenaz is to be identified with . . . a people who, in the time of Jeremiah, had settled near Lake Urmia in the region of Ararat." Here we have both biblical and extra-biblical references to suggest that the ancient land of Ararat lay, at least in part, in modern-day, northwest Iran (see map, pg. 72).

ARMENIANS IN ARARAT

The Armenians migrated into Ararat from Phrygia as early as 522 B.C., according to Lloyd Bailey, associate professor of the Old Testament at Duke University. Quoting fourth-century historian Jerome, Bailey defines *Ararat* as "a region in Armenia on the Araxis . . . at the foot of the great Taurus Mountain."[3] He agrees that, for geographical purposes, Ararat and Armenia existed as different versions of the same kingdom.

Through these and other accounts, we can approximate the likely site of Ararat/Armenia as a rugged region between Lake Van in southeastern Turkey and Lake Urmia in northwest Iran. Still, this gross oversimplification ignores the fact that, while the two regions certainly overlapped, the specific limits of each differed markedly. The discrepancy can be seen most vividly in the centuries at the beginning of the Christian era, when certain Bible translators freely, and, it seems, randomly, substituted Armenia for Ararat.[4] The lively interchange between supposedly synonymous terms not only skewed the bounds of their respective frontiers but altered for future generations the whole notion of the ark's likely landing place.

The impact of this on the modern search for the ark can only be described as profound. According to Bailey, modern theories of the ark on Mount Ararat in Turkey began to circulate in earnest only after early Bible translators began to intermingle the two proper nouns.

In his insightful book *Noah: The Person and the Story in History and Tradition,* Bailey writes, "By the time of the conversion of Armenia to Christianity (fourth-century A.D.) . . . and the introduction of an alphabet, so that the Bible could be translated into Armenian (fifth-century), Armenia was a semi-independent kingdom whose religious and administrative centers were concentrated in the northern part of the country. Thus when some persons read in the early translations that the ark had come to rest in 'the mountains of Armenia,' and when Armenians in particular read this in their own Bible, they might understand it in a much more restricted sense than the writer of Genesis intended."

This flawed interpretation, Bailey asserts, drew inappropriate attention to Ararat's northern limits, where Agri Dagi (the traditional Mount Ararat in Turkey) served as a conspicuous landmark. What resulted was an understandable, if mistaken, tradition, promulgated several centuries after the writing of Genesis and running counter to earlier Bible translations. The Syriac Peshitta and the Aramaic Targums of the first century A.D., for example, "understood the word 'Ararat' in the wide sense," Bailey continues, and translated the word in a way "that exempts Agri Dagi as the prime candidate for the ark's landing place." These early translations, he adds, correctly placed the ark "in the Qardu (Godyene) Mountains, south and east of lakes Van and Urmia, but still within the boundaries of Ararat."[5]

Such distortions persisted into the seventeenth century, with the A.D. 1611 translation of the King James (KJV) Bible. Here, for unexplained reasons, translators updated Ararat to read Armenia in some instances but left it alone in others. We see in both 2 Kings 19:37 and Isaiah 37:38 that translators supplanted Ararat with Armenia, apparently thinking "modern" Bible students wouldn't know where the kingdom of Ararat was. Yet in Genesis 8:4 and Jeremiah 51:27, the King James Version inexplicably sticks with the old term Ararat.[6] Nearly four centuries later, when the New King James Version came out, Armenia had been changed back to Ararat in all four verses. (The New International Version still uses "Ararat" exclusively.)

Such biblical updates and reversions simply highlight age-old misconceptions. Armenia came to prominence some four centuries after Ararat faded from the scene.[7] Yet, according to the ancient record, Armenia occupied a much more restricted area than the author(s) of Genesis intended. Ararat implied a broader, mountainous kingdom with an extensive political reach. So while the terms Ararat and Armenia referred, through the ages, to the same general region, it's easy to see how even minuscule deviations could skew the search area for something as small as an ark.

My research gave me a more realistic grasp of the region's parameters and helped me visualize these ancient lands from a clearer vantage. If nothing else, deciphering the origin and chronology of these shifting bits of data gave me a new starting point. Still I lacked a layer of understanding.

I knew I needed to go back further, to investigate Ararat's earliest history. What did Ararat imply in the centuries before the Armenians drifted into the territory and appropriated the name?

DEEPER INTO THE PAST

Piecing together chips and fragments from an odd array of historical texts, a mottled portrait began to emerge—that of a much older society, one established long before anyone uttered the word Ararat. I found, for instance, that the term grew out of another, far older term.

Ararat entered our nomenclature as an almost arbitrary by-product of a twisted linguistic evolution. Taken back to its earliest root, Ararat sprang from a Hebrew word referenced in Assyrian records as Urartu.[8] Bill Crouse, author of the Ararat Report, explains that the original Hebrew term for the mountains where the ark landed was not, in fact, *Ararat*, but simply *"rrt."* Ancient Hebrew did not write out its vowels, only its consonants; later scribes added the vowel "pointings" we see today. Only over time did "rrt" evolve into the word we now know as *Ararat*. Both words—Urartu and Ararat—share the same consonants (rrt). Only the vowels have changed. Urartu, then, is the true Asiatic forerunner to Ararat/Armenia, a one-time powerful kingdom centered around Lake Van in southeastern Turkey (see map, pg. 110).

In fits and starts my knowledge of the land Noah once walked came into focus, my understanding refined and enlarged. A once vague and confounding concept had crystallized before my eyes into a noble mountain kingdom the ancients called *Urartu!* This is where my search for the ark must begin.

With new knowledge comes new urgency. I kept turning the pages, eager to learn more about this obscure corner of the world—a world that, in my mind, had long cloaked itself in darkness and confusion. With each small revelation, I felt as if the shadows of cloudy thinking were steadily parting, elevating me to the threshold of a broad, well-lit place.

Λ

Thirteen

DISCOVERING URARTU

From fractured bits of truth, a compelling picture had begun to emerge. I'd come abruptly to understand that Noah's ark came to rest in the mountains of *Urartu;* Sennarcherib's assassins fled into the land of *Urartu.* Going all the way back to Genesis 8:4, I could now see that the ark settled somewhere in the dark ravines and beetling cliffs of a mountain kingdom above ancient Assyria known as Urartu.

So now the question became, which mountain range, or ranges, aligned most closely with this primeval kingdom? The question had no easy answer, for the passage of time and Urartu's own obscure beginnings rendered this intriguing kingdom almost invisible to modern sensibilities. Still, I knew that to understand the ebb and flow of Urartu's rise and fall, expansion and decline, meant whittling down the scope of the search for the *true* mountains of Ararat—and thus, the search for the ark.

Yet many questions remained. How, for instance, had a ragtag alliance of towns and kingships known as Urartu melded over three centuries into a regional power? How, from its early pedigree as the Kingdom of Van to its zenith around 850 B.C., did Urartu elbow its way to center stage in a violent, global struggle for world power with its arch-rival Assyria?

RISE OF A REBEL

By the time Urartu first surfaced as a geographical term in the thirteenth century, its southern neighbor Assyria carved a wide, vast swath north and east of ancient Babylonia. In those early days Urartu seemed little more than a vaguely troublesome rebel state rattling its saber southeast of Lake Van. Assyrian king Shalmaneser I, for example, dubbed Urartu a renegade upstart of such trifling stature that he once brought it into submission in a mere three days.

Yet from those humiliating beginnings, Urartu transformed itself in two generations into the most powerful state in western Asia.[1] How did this happen? It succeeded through an often brilliant and aggressive policy of military conquests and strategic alliances that engorged its territories from a small mountain enclave to much of what is now eastern Turkey, northwest Iran (Iranian Azerbaijan), and the Republic of Armenia.

Powerful yet obscure, forged under unusual political and geographical conditions, Urartu's legacy remains one of the most enigmatic civilizations of the Near East. Its archaeological imprint includes massive architectural projects, intricate irrigation works, and stone-carved cuneiform inscriptions in the Kufi language. And then suddenly, on the heels of a spectacular rise to power, Urartu collapsed, swiftly and violently. By the sixth century B.C.—less than two hundred years removed from its heyday—invaders from the north plundered its territories. First the Medes, then the Persians routed its armies, leaving scant trace of Urartu's awesome political, economic, and artistic achievements.[2]

103

Ironically, the record of Urartu's rise and fall comes not from Urartian scribes but from those of its fiercest rival, Assyria. Today we see the growth of Urartu's political, military, and geographic reach through the detailed journals of Assyrian generals, who between 781 and 774 B.C. waged no less than six military campaigns against the maverick empire. Twelfth-century records of Tiglath-pileser I describe an obscure kingdom west of Lake Van (in southeastern Turkey) called "Nairi," a collection of small chiefdoms across Assyria's northern frontier. Yet by the ninth century, at a time Urartu was engaging in military adventurism on all fronts, Assyrian records tell us Nairi had been absorbed by Urartu. It ranked as a military merger of major consequences and helped to usher in a stunning, albeit temporary, season of Assyrian decline.

The ninth and eighth centuries B.C. saw Urartu's influence reach a pinnacle, its borders stretching east of the junction of the two branches of the Euphrates River on the west, down to the western Taurus Mountains on the south, and southeast to the northern reaches of the Zagros Mountains and Lake Urmia. Its northern border draped lazily over the plain of the Araxes River, which today separates modern Turkey from the former Soviet Union (see map, pg. 110). Biblical writers might well have been referring to an immense territory in their use of the word *Ararat*, or, in earlier times, to a much smaller region. The Assyrian General Mutarris-Assur marched into the "Lake Urmiya" region in 821 B.C. to thwart an aggressive southward advance of Urartian King Ispuini; at the time, Urartu occupied the entire territory between Lakes Van and Urmia.[3]

By these records we see that, whatever its size, Urartu posed a terrible threat to Assyria's northern flank. *The Cambridge Ancient History of the Assyrian Empire* notes that "most of the reign of the Assyrian King Shalmaneser IV (782–772 B.C.) was occupied in wars with Ararat (Urartu)."[4] But then, in a power swing as dramatic as its stunning rise from obscurity, Urartu fell. In 714 B.C., Assyrian King Sargon II attacked and routed Urartu in a region east of Lake Urmia (in the vicinity of modern-day Mount Sabalan): "By forced marches Sargon moved northwards along the eastern shore of Lake Urmiya."[5] This crushing defeat pushed Urartu back into its own territory and foreshadowed an inevitable, spectacular collapse.

Politically, Urartu's influence bottomed out in the early seventh century, when invading, nomadic Cimmerian horsemen and plundering hoards of Scythian warriors routed its armies. These warrior bands "poured into Urartu from the southern slopes of the Caucasus Mountains," and by the early sixth century, the former military juggernaut had been reduced to ashes by rampaging Medes.[6]

104
Λ

URARTU IN BIBLE TIMES

Since Genesis 8:4 tells us, in effect, the ark came to rest in the mountains of Urartu, it's important to know its general boundaries at the time Genesis was written.

Bill Crouse, founder of the *Ararat Report,* raises some interesting questions about Urartu's size and influence when the first book of the Bible was authored. Traditional scholars and evangelicals believe the first five books of the Bible (Pentateuch) were written by Moses in the mid-fifteenth century B.C. (or about 1440 B.C.). If so, then the Urartu of Moses' day remained in its infancy—perhaps even its prehistory. For in 1440 B.C., Assyrian records depict Urartu as little more than a loose confederation of invading tribes—hardly the political power it would become six centuries later.

Though Crouse cites evidence that Egypt and Urartu conducted obsidian trade in the mid-fifteenth century B.C.—at or around the time of the Great Exodus, depending on which scholarly tradition one cites—in that day Urartu's boundaries may have been restricted to an area around Lake Van (near present-day Mount Ararat in southeastern Turkey). Ancient Persian sources beg to differ (see chapter 25), however, and place early Urartu squarely in the Lake Urmia region.

On the other hand, many liberal scholars believe in a post-Mosaic authorship of the first five books of the Bible, or roughly around the ninth century B.C., some time during Solomon's reign. By then Urartu would have risen to its political and geographic peak, a global power whose borders would have encompassed the entire mountainous district north of Syro-Mesopotamia, including northwest Iran.

The truth may lie somewhere in between. The *Harper's Study Bible* suggests that while conservative scholars support Mosaic authorship, they generally concede that through time, changes and minor editorial insertions have been made to the original Pentateuch. To help clarify terms and explain certain expressions and historical situations in a relevant, timely light, such editorial insertions might have revised or updated the terms Urartu, or Ararat, to describe the region in a broader, latter-day sense of the kingdom's boundaries.

THE MOUNTAINS OF URARTU

Urartu captures the imagination not only because of its connection to Genesis 8:4 but also because of its rocky, mountainous profile. I found it fascinating that Urartu *never* flourished as an imperial power outside of a mountainous environment. Historian Paul Zimansky says Urartu remained a mountain empire because it "lacked the manpower to operate as an offensive force in the populous territory south of the Taurus mountains."[7] Perhaps Uratu remained a mountain empire because it lacked manpower to do battle in the more populous territory south of the Taurus Mountains. Its strength came from its base as a mountain fortress, and its vital backbone seemed to run along the intersection of the Taurus and Zagros mountains. Their meeting place today, in the scalloped pinnacles and craggy heights of northern Iraq, southeastern Turkey, and northwestern Iran, can best be described as an interminable badlands.

In his great campaign against Urartu in 714 B.C., Sargon II described those mountains as a "netherworld; which, like the spine of a fish, has no passage from side to side and whose ascent from back to front is difficult; on whose flanks gorges and precipices yawn, whose sight inspire fear."[8] The remote, desolate confluence of these massive ranges divided the landscape into sheer canyons and isolated, impregnable passes that thwarted countless Assyrian campaigns.

For me it presented a dark, foreboding frontier of new possibilities for where the ark might have landed.

The shadow Urartu cast narrowed my target area considerably, reducing it to an oblong-shaped bubble encircling the northwest portion of Iran, northeastern Iraq, and extreme southeastern Turkey. Certain old parameters still applied, yet with a new twist. I now had to determine which mountain, or mountains, sat east of Shinar yet still fell within the former kingdom of Urartu.

By these rough coordinates only a handful of viable options remained. From my reading of Genesis 8:5—describing how the flood waters subsided in the tenth month, when "the tops of the mountains became visible"— Noah's mountain had to be one of the tallest (if not *the* tallest) mountain in the region of Urartu. Genesis 8:5 says other mountain peaks became visible to Noah *subsequent* to the ark's landing in the "mountains of Ararat." This strongly suggests that the ark landed on what must have been the highest mountain in a mountainous region. (Recall: Mount Ararat in Turkey sits not in a mountain range but stands alone in the vast Anatolian Plain).

Only one mountain I knew of met all the criteria: the relatively unknown (to western minds) and comparatively unexplored Mount Sabalon in northwest Iran (see map, pg. 110). At sixteen thousand feet, this peak, sitting just east of Lake Urmia, easily ranks as the highest peak in the mountainous region of Urartu. It lies east of Shinar and stands high in a rugged territory within the ancient realm of Urartu.

This latter point I knew beyond a shadow of doubt, and not merely from Assyria's military archives. A recent article pulled off the Internet, released by the Iran News Tourism Desk in Tehran, spoke of extensive excavations in east Azerbaijan Province. Archaeologists there had unearthed an inscription in Kufi belonging to the ancient Urartian Dynasty and written by Gishti Par Rusa, the sixth ruler of the Urartu Dynasty. The release stated that two other of Rusa's inscriptions, describing his regional conquests from about 680–710 B.C., surfaced in east Azarbaijain. Known as the "Razliq" and "Nashtban" inscriptions and unearthed in "Sarab," they were found in the immediate vicinity of Mount Sabalon in northwest Iran. This timely discovery by Iran's top archaeologists all but sealed my opinion of Mount Sabalon as the most compelling candidate for the final resting place of Noah's ark.

CUDI DAGH

Still one other mountain in the region merited consideration: Cudi Dagh, a peak perched between the Taurus and Zagros chains, two hundred miles due south of Mount Ararat along the border of northeastern Iraq. At seven thousand feet, however, Cudi Dagh doesn't cut a very imposing picture. Not even remotely ranked among the highest peaks in ancient Urartu, it can't be described, even in the most reckless terms, as sitting "east of Shinar." Cudi Dagh's berth almost due *north* of ancient Babylon nonetheless overlooks the all-important Mesopotamian Plain, and does lie within the biblical parameters of Ararat/Urartu.

Some researchers, like Bill Crouse, favor Cudi Dagh for its vague association with the oft-mentioned "Gordian Mountains" of ancient history. From about the first century A.D. on, scholars and historians like Flavius Josephus, Berossus, the writers of the Targums, Epiphianus, and Eutychius, variously cite the Gordian, Qardu, Gordyene, or Gordyaean mountains as the ark's landing site.

The problem is, to this day no one knows for certain the exact location of these mountains. Still, Cudi Dagh—notable for its many archaeological ruins (including various shrines and monasteries devoted to the ark)—remained for me more than just a passing curiosity.

FINE STRANDS OF LIGHT

So many fine strands of light; so many snippets of clues. But how does one find an ark the size of a soccer field in a territory the size of Canada?

To illustrate the point, I refer to the April 1997 disappearance of an A-10 Thunderbolt attack jet high in the Colorado mountains. The pilot, Craig Buttons, crashed his jet in an apparent suicide. While radar gave air traffic controllers an idea of the jet's general vicinity when it went down, not even the combined efforts of the United States Air Force—using spy planes and the most advanced military detection technology available—managed to pinpoint the crash site during a full-scale, eighteen-day search. As so often happens in the search for archaeological treasures and biblical artifacts, it took an unwitting passerby named Sonja Webb, driving down the road in a car, to notice a scorched patch of snow high on a splintered peak. She spotted the crash site by pure accident and alerted authorities to its whereabouts. So much for high technology and the consolidated efforts of the military's best minds!

In the case of the ark search, likewise, expertise and scholarship can take one only so far. One can put only so much stock in the accuracy and integrity of Assyrian military records more than two millennia old, or in the timeworn journals of long-forgotten scribes. Regional terminology and the global worldview fluctuate drastically from century to century; imagine the change from prehistory to the modern day! Yet my instincts told me enough strands of light remained to keep me pointed in the right direction. By now I'd eliminated several possibilities and in a relatively short period of time targeted an exclusive neighborhood for the mountains of Ararat. An ever-shrinking target zone kept narrowing to a fine bull's-eye tucked away in the heartland of legendary Urartu.

Armed with new evidence and a fresh perspective, a second trip to Iran seemed inevitable. This time I'd get a research team to assist.

I began to formulate a plan. We'd start out near Khorramabad, do a quick sweep of the west-central Zagros, then shoot north to inspect the high mountains of northern Iran. The thought of standing atop Mount Sabalon piqued my imagination. Suddenly I couldn't wait to return to Iran, couldn't wait to see what this remote region might divulge of Urartu's long-lost secrets. I marked September 6, 1999 on my calendar—the day I would return to Persia.

Part Four

IRAN, ROUND TWO

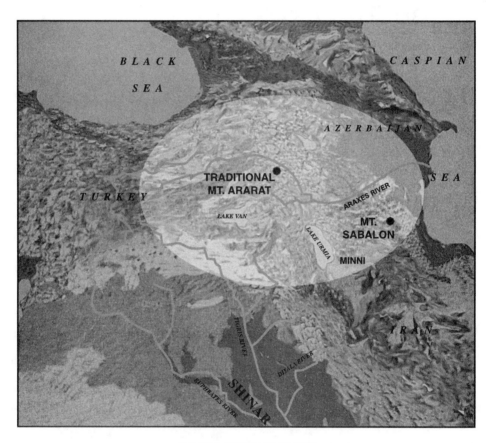

GENERAL REGION OF URARTU

FOURTEEN

TURKISH DETOUR

Pink flares lit up the ink-black sky. Attack dogs wailed above the distant shouts of Turkish soldiers and, farther back, the sirenlike groan of a midnight military convoy. The dense, moonless night found us scurrying across the sharp stubble and creeping shadows of the vast Mount Ararat plain. My swollen tongue stuck to the roof of my mouth and felt like a piece of tar from a Texas highway. Barely able to swallow, I wondered, *Am I dying of thirst?*

Lurching and stumbling through blind gulches and invisible ruts, we bounded along, trying to stay clear of the beacon flares. If spotted, we'd likely be shot. Our Kurdish guides raced out in front, scared to death, jerking at the reins of our pitiful, spindly horses and urging us on with muffled commands.

What in the world am I doing back in Turkey, I wondered, *scrambling down a hideous horse path on the north slope of Mount Ararat?* Four days of relentless climbing, crossing this sea of black without flashlights, dogs howling and flares exploding overhead, had become the most painful ordeal of my life.

By rights I should've been back home in Colorado Springs, packing for my September 6 trip to Iran. Instead I found myself back in Turkey, fleeing for my life, desperate for a sip of water on a mountain whose slopes had given birth to a recurring nightmare. With wooden, mechanical resolve, I forced one leg in front of the other, recalling bitterly how this disastrous detour began. *If not for that infernal phone call . . .*

TURKEY CALLING

On August 14, three weeks from my Iran departure date, I'd received a phone call from my old friend Dick Bright. Calling from Erzurum, Turkey, he sounded breathless with what seemed like urgent news. Buoyant and elated, fresh off a weeklong expedition to Mount Ararat, he spoke with a giddy flutter in his voice. For the gruff, stoic Bright, who typically sounds like General Patton gargling with gravel, it struck me as wildly out of character.

"Bob," he said, ebullient. Long pause. "*I think I found it!*"

The words didn't immediately register, but after a short delay, I practically yelped, "Found what?"

"*The ark!*"

"Where?" I asked.

I knew Bright to be a devout man of God. He'd enjoyed a long career as a pilot for Continental Airlines and held a Ph.D. in theology. Back in 1984, he took a keen interest in the ark search, and, to date, had traveled to Turkey upwards of fifteen times. He'd climbed, flown over, and led enough treks up Ararat to know better than to make such rash pronouncements. Known in ark circles as the "bulldog" for his steely determination and stubborn refusal to quit, Bright could always be counted on to stay balanced and objective. But now he sounded cocksure, almost defiant.

"*I found it!*" he repeated again, setting me further back on my heels.

Measuring my tone, I casually asked where his sighting had occurred, up high, near the Abich II glacier? Or down low, in . . .

"The Ahora Gorge," he blurted out, "low into the Abich II glacier, imbedded in the cliff face." Then he added: "I've got a *picture*. I'd like you to look at it."

Fumbling for words, I said, "A *picture*? What's that you say, Dick? A *picture?*"

I'd lapsed into a full stall, deeply skeptical, searching for a diplomatic response. I'd made extensive (and expensive) plans in diametric opposition to such news. I'd booked flights, hired a videographer, and raised financing for a team bound for Iran. Northwest Persia, the ancient land of Urartu, sat firmly in my sights. To sit mute as Dick Bright crowed about his discovery in the Ahora Gorge seemed distressing, to say the least. His next statement only compounded my confusion.

"Bob," he chirped. "I want you to go back up with me, to help me *verify* it."

Me—go back to *Turkey*? What bizarre, unseemly stream of events could've conspired to put me in this bewildering position?

"I don't *think* so, Dick," I replied, flustered. Awkwardly, I tried to explain that I was making final preparations for an expedition to Iran, and that it simply didn't make sense to change course at such a late date. But Bright dug in his heels, flagrantly indifferent to my protests.

"Listen, Bob, don't make a decision now. I'm sending a picture express mail. Look it over. I'll call you back in a few days." Then he hung up.

I continued to put last details in place for the Iranian expedition. When Bright's package appeared at my door, I ripped it open and curiously scanned his "discovery." Indeterminately dark and grainy, awash in the canyon's bleak shadows, the photo framed a section of a fractured rock face overlooking a ledge scattered with boulders. At center, an angular, flint-edged object of uncertain size initially looked vaguely boat shaped. I'd seen hundreds of rocks just like it scattered across Ararat's face. Everyone mistakes rocks for boats on the mountain. A closer look indeed revealed it to be nothing more than a boxy, pointy-shaped *boulder*—striated here, tapered there on an edge—yet little different from the dozens of "mysterious objects" I'd seen frozen on film. Knowing the gorge as I did, I immediately tabbed it a typical hunk of basalt with an ice-chiseled, prow-shaped nose. The phone rang just as I decided to give the photo, and the trip to Turkey, an enthusiastic thumbs down.

"What do you make of this photo, Bob?" asked my friend on the other end of the line, master climber Bob Stuplich. Bob already had signed on as the lead climber on my Iranian expedition, and now he was calling from Crested Butte with a print of Bright's photo in his hand. A wily veteran of numerous Ararat expeditions, Stuplich knew the terrain of the Ahora Gorge more intimately than any westerner I knew, so it relieved me to hear him debunk Bright's "ark" photo outright.

"I looked at it a long time," he said, "but I finally had to call Dick and ask where the *boat* was supposed to be. He told me where to look, and I said, '*You're kidding!* You took a picture of a *glacier.*'"

Either way—a rock? a glacier?—Bright's request posed a problem. "I'm telling you, this is Noah's ark," he kept saying. "I was *there.* Come over, and you'll see it, too."

But I'd already packed my bags for Iran, with a four-man team chomping at the bit to test *my* theory of the ark's landfall. Meanwhile, Bright sat in Turkey, circulating murky photographs that defied positive confirmation. What should I do?

When Dick called back, he practically pleaded with me to meet him in Erzurum. "When you see it in person, Bob," he said, "you'll know what I'm talking about. It looks like an old boat; you can even see the beams."

Stumped and disbelieving, I steadfastly did not want to return to Mount Ararat. Yet, strangely, the more I churned it over in my mind, the less I abhorred the idea. After all, going brought some subtle benefits. Bright defined the meaning of "credible witness," with both a Ph.D. and a commercial pilot's license. Hundreds of less credible eyewitnesses had seen similar boat-shaped objects across Ararat's face, but to chronicle Bright's quest for the ark on video during one of the driest, ice-free seasons on record, would help demonstrate what I'd been saying: the mountain's phantom shadows, jutting faults, and fractured joints can fool the most ardent

113

explorer—even one with impeccable credentials. For centuries these mirage sightings have skewed objectivity on Mount Ararat. (I have no doubt that hundreds of years from now, people will still be climbing up and seeing "arks" all over that mountain.)

After more thought I finally decided. How could I lose? Traveling back to Turkey to confirm that Bright had seen just another phantom ship would only strengthen my theory about Iran. And if, on the outrageous chance we found something (which now seemed about as likely as Bill Gates doing the Macarena in high heels), I'd be there to see it for myself. In any event, climbing Ararat on foot would give me a new perspective. To this point I'd only surveyed it by air.

After some quick calculations I decided to take a second cameraman to Turkey while the Iran team went ahead to Tehran. We'd climb Ararat, shoot some video of the Ahora Gorge, and add it to my file footage. To my knowledge, in the past decade no one had climbed or filmed on Mount Ararat. So what initially seemed like a costly, dangerous detour, began to look like a great opportunity to bolster my research. If all went well, I'd scurry off the mountain and catch a next-day flight to Tehran, on schedule.

I called Stuplich and said, "If we're going to go, we've got to go *now*."

With those words I flung us headlong into a flurry of last-minute preparations: reordering our flights, tightening timetables, revising visas, repacking gear. I'd wrangled a quick deal with another veteran videographer, Tucson-based cameraman David Banks, to shoot the Turkish leg of the trip. Fifty years old and an experienced climber, he expressed some reluctance. His ailing wife was about to start her first round of chemotherapy. But then he called back and said, "My wife told me it was the opportunity of a lifetime and that I had to do it. I guess I'm going."

With Banks on board, it seemed only hours before I found myself stepping on a plane bound for Istanbul, via Frankfort and Munich. I'd devised a simple itinerary: We'd do a quick, three-day climb of Mount Ararat, check out Bright's sighting, then climb back down and hop a plane to Tehran. If we found something interesting, great; if not, I'd revert to Plan A without missing a beat. The downside? I knew such a rushed, crazy schedule would impose *massive* added hardships on an already grueling ordeal; it would stretch my physical and mental limits to the breaking point. I wasn't at all sure my training regimen (involving daily jogs to the top of nearby Cheyenne Mountain) had prepared me for the task.

BACK ON TURKISH SOIL

Rumpled and jet-lagged, Stuplich and I set down in Istanbul, where we hooked up with our photographer, David Banks, then caught a quick flight to Van on the shores of Lake Van. Dick Bright met us there with a confident grin, quickly herding us into a van and driving us straight to

Dogubayazit, a small frontier town on Mount Ararat's southern foot. "Everything's taken care of," he assured us. "I've made all the arrangements."

I understood it to be both good and bad news—meaning, for one, we wouldn't have to wait indefinitely for the Turks to grant us permits. But Bright's comment made it clear other "nonofficial" arrangements were in place. This usually meant a payoff (a bribe), which set me on edge. Such arrangements had a way of blowing up in your face. My assumption was that some sort of "gratuity" had passed through unofficial channels, most likely through Bright's savvy, well-connected guide named Micah—to the oily palm of some faceless Turkish official, who evidently had clout to convince the entire Turkish military to turn its head long enough for us to complete our mission.

Bright remained elusive, refusing to go into details of his "special arrangement" but assured us nonetheless that it would allow us to climb the mountain, even though a civil war of sorts now raged on the slopes of Mount Ararat.

I groaned inwardly. Turning to Stuplich, I whispered, "How many Kurdish entrepreneurs have made their fortunes off us dumb Americans looking for the ark?"

"I just hope this Micah chap puts Bright's 'special arrangement' to good use," he whispered back, "and doesn't stuff it in his early retirement fund. If this plan doesn't work, we'll have a short, one-way trip up the mountain."

MOUNTAIN REFLECTIONS

We spent the night in Dogubayazit, in clear view of haze-covered Mount Ararat. I hadn't seen it in more than ten years. With its summit framed by a brooding, rose-peach sunset that seemed like writhing flames of a live volcano, it stood as proud and breathtaking as ever.

Seated at an outdoor cafe to enjoy a classic Turkish feast of lamb kabobs, vegetables, and rice, our anticipation turned the conversation into a testosterone-charged patter of aging men glorying in their most harrowing exploits. The animated dialogue, fueled by our exotic surroundings, scintillating views, and spicy fare, set our minds to reeling with the agonies and ecstasies of the painful mountain. Many a dashed dream littered Ararat's slopes, some of my own among them. Although I'd never climbed the mountain (and therefore slipped low in the table-talk pecking order), I knew well Ararat's reputation as one of the most inhospitable places on earth. Many a climber had simply disappeared up there, swallowed up by its icy crevasses. And of the stout men to make it up and back in one piece, most vowed never to return.

Amid the spirited talk, memories of Jim Irwin flooded back. I missed the calm, low-key humor he always lent such moments. How doggedly that

115

slight man had prowled Ararat's unforgiving heights—even in failing health. He remained indefatigable in his quest for the ark. He'd suffered a series of heart attacks leading up to the one that finally killed him in 1991 while biking in the Colorado Rockies and once explained how his heart had been irreparably damaged by the frantic, fevered pace of his historic 1971 moon walk. For eighteen hours he and Commander David Scott hustled around the lunar surface in stifling hot, unvented space suits, collecting rocks and charting the terrain. Irwin pushed himself beyond the point of collapse to execute an exhaustive task set, and by the time he returned to the Lunar Module, his own body sweat filled his boots shin-deep. On the flight home NASA detected a serious heart murmur from which he never fully recovered.

The memory left me queasy. I was nearing fifty myself and, staring up at the rocky behemoth filling the eastern skyline, doubting my own fitness. Would my middle-aged heart weather Ararat's arid, oxygen-starved conditions this late in the game?

116

Λ

MOUNTAIN MAN

Glancing across the table at Bob Stuplich—tanned, tall, tawny—I saw a man of supreme confidence and swagger. If anyone could boast self-assurance on the eve of our climb, he could. Yet back in 1975, he, too, had vowed never to return to Mount Ararat. As an idealistic, twenty-five-year-old Christian ski bum from Wisconsin, he'd dropped out of Biola College and taken his religious studies—and skis—to L'bri, Switzerland, where he demonstrated an instant affinity for sheer cliffs and soaring summits. When he learned that his hero—Noah's ark scholar, author, and biblical apologist, Dr. John Warwick Montgomery—had a visiting professorship up the road in Strasbourg, France, he wheeled across the border and presented himself at Montgomery's doorstep, insisting he could help the professor conquer Ararat. A fast friendship formed, and Montgomery took his young protege at his word, inviting young Stuplich to drive a Jeep filled with mountain gear to Dogubayazit for the summer.

Stuplich spent the month fishing, working the fields below Ararat, and generally getting acquainted with the local Kurds, while Montgomery sat back in Ankara waiting for permits. Stuplich made the most of his Turkish holiday, earning the local Kurds' trust, learning how to negotiate (and often bypass) the official permitting process.

"In those days," Stuplich recalled, "the Kurds laughed at the concept of getting *Turkish* permission to climb the mountain. The *Kurds* controlled the mountain, and I knew them all by their first names. It put me in immediate demand as the leader of several expeditions."

All that would change in 1975, when, as Stuplich recalled, "the Turkish-Kurdish situation went bad." In his years of scaling Ararat, Stuplich had weathered every frightful condition the mountain had to offer—including being taken for dead in a 1974 blizzard on the Parrot Glacier. Even that didn't prepare Stuplich for the nightmarish summer of '75, when, fearing arrest by Turkish authorities, he and a friend leaped from a second-story hotel window and made a mad dash up Ararat's south face before fleeing the country. "I was so scared," he recalled, "I told myself I'd never go back to southeastern Turkey. Getting thrown in jail in Turkey is about as bad as standing before a firing squad."

Stuplich's resolve lasted six years, when his name unexpectedly showed up in one of Montgomery's books as "my intrepid advance scout." It amounted to a lofty endorsement from a leading ark scholar, and Stuplich found himself once again inundated with lucrative offers to head up expeditions. He reconsidered his pledge and, in the end, couldn't resist the mountain's potent call. He still regards southeastern Turkey as one of the "scariest places on earth—the wild, wild west," an outlaw outback where one of the world's more disturbing new undercurrents pose a constant threat to life and limb.

"Anytime you have an ethnic group (the Kurds) occupying a land governed by another country (the Turks)," he explained, "you have a political and military dynamic like that in Bosnia and the Balkans. At any time the situation can explode into sudden, unpredictable violence.

"The Kurdish concept of life," he continued, "can be described, quite literally, as 'give me liberty or give me death.' Our forefathers lived and breathed this concept, but over here you can *feel* it. The Kurds will eagerly die for their ethnic group and for the land they believe belongs to them. And in certain, dicey situations atop Mount Ararat, one can find himself in a position where they expect *you* to die for their ethnic group."

In this sense we'd *all* been repeatedly fortunate as we toured hot spots around the globe. But sitting at dinner, listening to Bob spin his tales, I lamented that I'd never see this land through his eyes. He *knew* Ararat, knew its people. For me, simply sitting at a cafe at the foot of Ararat—site of some of my greatest disappointments—seemed cruelly ironic.

But in the leaden humidity of the Anatolian dusk, watching the molten sun dissolve in the west, I felt a certain flicker of suspense. Confronted anew with the daunting challenge of Agri Dagh, I gave in once more to a familiar, rippling awe.

"Painful mountain," I whispered under my breath, *"here I come!"*

Fifteen

IN COUNTRY

Micah dropped us off at the mountain's western edge well after sunset. Each team member crouched low in the back of the van, seated like wooden soldiers atop our backpacks. My watch said 9:30 P.M. As we stood to step out, a set of headlights appeared on the crest of a nearby hill.

"Close the doors. . . . Close the doors!" Micah shouted.

We all hunkered down again, just as a Turkish military police car passed us going the other way. Micah sped off into the dark, making me wonder: *Why all the fear and secrecy? Hadn't someone been paid off?*

No one but Dick Bright and Micah, his Kurdish go-between, knew the details of our "special arrangement," and Bright told us not to ask questions. Yet he gave the distinct impression that some ranking officer within the crack Turkish Army division charged with patrolling Mount Ararat had agreed to divert the troops long enough to grant us access to the mountain. Judging from Micah's paranoia, we'd been given an extremely narrow window.

We'd waited all day at a seedy youth hostel outside of Dogobyzit to hear that the coast was clear. Word finally came at dusk. Micah rushed in and told us to load our gear in his van.

"*Quick! Quick!*" he said, as we crowded into the back.

Micah drove us out of town, past a large convoy of Turkish troop transport trucks headed in the opposite direction.

"See that?" Stuplich whispered. "Our payoff at work."

Micah circled around and dumped us off at the previous drop-off point, but pitch darkness now made it impossible to see five feet beyond the door of the van. We stood up, waiting tensely for Micah's signal to go, when our other Kurdish guide, a young fellow of about twenty, saw another set of headlights coming and screamed, *"Out, out, out!"* He leapt from the van, landing headfirst in a shallow ditch beside the road. Staring unbelieving at his fearless dive, I took a deep breath, glanced over at Stuplich, and jumped into the ditch alongside the Kurd. Seconds later, our entire team lay sprawled in the scrub-filled ditch, the oncoming truck's high beams shaving the tops of our heads.

Micah sped off down the road and out of sight. I hated to see him go—an experienced climber himself who spoke good English, he might have led us up the mountain. He chose to stay back and keep us posted of Turkish military movements via cell phone.

"I'll do you more good down here," he said, as we jumped from the van one by one, like army paratroopers.

As both truck and van vanished in the distance, we picked ourselves up and began scrounging in the dark for our packs and supplies. Half of our gear ended up on the opposite side of the road, and, without flashlights, we gathered up what we could find and sprinted en masse across the road into the plain, trying to keep up with the young Kurd. Bright whispered that horses waited for us up ahead, some three hundred yards into the fearsome darkness.

A howling wind chilled me to the bone, and the soupy blackness struck dread in my heart. With only stars above, we had no shadows or visible contours to guide us across the knobby plain. Worse, I knew dangerous predators—bears, wild dogs, an abundance of poisonous snakes—roamed the peak's marshy lowlands. I could deal with the dogs, but the prospect of stepping on a snake filled me with terror. With each step I imagined crunching down on the head of a nesting asp, feeling its fangs latch to my shin. I plodded on anyway, tripping down blind gullies and up invisible hillocks until we finally saw the black silhouettes of five nervous horses prancing in the distance. We arrived to find an elderly fellow (the lad's father, I assumed) fighting to keep them from spooking.

A thick tension filled the air. The horses, rearing and snorting against their bits, felt it, too. For men who'd supposedly garnered assurances of safety from ranking authorities, our guides seemed scared to death. They behaved as if the slightest noise would call down a Turkish battalion on our heads.

Lashing our packs haphazardly to the horses, we stumbled off into the night. "Wait!" Stuplich shouted, "I can't find my backpack!"

He ran from horse to horse, fumbling feverishly in the dark for his pack. The Kurds tugged angrily at the horses, but Stuplich jerked back. "I'm not going up that mountain without my backpack!" he said angrily. He knew well the terrors of Mount Ararat, where summit temperatures can dip as low as 40 degrees below zero and where winds can scream by at 150 miles per hour. As he frisked the horses, I reached for my flashlight, cupping my hand over the bulb so we could see a few inches in the dark.

"No lights!" the elder Kurd hissed, bounding over and ripping it from my hand.

Stuplich finally found his pack strapped awkwardly to a horse. At last we resumed our manic flight into the Anatolian steppe. I'd never seen such a chaotic, panicky start to an expedition.

"Why are the guides so petrified?" I asked Bright between breaths, "if the Turks were compensated for our safe passage?"

He just shrugged and said, "We've just got to keep going."

FAST HIKE

Our traveling party consisted of myself, Stuplich, Bright, photographer David Banks, Canadian fireman George Kralik (invited along as our medic), and the two skittish Kurds. We hiked fast, blind to all but the plain's most obvious shapes and forms. I navigated by sound, keeping pace and staying on track to the muffled clop of horse hooves. I'd regained a degree of composure, having momentarily forgotten about the snakes and, for long awestruck moments, simply stared up at the mountain, now eerily silhouetted against the starry sky like an enormous, glowering pyramid. It seemed so far away, so impossibly distant, that it appeared almost unapproachable.

Was it a mistake? Had we been dropped off at the right spot? Untold miles of hiking remained just to get to its base, where we could finally *start* climbing.

"It's going to take us *forever* to get there," I complained to Stuplich. "This can't be right."

"Shhhh!!!!" the elder guide spit back through the pall.

Stuplich seemed strangely amused by my naivete and whispered sarcastically, "What did you expect, Bob? This is the deal. If you want to climb Mount Ararat, it's a killer walk start to finish."

"Shhhhh!!!!" hissed the younger Kurd.

Suddenly I *didn't* feel like climbing the mountain but kept walking anyway. We trudged five miles across the plain—trekking through an endless, meandering network of rugged ravines girdling the lower basin—before even starting a mild ascent. Climbing ever farther into the dense mantle of darkness, walking, walking, fjording sharp, invisible draws, and shuffling down into rocky washes and dead-end cul-de-sacs, each step began to take a toll on our cramping legs and backs. For a few miles we stayed together, keeping a compact perimeter about the horses, but as the hours passed, we each found our own stride, and slowly the team spread out across the slope. At times it felt like climbing alone, marching silently in the dark. I'd occasionally fall off pace and have to stop to listen for . . . yes, the faint sound of a hoof or boot kicking a stone or trampling brush. All night I stared up at the mountain, still so mystifyingly far away. At this snail's pace I didn't see how we'd ever make it to the top.

At about 1:30 A.M., just as we began to enter the lower foothills, the moon came out and illuminated the entire plain. It seemed a miracle, this thin, glowing wafer, brightening the flats bright as day. To eyes dilated by numbing darkness, it ignited the heavens like a supernova. We walked non-stop for ten weary hours up Ararat's western haunch, stopping to rest only when the first threads of dawn danced drowsily over the eastern plateau. By 5:30 A.M. our furious pace had paid off. We'd chopped a sizable chunk out of Ararat's interminable plain. What a few hours earlier had seemed an insurmountable gap, in the cheering light of morning showed itself a doable climb. Standing exhausted on a flattened patch of meadow at nine thousand feet, we pulled off our boots and unfurled our sleeping bags. Then we collapsed on the ground, as if drugged, for a quick nap.

121

WILD DOGS AND GREEN SHALLOWS

I didn't remember falling asleep, but I woke to see three huge Kongal sheepdogs circling us on the small knoll. These were the wild dogs of the mountain I'd heard of, trained to kill anything that moved. Jim Irwin once told me these sheepdogs struck more fear in him than either the mountain or the military, and from the thin veil of my sleeping bag, I saw what he meant. They kept circling, drooling, and growling over us like they saw breakfast—square-jawed beasts, bred for battle, looking as stout and muscled as diesel engine blocks. Each wore a spiked collar and had jowls like a coiled-steel bear trap.

To a man we played dead, tucking our heads inside our sleeping bags until we heard a faint voice calling out from below the ridge. After a few moments a bedraggled-looking Kurdish shepherd hiked up from the meadow and whacked the dogs on the head with his staff. The filthy mongrels instantly retreated, cowering in the grass like scolded pups.

Struggling to my feet, my back stiff and sore, we thanked the shepherd for his timely entrance by offering him some tuna and water from our packs. He hungrily accepted, devouring a tin of tuna in seconds. We all joined in, digging into our rations. After the marathon hike, our bodies craved protein, and the tuna tasted like prime tenderloin. I rolled mine up with bread like a burrito, devouring two cans in short order. I dreaded the brutal climb ahead, but the food and short nap revived me. Ararat loomed directly above us now in all its craggy splendor, lavender clouds caressing its high mountain passes. Her majestic, ice-capped peak filled the morning sky; her bright glaciers taunted us, glistening like blue razors in the sun.

With our cranky horses now bristling against our every move, we set off on a slow, ponderous climb up a tortured sequence of jagged slopes, cutting through loose rock and steep, scree-covered upgrades.

"Watch your ankles," Stuplich cautioned. "The rocks up here are like bowling balls—always rolling out from under you."

For the next two hours we rolled with them, hacking out a random path to Lake Kop on Ararat's northern flank. I'd seen the lake from the air and knew the glacier-fed pool as the traditional low base camp of veteran ark searchers. It also serves as a crucial first water refill stop, and we arrived just in time. At our blistering pace, we'd literally burned through our water supplies, and we all anticipated drinking our fill at Lake Kop. The moment the horses caught the scent, they charged toward the lake and started sucking like industrial Shop-Vacs. We arrived seconds later, ready to follow suit, but stopped short. Instead of the crystalline blue, pristine mountain lake we'd expected, we stared, disbelieving, at a slime pit pocked with hundreds of sheep hoofprints.

Kop's shallow waters, less than an acre in circumference, looked as thick and green as pea soup, its filmy surface freckled with floating dollops of sheep dung. The sight alone, not to mention the smell, made me nauseous, and though we felt dead on our feet—with only a few swigs left in our bottles—we turned away. There would be no refills at Lake Kop. Our guides spoke confidently of another stream bubbling out of the mountain at eleven thousand feet, so we wrestled the engorged horses away from their soothing oasis and resumed our climb into a curtain of cloud.

An hour, and one thousand feet later, we crested a hard rock plateau to hear the joyous song of a gurgling glacial stream. I left my horse and walked toward the sound, a small rivulet, about ten inches wide, tucked behind a stand of boulders in a shallow gully. Shimmering in the sunlight, its milky gray waters flowed fifty feet down the slope, then vanished into the volcanic turf. With our compact, reverse-osmosis filters, we pumped a few cups, repeating the process until the water filtered relatively clear and sweet. After pumping several quarts, we sat on a rock drinking until our heads hurt and our bellies swelled as hard as cast-iron kettles.

Even in fire-baked Saudi Arabia, where it's impossible to quench one's thirst, water never tasted so good. I could *feel* it replenishing my dehydrated body, inch by inch. Finally satiated, we pumped three more quarts each for the next leg of the hike, stuffed them in our packs and commenced climbing—up, up, up one backbreaking switchback after another.

MUTINY ON THE MOUNTAIN

The horses had now become a major concern, proving more a hindrance than a help. Slack-jawed and emaciated, their ribs sticking out like the strings of a harp, each looked as if it had just been plucked from

Auschwitz. Their spindly legs kept buckling under the weight of our packs, and on several occasions one or more would simply collapse to its knees. Tugging on their reins up each step of an endless stairstep of serrated passes, we found our progress came agonizingly slow. I looked over at Kralik—his walking pole bent and twisted from whacking his horse on the haunch to keep it moving.

"We should have left the horses behind," Stuplich complained. "It would have been easier climbing on foot."

I believed him. You can't just take a horse straight up the side of a mountain; you have to find the right path. I lost track of all the dead-end box canyons we had to fight our way out of just to gain fifty feet of altitude. Less than a day in, the horses looked like they might drop dead at any moment.

The Kurdish guides proved only slightly less bothersome. Whenever the going got especially rough, they'd go ballistic, throwing their hands in the air, jabbering and complaining that they couldn't go on. For Bright, who never could suffer fools, such antics didn't wash. He'd paid handsomely for horses *and* guides and expected both to perform. At each sign of mutiny, he lost his temper, turning red in the face: *"I'm paying you $7,000! You turn back, and you won't get a penny!"*

I hadn't seen this side of Bright before. He always struck me as unfailingly polite, even mildmannered, under stressful circumstances. But he hadn't earned the nickname "Bulldog" for nothing, and our whining, high-maintenance Kurds, behaving like fussy old women, drove him crazy. So it went, hour after hour, on and on, under the constant threat of insubordination, squeezing our way up through massive boulder fields, scooting across ankle-cracking moraine, yanking on the horses' reins only to feel the bits fly out of their mouths. Then we'd walk back down and start over.

I'd never endured anything more maddening in my life.

By 7:30 P.M., as the sun sank into the plain behind us, we arrived at twelve thousand feet to a flat patch of wind-battered grass nestled in the shadow of a cold cliff wall. We'd been charging hard for twenty-two straight hours with only one short rest; we needed water again, and our bottles ran empty.

Too tired for words we threw down a makeshift camp and dragged out our portable gas stove to heat a dinner of freeze-dried chicken casserole. With everyone else sprawled on the tundra, too exhausted to move, I climbed the remaining fifty yards, over a small rise, to a large slab of melting ice wedged in a stand of boulders. Below it, just as the Kurds promised, sat a drizzling pool of melt-off, ten-feet wide, but . . . *oh my gosh!* . . . it brimmed with hoofprints and sheep dung. This emergency water source reflected the same sickening smell and pea green color we rejected at Lake Kop.

If I drink this, I thought, *I'll have Montezuma's revenge until the year 2010.*

Yet as far as I could see, I had no other choice—I didn't expect to find a water fountain up this high, and the guys below, cracked-lipped, cotton mouthed and dispirited, needed rehydration . . . *fast*. We wouldn't make it another hundred yards without water, so, against my strongest impulses, I knelt down and stuck my filter into the turbid pool, siphoning out as many pollutants as possible before filling our plastic liter bottles. Returning to camp, I didn't have the heart to tell the others the condition of the water they so greedily guzzled. *Ignorance is bliss*, I thought, and they didn't seem to mind.

Over the next hour I prepared and cooked our dinner, serving the others but feeling too nauseated to eat myself. Either the water or the altitude had finished me for the day. The others nibbled a few bites and crawled sheepishly into their tents. My own sleep came hard and fitful, fraught with strange, high-altitude dreams of cracking crevasses and exploding avalanches. In one I drank gloriously from crystal mountain springs; in another I battled angry nests of spitting snakes. I slept nonetheless, and that's all that mattered. Tomorrow would be harder than today and far more dangerous. We had half a day to reach the lip of the Ahora Gorge, where Bright's ark supposedly lay.

Sixteen

TO THE SUMMIT!

I woke to the grating sound of Dick Bright and the Kurds bickering loudly. Sometime during the night's subzero temperatures, our guides had decided, without telling us, to retreat down the mountain with the horses. They had already packed and were ready to go when Bright, half-awake in his frost-glazed parka, began to boil.

"*No money!*" Bright shouted. "*Do you understand me? No money!*"

The $7,000 Bright offered the Kurds would allow them both to retire in luxury, but so far they hadn't acted even remotely as if they intended to earn it. The cruel rigors of Ararat seemed too high a price for even a once-in-a-lifetime payday, and I could see by the veins bulging in Bright's neck he meant to fire them without a cent.

Stuplich, already up and packing for the day's climb, walked over to calm things down just as Bright clenched his hands around the youngster's collar.

The young Kurd's eyes turned fierce—wild. He clearly wanted to throw the old codger off the cliff.

"That's *enough!*" Stuplich bellowed, separating them. "We're a *team.*"

Bright and the Kurd backed off, brought to their senses by the word "team." Even the young Kurd understood: on these dizzying Alpine tracks, no man lives unto himself. To abandon us up here would violate the supreme rule of the mountain. Such heights must be scaled not by individuals but by parties—*teams!*—and every member of the party is part and parcel of every other member. As the venerable Christian essayist F. W. Boreham once said, "No brotherhood could be more real, more practical, or more imperative. The murky mists of the valley often obscure the fact that we are, in deed and in truth, members one of another."

Suddenly the young Kurd lunged at Bright—yet instead of flinging him off the ledge, he wrapped Bright in the tightest bear hug I'd ever seen, then kissed him on the cheek. Bright stood there, speechless, and we all felt deeply relieved that the Kurds had come to their senses. Walking away, Stuplich whispered sardonically, "I think they saw their nest egg passing before their eyes."

The uproar rousted Banks and Kralik, sleepy eyed, from their sagging tents. With the morning's crisis over, Stuplich and I crammed a couple of power bars and bottles of green-tinted water in our packs, then marched quickly out of camp. Frustrated by the sluggish, fitful pace, we intended to set out early and scout a feasible route up to the Parrot Glacier in advance of the team.

All this quarreling over horses and turning back had cost us valuable time. Since we could move only as fast as our slowest man, we hoped our quick departure would incite the troops to strike camp and get moving. As the intrepid mountaineer, George D. Abraham, once said: "In negotiating a difficult pass, in clambering up a perilous face, or in attempting a forbidding ascent, it is the weakest member of the expedition whom all other members must consider. His failure would be the failure of all." From here on in, we needed everyone working as a unit, for to squander even a minute could prove fatal.

We turned in time to see Bright again challenging the Kurds about the horses; Kralik, eating a spare breakfast of dried apricots and granola; and Banks, tending to his tripods and cameras. The latter two waved as we went by.

"We'll be right behind you," Banks said.

"Don't hold up the train," Stuplich snapped. "The days up here are short."

Still wrapped in morning mist and surly with whipping winds, the summit towered before us. The sun rose quickly, warming our stiff muscles as we climbed toward the bulging humpback of Parrot Glacier and quietly pondered Ararat's stark solitudes and glacial heights.

PARROT GLACIER

Climbing separately up a steep, rugged field of teetering, cabin-sized boulders, Stuplich and I separated in hopes of finding the best route up. I arrived first at the stony ridge running east alongside Parrot Glacier, and, as I waited in the harsh morning sun, turned to behold the vast, icy colossus in quiet repose.

This leviathan block of ice got its name from professor Friedrich Parrot, who in 1829 became the first foreigner in modern times to reach Ararat's stormy summit. In coming years Parrot Glacier became a familiar haunt of ark searchers who theorized its prodigious ice cap made a logical grave for the ark. Spurred on by frequent phantom sightings, in 1955 French explorer Fernand Navarra bore into the glacier to find what he claimed were shards of "ark wood." Subsequent carbon-dating determined the chips were of far too recent origin to have come from the ark, and others—myself included— often noted how the Navarra site approximated where professor Parrot, more than one hundred years earlier, planted two heavy wooden crosses to commemorate his triumphant ascent.

Seeing the glacier up close had a strangely disorienting, even hypnotic effect. Something about its glistening immensity seemed surreal, almost mystical. Set against the indigo sky, it seemed almost alive—a living, breathing organism yawning awake after a long hibernation. Every few minutes or so it would let loose a deep, guttural groan as if protesting our presence, shattering the pristine, breezy quiet. First came a high-pitched creak; then an elongated *craaack;* then, a clattering, quaking symphony of pings and pongs followed by a booming thunderclap—a spectacular, ear-splitting tantrum of shattered ice, triggering hideous echoes and sudden rock slides hundreds of yards below. My heart lodged in my throat watching this glacier snapping and popping with such monstrous force. I felt like an insect, helplessly exposed, about to be swallowed whole.

"Bob!" piped a voice behind me.

I turned to see Stuplich, sweating profusely and looking concerned, strutting toward me on the ridge. "I found you," he said, gazing intently back down the slope. "It's taking Bright and the others *way* too long to get up here. . . . It'll be touch-and-go now if we make it up to the gorge and back down to camp before nightfall."

Inhaling huge gulps of thin mountain air while keeping an eye on the lower slope, he turned momentarily quiet. Then he pointed west, toward a wide, icy moraine framing the eastern rim of the Ahora Gorge.

"See that?" he said between breaths. "That's the boulder field where Jim fell and nearly killed himself back in '82."

I knew the story by heart, the time Jim Irwin and Stuplich spear headed one of the first ascents of Mount Ararat since the mid-seventies. That expedition opened Turkey's doors to dozens of subsequent Ararat expeditions in the eighties, but Stuplich noted it for something far more personal. At fifteen thousand feet, he and Irwin clashed over Jim's indifference to mountain etiquette.

"It's a gross understatement to call Jim a very independent man," Stuplich recalled. "Every so often, as the team went one way toward the summit, he'd go wandering off by himself, looking for the ark. We'd already reached the Cehennem Dere Glacier when someone said they saw something on the other side of the Ahora Gorge. Jim decided he was going to get a closer look and told us he would climb back down to high camp, then climb back up the other side to look into the gorge."

Grinning at the memory, Stuplich added, "I confronted him and told him he couldn't go, that to climb down by himself would be far too dangerous." Then Stuplich shrugged sadly. "I essentially yelled at him in front of the team and ordered him to stay with the group—which was a mistake. I didn't understand the military chain of command, and I think it caused him to lose face; I embarrassed him in front of the others.

"So Irwin stormed off down the mountain. We didn't hear from him again until the next morning, when the folks down at base camp found him at the bottom of the moraine, ripped to pieces."

Irwin had slipped on the ice, then slid out of control down the ice field, slamming headlong into the rocks at the bottom of the moraine field. The fall knocked him unconscious, shattered four teeth, cut his hands to ribbons, and opened two gaping cuts in his head. The search team found him curled inside his sleeping bag at the bottom of the moraine, nearly dead from exposure and blood loss.

"He only survived because he regained consciousness long enough to crawl inside his sleeping bag," Stuplich noted. "He was a bloody mess when we found him, so we patched him up, put him on a donkey, and rushed him down the mountain to a hospital. He was hurt *bad*, but I'll never forget how upbeat Jim was, trying to make light of it."

Stuplich's countenance brightened. "He was trying to make *us* feel better."

To this day Stuplich said he cherishes the memory of Irwin showing up unannounced in Crested Butte a year later to ask forgiveness for getting angry and ignoring his warning.

"He was a good man," Stuplich smiled, "—a *great* man."

Up here on the Parrot, nearly every boulder and crevasse triggered some memory for the veteran climber. Stuplich raised a hand to the east, pointing out the albino hump of Parrot, its back cracked and scarred by a lattice of sunken crevasses. Back in 1974, Stuplich tried three times to find Navarra's "ark wood" inside those yawning trenches. At the bottom of one, he even located what appeared to be a huge, dark object—perhaps the remains of a large ship—yet it sat submerged beneath one hundred feet of glacial water, well out of reach.

But Stuplich is nothing if not doggedly persistent. He climbed down off the mountain, returned to Switzerland to get married, then immediately returned to Ararat with scuba gear and a wet suit. While his new bride waited out the first days of their honeymoon in Erzurum, Stuplich raced back up the mountain with his face masks and fins to probe the depths of the crevasse—but before he could dive, a huge blizzard blew in and stranded him for five days on the ice cap. Word reached his wife below that her new husband had perished in the storm. Fortunately, those reports failed to take into account his exceptional survival skills. He calmly weathered the storm in his North Face tent and climbed down through deadly snowslides and avalanches to retrieve his wife.

"I don't think my wife fully appreciated our honeymoon," he recalled, deadpan.

THE CEHENNEM DERE

Bright and the others finally joined us on the ridge, without horses. Stuplich waved them over.

"You took your sweet time," he said. "Now we've got to hurry, or we'll never make it back to camp in time."

We each took a sip from our bottles and grabbed our packs, preparing to leave, when from below the ridge we heard the menacing WOMP, WOMP, WOMP of helicopter rotors speeding up over the rise.

"*Get down! Get down!*" Bright yelled, and like panicked deer we ditched our packs in the rocks and wedged ourselves under a granite overhang. I knew if the Turkish military chopper—likely searching the peak for Kurdish rebels—saw us or mistook us for Kurdish freedom fighters, they'd blast us off the mountain.

"Pray them away," Dick whispered desperately under his breath. "Pray them away."

For an hour and a half the chopper buzzed overhead, skimming Parrot Glacier to the fringe of the gorge, then all the way up to the summit. When the whirl of rotors finally faded below us and disappeared, we couldn't believe our good fortune. (The next day Micah contacted us on his cell phone and told us that the Turkish military had ambushed several Kurds near Lake Kop just hours after we left the area. The subsequent gun battle left seven Turks and four Kurds dead on the mountainside.)

We had suffered another devastating delay.

With daylight melting away, we pulled our packs out of the rocks and set off up a harrowing path through new vistas of sharp, rolling scree. For another two hours we climbed into the stratosphere, fighting against an unseasonably hot breeze that surprised Stuplich, who'd been blown off the peak by icy blasts at this height. The younger Kurd said he'd never known such dry conditions up so high, and while the heat, preferable under any circumstances to rain or snow, gave us good climbing conditions, it nonetheless forced us to drain our water reserves prematurely. At the glacial pool where Stuplich dipped his cup on a prior trip, we found nothing but an alkaline dust hole. We inched higher up the ridge toward a cluster of ice cliffs hanging from the North Canyon, when Banks suddenly declared, "I hear water rushing."

We climbed another one hundred grueling yards up the crumbling slope to find a tiny puddle of glacier melt-off, and, like our crazed horses at Lake Kop, I charged toward the water, kneeling down to drink.

"Wait, Bob!" Stuplich shouted, yanking me back by the cuff of my jacket.

"What?" I asked irritably. He pointed to a faint, pinkish hue imbedded in the ice.

"See that pink?" he asked. "That's bad bacteria. Drink that unfiltered, and you'll be so sick you'll want to die."

I spat out the water and tore open my pack, looking feverishly for my filter. After pumping another few liters, we all drank deeply, took a few deep breaths, and began struggling back up the last stretch of icy ground to the overhanging Cehennem Dere. I'd seen dozens of pictures of it, but nothing could have prepared me for the visual impact of this colossal cleft of ice rising dramatically into the skyline. It seemed precariously perched on the crater-edge of eternity—an arctic platform to the heavens, and from its enormous floor we caught our first stunning glimpse of the Ahora Gorge. Strapping on our crampons, we began treading carefully across the huge, sloping dome of ice, carefully lifting, then planting one foot in front of the other on the slushy, water-glazed surface.

"It's like climbing across an ice-covered basketball," I carped to Bright, aware that the tiniest slip would send me sledding feet first into the gorge's hungry maw.

Under normal circumstances we would've roped ourselves together for safety, single file. And for a few hundred yards we let Bright, tethered to a cord, lead us across the ice.

"If you fall in, we'll reel you out like a fish," Stuplich promised—but with the late hour and our ploddingly slow progress, Stuplich made an executive decision. He untied the rope and told us to set off on our own.

"What if someone falls?" I asked.

He turned and said, without a trace of sarcasm, "Don't fall."

Step-by-step we traversed the Cehennem Dere, padding alongside creaking crevasses, over fragile ice bridges and down into bowled-out ice pockets. In one windblown snowdrift we came upon the frozen, mummified remains of some unrecognizable one-horned beast, half-protruding from the ice. Its long, serpentine horn, we surmised, once belonged to an ibex: a rugged, wild goat of the mountain, uniquely adapted to these sullen heights. Continuing upward, I shuddered to think, *If Ararat proved too much for that poor beast, what chance do I have?*

By now our legs cramped from oxygen deficit, our faces burned red and blistered from the arctic glare. Momentarily dazed from exhaustion, I carelessly clicked my crampons together, releasing the spring lock on my right ice boot. Before realizing what happened, I found myself staring into the black hole of the gorge, standing one-legged on the ice dome, my crampon dangling by a strap. I couldn't sit, couldn't plant my foot, and didn't dare move. One touch of boot rubber on ice would send me hurtling into the gorge—at the exact spot where Stuplich warned us that many had been swept off the mountain.

Breathing hard, trying not to panic, I started to teeter and lose my balance. Suddenly Stuplich appeared from nowhere and lent me his shoulder. Balancing myself against his body, I very slowly, methodically, reached down and, with trembling fingers, reattached my crampon. Then I stood up and exhaled deeply, knowing that, in all likelihood, he had saved my life.

"Thanks, Bob," I said, but without a word he just nodded and kept walking.

THE GORGE

Our team, spread out now across the Cehennem Dere at intervals of fifty to one hundred yards, treaded lightly over a series of fragile ice bridges and crevasses made nearly invisible by the swirling clouds and fast-descending shadows. At fifteen thousand feet, with most of us suffering from severe oxygen deficit, our eyes played tricks on us, blurring the gorge's fatal edge.

Suddenly Bright called out from beside the lip, "This is the place!"

Stuplich and I and the others walked over to see.

"That's where I saw the ark," Bright said, pointing down into the breathtaking canyon. We followed his pointing finger along the ice, peering over the edge into a chasm, two miles wide and two miles deep, that dwarfed the Grand Canyon. Its jolting contours and depths seemed distorted and out of scale, and I found it hard to focus. Sensing my vertigo, Stuplich placed a steadying hand on my shoulder.

"Don't sweat it," he said. "Most men's knees turn to mush at their first sight of the gorge."

We stood there for a long while, doing our best to scan the flinty cliffs and shadows. At long last Bright spotted his target: a large, angular object imbedded in the opposite cliff face. It appeared sharp and nautical nosed, angling down from the side of the gorge, as in the picture. We surveyed it from several angles with our binoculars, but, as expected, it proved to be nothing but ice-covered rock sticking out from the canyon wall.

I climbed all the way up here for this? I thought.

Coming as it did at the end of an exhausting journey, the sight struck me as depressingly anticlimatic. It made me want to get off the infernal peak as quickly as possible; but even so, we stayed on the rim as long as we could, taking the opportunity to scrutinize the gorge from every angle. We scoured the cliffs, probed its trenches, videotaped the canyon from top to bottom, but saw nothing—no ark, no boat, no object warranting any further time and attention. Though I'd doubted Bright's claims from the start, my heart sank to realize I'd been right. So much pain and effort for *nothing*.

My vague sense of disappointment couldn't compare to Bright's. He now stood glassy-eyed and crestfallen on the rim of the abyss, having climbed this heartbreaking slope three times in the past two months. He didn't want to go down, but to stay a minute longer would be our undoing. As the sun banked slowly below the summit, the temperature began to plummet.

I knew it: we'd stayed an hour too long. We'd never make it down before dark. Desperately thirsty, hungry, and exhausted, the threat of mental lapses now loomed large; oxygen deprivation could slow our progress or even send someone walking absently off a cliff.

With time running out, we gathered our resolve and began painstakingly to retrace our steps back across the Cehennem Dere, knowing that to stray a step or two outside of our tracks could kick out a hidden crevasse.

My watch said 4:00 P.M. Dense clouds and cold settled in about us. It would be pitch dark by 7:30 P.M., yet we still had a four-hour descent to high camp. The math didn't look good, and thanks to the Turkish army, we couldn't use headlamps or flashlights. Imagining our bedraggled crew down-climbing this tortuous route in the dark gave me the cold shakes.

"Let's go, men!" I shouted. "Wake up! Let's get moving. We're in a race against darkness!"

132
Λ

SEVENTEEN

RUGGED DESCENT

Cruising down off the ice cap, shooting video of the sunset, David Banks and I found ourselves in front of the others. Padding to the loose sand ridge below the Cehennem Dere and on to a vast boulder field, I realized that Stuplich, Kralik, and our guide had fallen some distance behind. Farther back still, Bright shuffled morosely across the ice, struggling mightily. Exhausted from the climb, demoralized by his failure at the Ahora Gorge, he'd lost his edge.

"I could've sworn it was the ark," he kept muttering as we turned back toward base camp.

I'd seen it all before: the gorge's shadowy depths, uncommon lighting, and basaltic geology could trick the most sincere observer into believing he'd seen the ark. Bright couldn't have looked more crestfallen. Shortly into our descent, his crampon speared the ice and flipped him head-over-heels down the glacier toward a huge crevasse. He somehow caught a crease with his ice ax at the last possible second and dragged himself to a stop, his legs flailing over the edge. Kralik raced back up the slope and pulled him out—a second fatality narrowly averted.

Now we were in trouble. Any hopes of making it back to camp as a group before dark had passed, a deadly prospect considering we couldn't use flashlights or headlamps for fear of the Turkish military. And then, something else to slow us down: Bright's boot had come apart. Picking my way down the boulder field, I turned to hear Stuplich screaming from above.

"Bob, we're hung up here. Bright's boot is falling apart."

It hardly surprised me. Bright's leather alpine boots, well past their prime, had served him nobly through the years. But this trip pushed them over the edge. Descending from the ice cap, the rubber sole of his right boot had split away and now flapped against the rocks. *What else could go wrong?* I wondered. We'd spent thousands of dollars on travel and equipment, and now the expedition's outcome hinged on a piece of bad footwear. Stuplich shouted that they might try to duct tape Bright's boot together and hope it lasted down one of the steepest stretches of one of the most dangerous mountains in the world—in total darkness. It didn't sound like much of a plan, but what else could they do?

"Are you guys going to be OK?" I shouted back.

"Go on ahead!" Stuplich yelled. "We'll get Dick down somehow."

For three days this potential disaster had been building; now the consequences of every delay, every argument, every horse spitting out its bit, stared us square in the face. Even in broad daylight Bright's predicament would've created a sizable problem, a costly momentum killer. But with darkness closing in, it meant people might die on the mountain this night. Too many blind turns and forked ravines lay between us and high camp to find our way back quickly in the dark. I didn't have the strength to climb back up, and I knew I would be of no use to the others from where I was. Surveying the terrain below, I realized our only hope would be for me to make a mad dash down to camp before the last flicker of sunset disappeared, then try to find some way to guide them in. Maybe, from below, I could do something to help.

I turned to Banks and shouted, "Can you make it on your own?"

"Yeah," he said, clearly too spent to keep up. "Go on. I'll wait on the others."

I knew they'd catch up with him soon enough, so I bolted off down the mountain, moving as fast as I could without killing myself, juking and stutter-stepping into the North Canyon to the narrow ridge beside Parrot Glacier. From above the glacier looked like a big, white serpent coiling into the valley, but my burning legs and lungs kept me from enjoying the splendid scenery. I knew I had to keep moving and not stop even to rest. During extreme circumstances in the past—countless desperate moments in remote locales when I felt like giving up—I learned simply to grit my teeth, block out the pain, and keep pushing, just to gut it out. I knew that to even entertain the notion of resting might mean the difference between surviving . . . or not. So I settled into a mechanical rhythm, mindlessly moving my feet, scooting from rock to rock and letting the "bowling" effect roll me from one point to the next.

Scrambling through the boulder field, it occurred to me that, prior to the 1800s, the Armenians thought it was physically impossible for a human to reach the top of Mount Ararat. Two centuries later, God willing, we'd be up—and *off*—in three days. I now knew, firsthand, why they called it the "painful mountain."

← During his stay in Iran, Davis (center) helped a local Iranian village build a water system, an act of friendship that made him privy to the village's ancient secrets, which held that a nearby mountain concealed the remains of Noah's ark. Accepting an invitation to visit the site, Davis ascended a peak whose name or location remains a mystery, stood upon a ledge and stared down into a steep gorge, where he saw a massive boat, broken in two, protruding from an ice flow—a sight that would change his life forever.

↓ Sergeant Ed Davis of the 364th Army Corp of Engineers, stationed in Hamadan, Iran, during World War II, assisted with the construction of halfway camps and supply routes linking Russia to the Persian Gulf.

↑ Whereas Genesis 8:4 states that Noah's ark came to rest on "the mountains of Ararat," tradition and numerous unconfirmed eyewitness accounts suggest that Mount Ararat—a solitary peak in southeastern Turkey's vast Anatolian Plain—is the true resting place of Noah's ark. This photo, shot by pilot Chuck Aaron in 1988, was taken during one of the first aerial reconnaissance surveys of Mount Ararat.

↑ Author Bob Cornuke, standing here on a 15,000-foot glacier above Ararat's Ahora Gorge, visited Turkey four times to investigate claims that Noah's ark lies buried among the clefts, canyons, and glaciers of Mount Ararat. Yet his search convinced him that, if Noah's ark still exists, it rests on a peak other than Mount Ararat.

⬆ Astronaut Jim Irwin, the eighth man to walk on the moon, introduced Cornuke to the search for Noah's ark. The Lunar Module pilot for Apollo 15, Irwin was the first man to publicly quote Scripture from the moon: "I lift my eyes up to the hills—where does my help come from? My help comes from the LORD, the Maker of heaven and earth" (Ps. 121:1–2).

⬆ Irwin also piloted Lunar Rover 1 (shown here on the lunar surface) and left a Bible on the pilot's seat at mission's end. It was while gazing at earth from the moon's surface that Irwin had a revelation about God and the truth of Scripture. He thereafter dedicated his life to uncovering historical facts and biblical artifacts to validate the authenticity of the Bible.

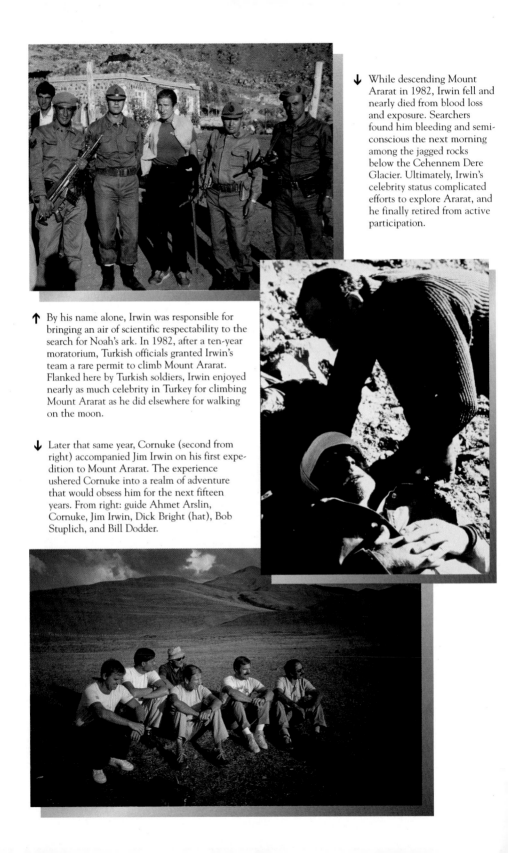

↓ While descending Mount Ararat in 1982, Irwin fell and nearly died from blood loss and exposure. Searchers found him bleeding and semi-conscious the next morning among the jagged rocks below the Cehennem Dere Glacier. Ultimately, Irwin's celebrity status complicated efforts to explore Ararat, and he finally retired from active participation.

↑ By his name alone, Irwin was responsible for bringing an air of scientific respectability to the search for Noah's ark. In 1982, after a ten-year moratorium, Turkish officials granted Irwin's team a rare permit to climb Mount Ararat. Flanked here by Turkish soldiers, Irwin enjoyed nearly as much celebrity in Turkey for climbing Mount Ararat as he did elsewhere for walking on the moon.

↓ Later that same year, Cornuke (second from right) accompanied Jim Irwin on his first expedition to Mount Ararat. The experience ushered Cornuke into a realm of adventure that would obsess him for the next fifteen years. From right: guide Ahmet Arslin, Cornuke, Jim Irwin, Dick Bright (hat), Bob Stuplich, and Bill Dodder.

← Bob Stuplich, shown here climbing an ice cre-vasse on Mount Ararat, and standing above the Parrot Glacier, has led more expeditions to Mount Ararat than any other western explorer. ↓

↓ It is common in southeastern Turkey to see women performing heavy physical labor, such as carrying enormous bundles of wheat and other products on their backs over long distances.

↑ Many villages at the base of Mount Ararat are off-limits to foreigners, especially western climbers, who often try to sidestep authorities in hopes of asking the townsfolk for information, local stories, and traditions about Noah's ark.

← By late 1998, Cornuke's research hinted that the real "mountains of Ararat" consisted of a rugged mountain range in northwest Iran. Located in the heart of the ancient "land of Urartu"—another translation for the Hebrew term *Ararat*—stands the towering 16,000-foot Mount Sabalon, itself the object of a rich local tradition as the true resting place of Noah and the ark.

→ In his efforts to scan every foot of Mount Ararat, Cornuke, in August 1988, surveyed the peak by helicopter with Chuck Aaron and Larry Williams. Here, Cornuke's foot is perched precariously on a helicopter skid while he probes the bowels of the Ahora Gorge. On this trip, during one of the clearest, driest summers on record, Cornuke decided the ark would never be found on Mount Ararat.

← In 1999, more than ten years after his last trip to Turkey, Cornuke and a small team, spearheaded by Dick Bright and including Bob Stuplich, took one last, clandestine trip to Mount Ararat to search for Noah's ark, hiking all night past dogs and military patrols to reach the peak's base.

↑ The group came across this frozen, unidentifiable carcass high on the Cehennem Dere Glacier, leading them to question their chances on the unforgiving summit.

↑ With nightfall fast approaching and a long climb back down to high base camp, videographer David Banks padded precariously across the massive ice cap that spills over into the Ahora Gorge.

↑ After barely making it down Mount Ararat in a frantic, midnight descent, Cornuke and Bob Stuplich immediately flew to Iran, where locals pointed them toward a well-known hot springs called Ghotor Suee (otherwise known as Sulfur City), nestled like a set piece from *Raiders of the Lost Ark* below the towering Mount Sabalon. In his interviews, Ed Davis consistently noted the smell of rotten eggs—or hot sulfur springs—on his mountain ascent.

↑ Though very protective of their legends and traditions, the locals of Sulfur City grudgingly divulged that the remains of Noah's ark indeed lay hidden high in a glacial gorge on Mount Sabalon.

← Having already been detained by Iranian police, Cornuke and Stuplich attempted a final-day, mad-dash ascent of Mount Sabalon, arriving at a pristine, glacier-fed lake near the summit.

→ Within minutes of their arrival near Sabalon's summit, however, a violent blizzard blew in, raining freezing ice on the exhausted climbers and sending them scurrying to lower elevations (R12). A year later, Cornuke and another team—using satellite images and topographical data matching Ed Davis's sketch of the terrain—visited Iran once more to explore the heights of Mount Sabalon, the peak Cornuke concluded Davis climbed to see the ark.

← The real "mountains of Ararat"? A vast expanse of rugged mountains surround the craggy peaks of Mount Sabalon in northwest Iran—a true mountain range—believed by the authors to be a far more likely landing place for the ark of Noah than Mount Ararat in southeastern Turkey.

↑ Todd Phillips (left) and Darrell Scott (right) banter with Sulfur City natives as an armed Iranian soldier watches closely in the foreground.

→ Government-sponsored, anti-American propaganda can be seen throughout the Iranian countryside; this sign located on the outskirts of Nir, a small town on Sabalon's southern base, inspired an impromptu photo shoot. From left: Paul Cornuke, Dan Toth, Todd Phillips, Larry Williams, David Halbrook, Darrell Scott, Bob Cornuke, and John Tomlin.

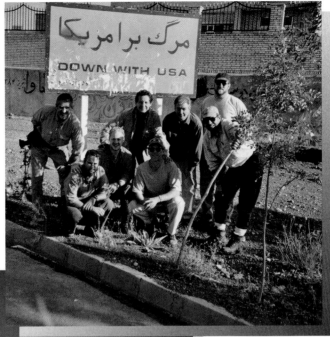

← Ex-Navy Seal Dan Toth (left) and guide Ali (right) debate with local drivers to determine the correct route to the target zone on Mount Sabalon's southern flank.

↑ Coauthors Bob Cornuke and David Halbrook measure the group's progress at one of numerous nomad's camps encountered throughout Sabalon's rolling highlands.

↑ A navigator's nightmare. Attempting to find the right road to the Camel's Back on Sabalon's southwest flank, Dan Toth (far left) engages in another round of negotiations with villagers scattered among the peak's confounding maze of dusty foothills.

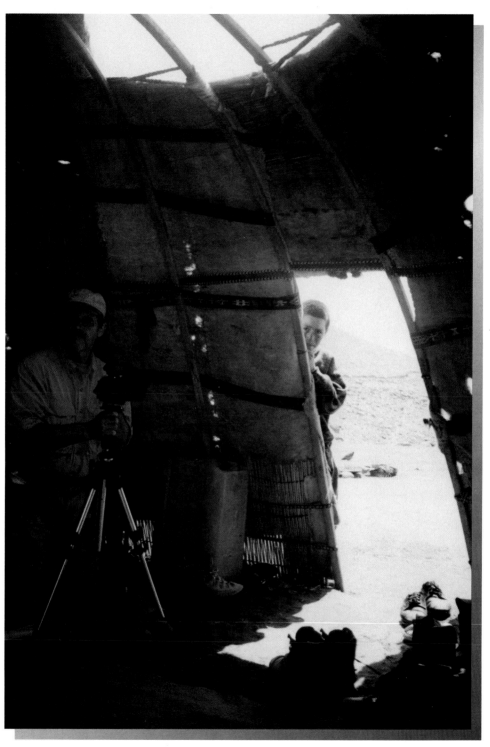

↑ Stopping for rest and shade among the hospitable dome tents of northwestern Iran's rugged shepherd culture, our contingent draws curious stares from startled nomad children. At left: Paul Cornuke, shooting video.

↑ At remote points on Sabalon's rugged southern heights, our vintage Land Rovers bogged down in high mountain streams and had to be pushed out.

↑ Early morning march toward the high ridge leading to Sabalon's Doomsday Rock.

↑ Man-made rectangular corrals found at Sabalon's upper altitudes suggest that the satellite-enhanced "target zone" lay too low on the peak, and remained far too populated, to be Ed Davis's canyon.

↑ Standing on Ed Davis's so-called Doomsday Rock, as the summit of Mount Sabalon looms in the background: (left to right)—Paul Cornuke, Bob Cornuke, John Tomlin, and David Halbrook.

↑ Descending Sabalon from the north, the peak's true summit appears far in the distance as three distinct, towering and treacherous peaks.

↑ Coauthor David Halbrook, knocking out final chapters in the dining room of the Hotel Sabalon, a rustic oasis in northwest Iran's holy city of Ardabil. Some local traditions say Ardabil and surrounding towns were built by Noah and his sons.

As night swallowed up the last pinpoint of sunlight, I staggered, half delirious, into base camp. Within minutes the entire slope vanished in a veil of black, obliterating any shadows or structures that might help the others feel their way down. The elder Kurd sat off by himself, away from the tents, casually smoking a cigarette, watching me in silence. I calculated the others would have reached the steepest part of the slope by now, perhaps perishing in the treacherous boulder field. Without a minute to waste, I groped about in the dark to find my tent, crawled inside, and ripped open my pack, rifling frantically through clothes and camping gear in search of a small, plastic medallion—a green, fluorescent light patch with an adhesive backing. This tiny camping light releases chemicals when you break the seal, emitting a soft, green glow. Stuplich laughed when he saw me stash it in my pack in Erzurum. "That's a waste," he said, "you'll never use it." Now it looked like our only hope: a light too faint to be seen by Turkish patrols below, yet, I hoped, bright enough to guide the climbers down. I found the disk and broke the seal, watching it glow to life as a soft, jade ember. I crawled outside and stuck it to the outside wall of the tent, facing uphill, toward the climbers, then sat down and prayed they would see it.

As I waited, exhausted from my high-speed workout, I felt so sick I couldn't even eat a bite of a power bar. So I sat there in dead silence for two hours, watching, waiting, listening. At about 9:00 P.M., I heard footsteps dragging heavily through the rubble. Slowly they appeared, one by one, like zombies in the night—Banks, Kralik, Bright, the young Kurd—staggering into camp, shell-shocked and dead on their feet. As they passed, each mumbled a grateful, barely audible, "Thanks," then either crawled into their tents or simply collapsed on their sleeping bags in the open night air. As expected, Stuplich brought up the rear, shuffling into camp like a weary shepherd trailing the flock. He walked over and put his hand on my shoulder.

"Bob," he said, "that's the best thing you could've done. I'm glad you brought that little light."

"No problem," I said, as we both joined the others, now snoring in their sleeping bags. No one moved until mid-morning the following day.

CHANGE OF PLANS

For the second straight day, I woke to the shrill refrain of bickering Kurds. Fearing Bright was at it again over horses or money, I rolled out of my sleeping bag and saw Bright, sitting by himself on a rock, looking gloomy. The Kurds had huddled off by themselves, near the horses, shouting into the cell phone.

"They're talking with Micah," Bright said. "He called to warn us—the gendarmes are on the mountain." I looked back at the Kurds, fussing and fuming, looking more agitated than ever. "They're scared to death," Bright

135
Λ

continued. "Micah, too. He says he's very afraid for us." Bright stared off into the distance, then added, "Micah says he won't be able to pick us up where he dropped us off. We'll have to go down a different way."

That grabbed my attention.

"A different way? What do you mean, Dick, a *different* way?"

"Remember the helicopter?" he asked. "There was a gun battle yesterday near Lake Kop; it stirred up the Turkish military, and now they're combing the mountain for rebels. They'll have the north slope wrapped down tighter than a drum." He sighed and glanced over at the guides. "We'll have to descend the southwest side of the mountain."

The southwest slope? I'd never heard of anyone descending the southwest slope. I doubted even Stuplich knew that terrain, but we had no time to debate the point. The Kurds had already packed the horses and begun shouting at us, "*We go! We go!*"

I started to roll up my tent, but suddenly remembered something.

"Wait!" I shouted, "we've got to filter some water."

We raced back up the hill and found the fetid puddle where I'd filtered water two days earlier; but when the others saw it, they insisted we not only filter but *boil* it. It seemed to take forever for our two little camp stoves to boil the water in our tiny cook pots, and even then it looked undrinkable. Kralik and Banks poured instant coffee crystals in their bottles to try to mask the rancid taste and scummy appearance, but they might as well have dabbed perfume on a warthog. In the end we had neither the time nor firepower to stock up on water. The Kurds seemed on the verge of a nervous breakdown and threatened to abandon us if we didn't get moving.

They'd been so combative and high maintenance, for a moment we contemplated letting them go; perhaps we'd be better off without them. But we quickly decided that going it alone would be a mistake. They certainly knew these slopes far better than we and understood how this latest dust-up with the Turks might affect our descent. We all agreed to keep the team together and trust the Kurds to guide us down safely. Strapping our packs to the horses, each man gripped his bottle of cloudy water as if it were vintage Perrier, knowing we had to find more below.

DRY TIMES WITH THE KURDISH UNDERGROUND

I hated to see the raw fear in the Kurd's faces. They kept rubbing their foreheads, wringing their hands, shifting their weight nervously from foot to foot. "*We go! We go!*" They droned on in a high-pitched squeal, looking like death-row inmates waiting for a pardon. I took their edginess with a grain of salt—after all, they'd acted like this the whole trip—but I knew our predicament had deteriorated when Bright kept repeating, "*Micah is scared for us.*"

We set off down the mountain at a steady clip, refusing to speak and keeping our eyes on the slope directly in front of us. Climbing down by this different route, however, soon made apparent that we would run out of water long before we reached bottom. No one knew when or if we'd pass any streams or glacial pools, and on Ararat's porous, bone-dry slope, chances of stumbling upon potable water looked doubtful. So we carefully monitored our intake, taking sips only when we couldn't stand it anymore and keeping our ears trained to the breezes, straining to hear the distant trickle of water.

The sun bore down as we descended into the small bowl of Lake Kop shortly after noon. Sweating and chafing under my load, I fantasized that its waters had somehow cleansed themselves, or that we'd been mistaken, that its foul appearance had been a cruel trick of the sun. Yet walking up to the bank, Kop's waters, if anything, stank more than before. The horses didn't care, and I envied them as they filled their bellies. We still had a few cloudy swigs left in our bottles, so no one thought to filter a bottle or two for good measure before we left—a decision we'd regret.

From Lake Kop we traced a jagged route over to the southwest side of the mountain, traversing high meadows and the bristly ridges of the upper foothills. The way down proved just as laborious as the trek up—pulling the horses down the steep grade; walking and pulling them up knifelike ridges and down ravines filled with loose rubble; proceeding foot by foot, hour by hour, mile by mile, into vast, unproven tracts.

Bright insisted on riding down on horseback. But lurching down a steep, uneven series of knobby switchbacks, his scrawny horse stumbled and nearly fell, pitching Bright headfirst into the rocks. He lay motionless for several moments as we all scrambled back up the hillock, fearing he was dead but cheered to see him still breathing. "He's alive," Stuplich said, touching his chest.

Suddenly Bright popped his head up, grinning like a catfish, and said, "I'm OK. *Piece of cake.*"

Piece of cake? How about, *Piece of granite!* An inch on either side and he would've split his skull open like a clam. I thought we'd lost him, and Bright himself, noting the lay of the rocks, chuckled nervously, "That was close." From that point on, he walked.

Every hour or so we crossed paths with a changing cast of Kurdish sheep herders, most mysteriously appearing from behind a bluff or over a rise to point us off in a new direction. "Go down that way," they'd point with their staffs, or, "Duck into this canyon and down that pass," and we'd shift course accordingly. I didn't immediately recognize it, but these silent messengers comprised Ararat's famous Kurdish underground—a stealth guerilla corps of sheepherders, villagers, and ethnic terrorists, invisible to outsiders but strategically choreographed for mountain warfare. It seemed similar to the European resistance movement of World War II, when local farmers assisted freedom fighters to sabotage the German army's advance. Up here everyone looked out for everyone else. These silent assassins led us from one camp to the other, sharing intelligence on Turkish maneuvers below. They always knew precisely where the Turkish military patrolled the foothills, and we passed three, then four, Kurdish camps spread across the mountain. Together they kept us out of harm's way.

We arrived mid-afternoon at another camp, where a smoky-eyed shepherd bid us to sit down for a cup of tea and a crust of brown bread. *Oh yes, thank God!* I thought. We each had only a few slugs of water left in our bottles, and, with miles to go under a hot, brassy sun, I'd worked up a raging thirst. Neatly constructing a little pile of sheep dung on the hillside and lighting it with a match, the shepherd fanned a hot campfire to brew a small pot of tea. It had a strong, excessively sweet bite, but it tasted so good I would've chugged the whole pot had he offered it.

"We'll be safe here for a minute," Bright said, removing his boots—and the sight made me nearly choke on my bread. His torn and blistered toes had turned black and blue and swollen up like a cow's udder. I couldn't see how he'd made it this far or, for that matter, how he could even *walk*. The duct tape holding his boot together had disintegrated, and he'd been walking for miles on a single, frayed layer of stocking. *How does this guy do it?* I wondered, marveling at the fortitude of a man older than any of us—and by the looks of it, not in the best shape. I'd trained hard for this trip, but his pudgy and stooped-over appearance belied an iron-man constitution. Mentally tenacious—a true human bulldog—he'd pushed himself through terrible pain on guts and determination alone. With feet like that (they looked as if they'd been through a plane wreck) anyone else would've given up long ago. Yet he never complained or lagged behind. In that moment my respect for Bright soared to new heights.

138

OVER THE CLIFF

Afternoon turned to dusk, steep canyons changed into high foothills, mild breezes gave way to sweltering heat. Traversing down the southwest side of the mountain, we entered a patchwork of smooth, wide pastures bleeding into long, lazy valleys. Even desperately thirsty and tired, this gently rolling southwestern route provided a pleasant surprise. It seemed, if anything, easier than the way up. *Why would the Turks ignore this mellow decline,* I wondered?

Arriving at a flat, grassy plateau, where another large herd of sheep grazed, a shepherd there told us to hunker down in the tall grass and wait for sundown. The pasture stood plainly exposed in broad daylight, and the adjacent slope, he said, had been crawling with Turkish troops all day. We waited for two hours, until the last rays of sun melded into a crimson sunset, and then, at dusk, walked the horses over to a wide ledge. Staring down at the steep drop-off, I asked, "What's *this*?" Bright peered out over the edge into the tumbling moraine.

"We've got to climb down there to reach the plain," he said sheepishly.

I suddenly understood why the Turks never patrol these cliffs. No fool would attempt an ascent up this suicide precipice. With a moonless night now upon us, we shimmied down off the ledge and found ourselves instantly slipping and clawing down a sheer granite cliff wall into a waking nightmare. The near vertical pitch would've made for treacherous climbing during broad daylight. But at *night*, with *horses*, our prospects could only be described as insane. I, for one, have terrible night vision and, without a trail, had to feel and fumble my way down every foot of slope, using my ski pole to probe the large, empty black spaces in front of me. Pulling the horse along, I'd take a hesitant step down into the rolling scree, probe the dark, take another baby step, then another, sometimes poking my pole where the next step should be and feeling nothing—*anywhere*. To step off in any direction would send me plunging off the cliff.

The horses, who *could* see into the darkness, whimpered and whined with each step, making pitiful crying sounds as they wobbled and heaved under their heavy loads. Skidding and clopping down the winding course, their hooves kicked up fiery sparks on the granite. I found myself following the sparks of the horse in front of me, keeping a hand on its bony haunch, tapping my pole for a foothold, then nudging the horse along and feeling my way down through the crumbling rubble.

If the Kurds knew a way down, they didn't share it with us. I could hear them chattering frantically back and forth in the distance, clearly petrified themselves, cursing the horses, refusing to wait on any of us. In the interminable darkness our team soon found itself spread across the cliff face like lost pups in the woods. It was now every man for himself.

For twenty years I climbed mountains and took risks, but this easily ranked as the most grueling, frightening seven hours of my life. Walking blind, without lights, my pulse pounded in my temples, and my hands and legs shook from horror.

"This is *mountain goat* country, not horse country," I complained to Stuplich, who, slipping along behind me, prodded his horse awkwardly down the terraced granite with terrible, loud crashes. At one point, hearing a horseshoe scrape violently across granite behind me, I turned to feel Stuplich's horse slam into me, knocking my breath out and sending me flying fifteen feet off a ledge into a ravine. Miraculously, it seemed at the time, I landed on my back in soft sand.

Dusting myself off and thanking God I hadn't hit my head on a rock, I wondered, for the first time, *Are we going to make it?* I didn't like my answer. *The odds aren't in our favor. First, I'm dying of thirst and sweating so hard my kidneys ache; we have no water; my next step could send me over a cliff, and we've still got hours to go in pitch blackness.* I scolded myself. *Why didn't we filter more water at Lake Kop? It didn't look so bad . . . I wish I had a gallon of it right now!*

But no matter how hard I prayed, I couldn't escape the awful fact we still had a long way to go. We still had to get these horses down off the cliff, and without lights.

Hour by agonizing hour we made our way down into the valley, where we encountered another sea of rocks. I kept praying for the moon to come out, like it had our first night, but the sky remained soupy black, so dark I couldn't see Bright walking five feet in front of me.

"It's not far from here," he said, trying to encourage me. "Micah should be waiting for us up ahead."

He didn't finish the sentence. I heard a soft *whump!* somewhere down below, and Dick was gone. I stepped forward and probed the darkness with my ski pole.

"Dick . . . Dick, are you *there?*" I whispered, standing in the creepy silence, waiting several moments for a reply. "Dick, are you OK?" I shouted again into dead silence.

Then, from the abyss, came the raspy response: "I'm OK!" Spitting sand from his mouth, Bright called up, "I fell off the lip of that wash and fell face first into this trench." Checking for broken bones, he said, "Piece of cake," then clambered back up the knoll, where we completed our transition to the plain.

We caught up with the Kurds in the valley and found them chattering on the cell phone with Micah. In yet another shocking bit of bad news, Micah said the military had formed a noose around the base of the mountain, and he couldn't pick us up where we'd originally planned. It meant walking another five miles across the plain to meet him at an alternate site. My heart sank, but I didn't have time to feel sorry for myself. In that instant, military flares exploded over our heads, shattering the midnight black in petrifying hues of pink. Dogs started barking, and we could hear trucks grinding their gears in the distance. The panicked Kurds set off in a wild sprint across the valley floor, screaming back at us: "Go! Go! Go!"

We raced after them, yanking our horses and straining to keep pace.

HOT FLARES AND WARM BEER

The final sprint across the plain nearly did us in. Miles back we'd all lapsed into the advanced stages of dehydration. I'd stopped sweating hours ago; my contacts had dried up and fallen out, so I put on my glasses.

I worried most about Banks, who'd gone without water the longest. His parched and blistered throat made it almost impossible for him to speak. He'd gone quiet; I could hear him breathing hard, counting his steps, and sensed he was in anguish over his decision to leave his wife, and now, possibly never returning.

"Bob," he finally said, hoarsely through cracked lips, "I'll make it, but . . . *my God,* I'm so thirsty."

Up ahead Bright haggled with Micah over the cell phone. "Tell him to bring water," I interrupted. "Whatever he does, don't let him forget to bring us water."

Trotting across the plain, flares exploding in the sky behind us, we stopped and listened. "Hear *that?*" I asked—the faint groan of gunning engines had gotten louder. So had the barking. The dogs had caught our scent, which set us running again across the plain, trying to stay out of range of the hounds, flares, and circling flashlights. At any second I expected a helicopter to zoom across the steppe and swoop down upon us, guns blazing. Whatever "special arrangements" had been made with the military had clearly broken down.

"We're open season now," Bright said between gasps.

I didn't know how much longer my body could hold out, but I kept pushing, trying to encourage Banks along. When we finally crested a small knoll and saw the flashing headlights of Micah's van, my watch said 2:00 A.M. The Kurds circled the horses to make sure no one followed us, and, as we approached the van, the doors burst open and five Kurds jumped out and grabbed our mounts. Without a word, our guides vanished with them into the night.

We hopped in the van, and Micah sped off down the road. No one spoke until we were safely out of range of the flares. Finally Micah turned and gave us a broad grin.

"Welcome home, gentlemen."

"Where's the water?" I demanded.

"I'm sorry," he said with a frown, "but the military stopped me earlier at a checkpoint. I had to give them all my water to get through."

I could feel my throat closing up. We still had more than an hour's drive to reach Dogubayazit. I looked at Banks, crushed by the news, and doubted he would remain conscious for another hour. Micah pointed at the floor of the van, to a dusty six-pack of beer.

"Help yourself," he said—and like starving men, Stuplich, Bright, and Kralik grabbed cans and ripped off the pull tops, spewing warm sprays of fermented foam across the van's interior. As they guzzled, I grabbed two cans and handed one to Banks. I could have gulped down that warm, flat beer without even opening the can. *Nothing* had ever sounded so good. But as I put the warm can to my lips, I noticed Banks wasn't drinking.

"C'mon," I said, "We *made* it. Time to celebrate."

The others, already lost in a giddy postmortem of our adventure, gleefully swigged beer and replayed our close calls and outrageous exploits. Banks stared at me helplessly, eyes vacant, his lips cracked and bleeding. With a voice reduced to a scratchy whisper, he said, "Bob . . . I . . . I . . ." then paused to compose himself. "I'm a recovering alcoholic. I can't drink that."

141

My jaw dropped. I lowered my beer as he continued: "I haven't had a drink of alcohol in fourteen years. My wife's waiting for me back home. She's undergoing chemotherapy. I promised her I'd never drink again."

He stared at the can in his hand, then handed it back to me and closed his eyes.

I couldn't believe my ears. My tongue and throat, my whole dust-caked, sun-parched soul screamed out, *"Drink! Drink, you fool! Drink the beer! For God's sake, you're dying of thirst! Drink the beer!"*

But I couldn't do it. I couldn't drink in front of Banks. Beer flowed generously at the front of the van, but for me to take a sip would be like teasing a starving man with a T-bone steak. I stared at Banks. His cheeks and eyes looked sunken, hollow. I put my can down.

"David," I said, reaching out and grabbing his hand. "We've been through a lot; we'll wait this out together."

I didn't yet know the outcome of this ordeal. My tongue felt dry as chalk and twice its normal size but with my final decision came a sudden, warm rush of optimism. It was as if the Spirit of God, pleased with my choice, settled gently upon me, soothing me, strengthening me, flooding me with a sense of transcendent calm.

I turned to Banks and said, too softly for the others to hear, "David, I want you to remember something. I've learned that *Jesus* is the water of life—not this beer. God knows we're thirsty, and He'll sustain us."

Banks's eyes stayed closed, so I leaned in closer, whispering: "He'll give us water, David, water that will well up inside of us as a spring of eternal life." These words were not my own, so I paused, unsure whether he could even hear me. "You and I, David—there's coming a day when we'll never thirst again."

With that he opened his eyes and whispered, almost inaudibly, "Thanks, Bob. I think you're right."

At that moment I knew he'd be OK. I lay my head back against the wall of the van as it bounced along washboard roads. And waited.

More than an hour later, Micah pulled into the old hotel outside Dogubayazit. A case of water sat on a table inside the doorway of a rundown cafe. Banks and I broke it open and drank to our heart's content. *We'd made it;* somehow, we'd made it, and now we guzzled enough water to float a battleship. And still we kept on drinking.

As I sat there, water running down my neck and shirt, feeling satisfied and secure for the first time in four days, it suddenly hit me: *Oh, brother! Tomorrow I fly to Iran.*

Eighteen

TRACKING ED DAVIS

The painful mountain behind me, I counted myself among those who vowed never to return.

We left Dick Bright in Erzurum to his obsession with Mount Ararat. Two weeks later I heard he climbed back up, still declaring, "This has *got* to be it!" Banks flew home to be with his wife; Kralik returned to Canada. Stuplich and I, slightly worse for wear, caught a late-night flight to Iran via Istanbul, landing in smoky, teeming Tehran in the dead of morning, the airport abuzz with crowds.

Passing through Tehran International Airport, we met our new guide standing amongst the curious, staring throng. He waved a placard that, typically, misspelled my name: "Mr. Bob Kornuk." Short of stature, soft-eyed, gentle—a tad on the nervous side— Ali seemed competent and eager to please. A Ph.D. professor of education at Tehran University, Ali would be able and qualified to interpret the country through the eyes and mind of a scholar. On my last trip I'd enjoyed and appreciated Fatima, but in a land of unbending gender class, it seemed far better to be paired with a man. And Ali (not the driver from my first trip) came highly recommended, with solid standing among the Iranian tourism autocrats who helped us secure our visas.

I found it mildly disorienting to be back in Tehran. Even at 3:00 A.M., huge crowds milled about, and passing through customs—where officers pulled Stuplich and I aside for an hour while they double-checked our papers—we drew intense stares from the other travelers. I'd forgotten that, in this land of social conformity, westerners stick out.

We took a cab to a downscale hotel in the center of town, where all I wanted was to collapse into bed. Every inch of my body ached from the rigors of Ararat, and my head felt heavy as a block of concrete. But before I could even take off my shoes, there came a loud knock at my door. I opened the door to see Larry Williams and Phil Trahern,[1] who'd arrived with our new videographer, Brad Houston, two days earlier. They'd been setting our itinerary and doing some preliminary research.

So far as I knew, we planned to drive directly from Tehran to Kermanshah, to begin phase two of my two-year plan to canvass the whole of Iran. It meant working our way systematically up the Zagros Mountains and interviewing as many Iranians as possible on legends and theories of the ark and then working east across the interior. Having already searched the southern Zagros on my last trip, this expedition would start in Kermanshah, in the central Zagros, then cut north toward Iranian Azerbaijan.

Even though it was late and I needed sleep, I invited them in. They seemed giddy for such a late hour.

"What's going on?" I asked. "What are you so excited about?"

They cried in unison: "We found *Casbeen!*"

This I had to hear and invited them in. I knew Casbeen from the Ed Davis interviews, in which he'd mentioned it often. He recalled how he and Badi drove through Casbeen—or someplace that *sounded* like it—en route to the mountain of the ark. This qualified Casbeen as a critical, albeit confounding, landmark, because we'd never been able positively to identify where, or what, Casbeen *was*. I'd always suspected that if we could solve this troubling mystery, it might give us a good starting point or at least point us in the right direction. Unfortunately Davis and Badi traveled without a map; Davis couldn't remember where it was, how it was spelled or even if it might be found on a map. It set us to guessing, and for the longest time I thought he might have meant "Cas-peen," as in Cas-pian, or Caspian *Sea*— but nothing clicked. Now, all of a sudden, Williams and Trahern claimed they'd found it.

When I asked how, they explained that, upon landing in Tehran, they hooked up with our new guide Ali and began asking him a broad sequence of questions, trying to catalog some regional characteristics, places, perhaps, that Davis might've visited. In interviews, for example, Davis spoke confidently of climbing to a spot on the mountain that smelled pungently of rotten eggs—or sulfur. So Williams asked Ali if he knew where they might find a hot sulfur springs near a large peak. Ali didn't miss a beat: "That would be Ghotor Suee," he said, "the hot springs at the foot of Mount Sabalon. It lies in Iranian Azerbaijan, in the northwest part of the country."

Mount *Sabalon?* I thought. What a startling coincidence. Of all the mountains and hot springs in Iran, Ali instantly cited the only place he knew of where both features converged—Mount Sabalon.

"Sit down," I told the pair. "This is getting interesting."

Next they queried Ali on possible sites for Casbeen, but when Williams pronounced "Caz-Been," he said Ali casually replied: "Oh, you must mean *Qasvin*. It is just north of Hamadan, due west of Tehran." Then Ali pointed it out on the map; it lay on the main route to Ardabil, near the foot of Mount Sabalon. Confronted by this bombshell, Williams said they just stood there, speechless, staring dumbly at the map.

"It seemed too easy," Williams said. "We'd never considered that, in Farsi, *v* is pronounced *b,* and the *b* sound is spelled with a *v*. But it made perfect sense. Casbeen was really 'Qasvin.'"

I stared at Williams, unsure in my foggy state what to think. "Bob," he gushed, "do you realize what this means? This is great news." He described how he and Phil took a drive to Qasvin the day before. "From what we could see," he said, "it fits Davis's account."

Now *I* went mute. We'd been trying to confirm these features for years, but, by the sound of it, they'd smashed a grand slam in their first at bat. On the map Sabalon sat 250 miles north of Hammadan, where Davis and Badi said they began their journey. As the tallest mountain in the region, it sat well within the prescribed "two days'" driving distance Davis described. At the very least they counted as compelling new leads: the hot sulfur springs of Sabalon and the identity of Qasvin. As far as I was concerned, it put us back hot on Ed Davis's trail in Iran.

This raised a problem: in Iran, you go only where you have permission and our visas would allow us to travel only south to Kermanshah, well out of range of Sabalon, and clearly taking us in the wrong direction. So with Williams and Trahern standing next to my bed, waiting for my response, I made a spot decision: "We're scrapping everything and heading to Sabalon. We've got to see this mountain."

"OH MY GOD!"

In Iran it's never a good idea to change one's plans abruptly—and for Americans it's a bit like hanging a pork chop around your neck and strolling through a kennel. You're bound to attract unwanted attention.

Simply to enter the country, foreigners must obtain visas, secure a government-appointed guide, then file a detailed schedule of activities with the authorities. Straying off course can only invite calamity. You might as well walk around with a sign saying, "Kick me out of your country," or, "Arrest me!" Given America's strained history with Iran, any U.S. citizen fortunate enough to procure a visa—even under today's supposedly "relaxed" tourism policies—is closely monitored, every movement tightly regimented. The fact is Iranian authorities still deeply mistrust all Americans, so when we informed Ali of our change of plans, his jaw dropped. When he saw I meant business, he slapped his forehead and hissed forlornly: *"Oh my God!"*

145

I felt bad. We'd created a touchy situation, and I understood his dilemma. Ali had superiors to report to—the *secret police*, for instance—who would hold *him* accountable for any irregularities. But I didn't have the luxury of wasting an entire trip touring the central Zagros when this new data clearly pointed us north toward Mount Sabalon. I apologized profusely, then said, "I'm sorry, Ali, but we *are* going to Sabalon. We leave in the morning."

"Oh my God!"

LAND OF DIVERSITY

Early the next morning, Williams, Stuplich, Trahern, Houston, and I jammed our packs and equipment in a white, ten-seater, chartered van, and headed northwest. Chiseled into the hot plains about Mount Sabalon, Ardabil sits 250 miles from Tehran. But traveling 250 miles in Iran can't be compared to 250 miles in the U.S. Iran's main roads, while mostly passable and often quite modern, feature a driving culture that requires plenty of stopping and loitering along the roadside to chat with the locals about the weather or such things. In our case it provided our driver ample time to check frequently under the hood, pour water in the radiator, buy a soda.

And while Iran is experiencing a modest political liberalization, the fact remains it has been locked in the 1940s for decades; over-the-road travel, as such, remains a hot, grinding ordeal. Driving the vast, rumbling byways north convinced me that Davis and Badi could never have reached Mount Ararat in Turkey in the required time. Traveling from Hamadan to reach Ararat on the rutted Iranian roads of WWII in a British Lorry, at a top truck speed of 35 m.p.h., would have taken Davis four, maybe five days.

The highway took us into Qazvin, a nondescript, dusty little town of shadowy shops and well-kept mosques. We drove ten hours through monotonous desert foothills and dry, stubble-filled prairies, en route to the south coast of the Caspian Sea, whizzing past rugged wheat fields and dreary, sodbusted farm plots worked by men in long sleeves and women in flowing scarves and ankle-length dresses. Yet nearing the southwestern fringe of the Caspian—less than sixty miles from Mount Sabalon—the landscape abruptly changed, and we found ourselves entering a countryside of wonderfully diverse climate and texture. From harsh, withering desert heat, we transitioned almost imperceptibly into a land deliciously lush and green, gorgeous with palms and ferns.

We stopped for the night at the town of Rasht, a pleasant village on the southwest coast. There at a balmy beachside villa reminiscent of the Caribbean, we enjoyed a delightful dinner of curry-spiced sturgeon grilled with fresh lime. From our patio deck we saw miles of wild, blossoming fauna, fragrant hillside tea plantations, and lazy, pristine beaches.

From Rasht we had but a short drive to Ardabil, nestled in the heart of Iranian Azerbaijan, eighty miles south of the border of Soviet Azerbaijan. Approaching from the southeast, we passed through an abandoned border-land of bygone wars—a desolate badlands interrupted every few miles by crumbling, derelict prisons, military compounds wrapped in rusty barbed wire, abandoned gun turrets, and sturdy watchtowers overrun by dense foliage and creeping vines. The cold war had long ended, and Iran now enjoyed a tenuous peace with her neighbors. Yet these rotting monuments cued us into the region's bloody past.

We arrived at Ardabil mid-morning and checked into the dingy Hotel Sabalon. Our rooms all shared an underlying aroma of raw sewage, seeping up from the ill-kept, one-holer squatter's johns punched into the floors. Regarded as a Muslim holy city, Ardabil's sidewalks teem with street commerce and humanity: women in hot, black chadors and men in dark slacks mill in and out of an endless tangle of shops and sandy mosques, minarets, colorful fruit stands, bakeries, barbers, and clothing shops sporting fashions not seen in the U.S. for decades. As in Ahvaz, every other street corner features a huge billboard eulogizing local sons who died in the Iran-Iraq War. To our guide Ali, Ardabil deserved its designation as a holy city. To me it seemed just like any other hot, dirty town you'd find in central California.

From Ardabil's brown hillsides one can behold Mount Sabalon's icy peaks. And, as I calculated it, only sixty-two miles separated Sabalon's looming crags from the beaches of the Caspian sea—a sixty-two-mile radius encompassing an incredibly diverse, uniquely condensed climatic zone. In this corner of Iran, one might tour everything from foaming surf to frigid peaks—and everything in between—in a single day.

"Did you notice that?" I asked Larry, as we placed cold, wet towels over the one-holers to stanch the smell. "The climates of the world have been squeezed into this little corner of Iran."

In all my travels I'd never seen or heard of anything like it. From a purely *biblical* perspective, I felt it resonated with the story of Noah; for practically speaking, after a great flood, the animals of the ark would've required a broad range of habitats. And this highly diverse, superconcentrated ecosystem would have given them all a place to settle and regenerate. Here about the green, sloping plains of Sabalon, I observed the perfect milieu for nearly every species leaving the ark—a range of climates in which to adapt to a new life, all in close proximity.

Watching from the window of our van, I noted with increasing fascination everything from hot, dead, undulating deserts, to verdant ocean wetlands, to dense tropical jungle. Densely packed within a fifty-mile radius sat luxurious beaches and world-class glaciers, spongy marshes and arctic tundra, tree-lined ridges and fertile meadows. *How could this be?* I wondered. But this much I knew: it had little in common with the region of Mount Ararat in southeastern Turkey. I just barely survived that mountain's inhospitable, oxygen-starved heights and steep, parched slopes. But *here*, in

147
Λ

Iran, Sabalon's slopes looked smooth and spring fed; its fertile lowlands stretched out green and inviting, capable of supporting everything from hippos to bears, snakes to mountain goats, foxes to crocodiles. Such diversity seemed divinely conceived—a land of contrasts mirroring a place I'd long imagined, the biblical land of Noah.

My mind kept flashing back to Mount Ararat, to that punishing hillside where, two days earlier, I felt my life ebbing away. The memory of those punishing slopes and waterless expanses gave me pause. On Mount Ararat I could hardly imagine a brawny Kodiak bear, much less a fragile butterfly, emerging from its heights unscathed. But here, in the hills and valleys about Mount Sabalon, I sensed the gentle, lingering traces of emerging life and new beginnings.

Пineтeeп

UGLY AMERICANS

"Oh my God!"

Pleading with us to abandon our forbidden course, Ali kept wringing his hands, slapping his forehead, and imploring Allah to intercede. I'd begun to share his concern, for a member of our team insisted on playing the part of the ugly American.

Our journey had taken us into the foothills of Mount Sabalon, where we visited villages and busily questioned folks about Noah's ark. Tragically, Phil Trahern kept strutting about and acting like a Navy commando, crippling our efforts.

I'd met Trahern, an ex-Navy officer, some months earlier through my speaking ministry. He apparently liked what he heard and became an energetic fundraiser and volunteer researcher for BASE. Over time he compiled some thoughtful research on Noah's ark; his interest lay in a peak mentioned in the Gilgamesh Epic as Mount Nissar, possibly located in the northern Zagros Mountains along the Iran-Iraq border. Though its exact whereabouts remains a mystery, Nissar had once been named as a possible ark landing site, and Trahern had it fixed firmly in his psychological viewfinder. When we changed the trip's focus to include Mount Sabalon, he balked and kept insisting we cross the border into Iraq to look for Mount Nissar. His antics began as a nagging concern but now threatened to sabotage our cause. He couldn't seem to grasp the fact that Iran lost thousands of men to its war with Iraq and that even to mention its name in these parts is like sketching horns on a picture of the Ayatollah.

We had a real problem on our hands. Born and bred on their government's venomous anti-American propaganda, Iranians behave cautiously around Americans as it is; but a Trahern acting like a desert assassin from the old *Rat Patrol* series set the shy villagers on edge, compromising my efforts to strike up a friendly rapport. I'd asked the team to dress and act conservatively—no loud colors, no Hawaiian prints, no flamboyant gestures of any kind to call attention to ourselves—yet, to my growing distress, Trahern sported pouched military pants, an Australian commando hat, and a broad-bladed Rambo knife in his waistband. No matter where we went, he'd stop and pull out his hand-held GPS (global positioning device) to check our coordinates or pull maps from the Russian-made military map case (slung over his shoulder like a sawed-off shotgun). Added to his habit of asking anyone within earshot how we might catch a flight to Iraq, I'm certain the locals suspected Trahern of spying for the CIA—or perhaps even planning an invasion.

In the land of the Islamic Revolution, Trahern stuck out like Ted Kennedy at the Republican National Convention—which meant, of course, we *all* stuck out. Once, while we were poking around at a Persian bazaar, a female passerby stumbled and fell; Trahern reflexively grabbed her, an act of chivalry that ignored the fact that, in Iran, it's a crime to touch another man's wife. The woman ran screaming from the bazaar, searching for her husband, who would have been within his rights to slit Trahern's throat. We didn't stick around to watch. Ali hustled us out of the area before the vigilantes arrived.

Trahern's antics presented me with a serious dilemma: while he had earned the right to come on the trip—I appreciated his research; he had a great researcher's mind—he just didn't *get* it. Locked in the military mindset, grossly insensitive to Iran's rigid social mores, his very appearance drew unwanted attention at a time when simply being in the region might get us arrested.

I'd traveled two thousand miles in Iran without incident, but I now found myself constantly on guard, never sure what Trahern might do or say next. The locals seemed cordial enough but deeply wary. I finally threw up my arms and decided to make the best of it, turning my attention toward calming Ali's growing anxiety.

Ali had grown increasingly panicky at the prospect of the secret police tracking our footsteps; it made me nervous, too. I knew he had his orders and wanted to do everything by the book. But, circumstances being what they were, I had no choice but to throw the book out the window. My brief time in Iran taught me that it's better to ask forgiveness than permission. I knew if we asked permission for every little thing, we'd never get anywhere. We had only a limited amount of time left; if we couldn't complete our survey of the region, we'd go home empty-handed. I couldn't let the trip be a complete waste.

"Ali," I insisted, looking him square in the eye, "we *must* continue. It is *compulsory*."

I turned back toward the van and heard the faint, familiar *fffwap!* of Ali's hand on his forehead, and his anguished, whispered groan, *"Oh my God!"*

SABALON SPLENDOR

The hills and valleys below Sabalon looked awash with life. Driving along the north side of the mountain toward Ghotor Suee—the smelly, hot sulfur springs Ali told us about—I marveled at the lush, abundant farmland. Mile after mile of its lower glades stood radiant with charming apple, cherry, and peach orchards, vast, bushy plots of tomatoes, melons, cucumbers, and most any fruit or vegetable you'd find at a gourmet American grocer's. And then acre after acre of thick, leafy, fruit-laden vines.

I turned to Williams: "Vineyards!" He nodded knowingly, acutely aware these vineyards filled in another hole of the Ed Davis story. Davis spoke frequently of ancient vineyards he saw at a remote village near the mountain's base, some plots so old their vines appeared thick and gnarled, like wind-twisted oaks. It never fit the profile of Mount Ararat, whose surrounding plain has no vineyards or *any* significant agriculture to speak of. But here in northwest Iran, beholding the agricultural riches at the foot of Sabalon, one had to wonder: could *these* have been the vineyards Davis saw?

The profound biblical significance of such vineyards can be found in Genesis 9:20, which states that, after the flood, Noah planted a vineyard. (He later drank the wine and got drunk—an indiscretion for which I could hardly blame him, having spent eight months sequestered with a boat full of animals in a global flood.) And the presence of vineyards about Mount Sabalon squares with the region's status as, perhaps, the cradle of modern civilization. Traces of the oldest wine, dating from about 5000 B.C., surfaced recently in northwest Iran. Archeologists excavating the ruins of Tepe Haiji Firuz, just below Lake Urmia, scraped wine residue from the inside of an ancient clay jar. This wine predated the next oldest known wine by some two thousand years,[1] certifying Iran as an undisputed birthplace of modern culture.

Admiring these gently sloping hills and quaint farming villages, noble orchards and majestic vineyards, I wondered: *Could these glistening fields of grapes, draped across the valley like a jade necklace, have evolved from Noah's virgin seedlings?*

SULFUR CITY

Our van driver pulled off the main road and steered us up a narrow, ascending dirt path into Sabalon's steep, vineyard-laden foothills. As we climbed higher, quiet glens of rolling orchards became turbulent swells of baby alps overlooking deep canyons. As we climbed higher and higher, I

151

GOD'S LITTLE HORSE

In 1965, a diminutive breed of horse known as the Caspian was discovered roaming a remote area of the Elborz Mountains, along the southern shores of the Caspian Sea in northern Iran. Some experts believe that, together with a growing body of new archaeological findings, the discovery adds to northern Iran's reputation as a leading birthplace of civilization. Others say it's further evidence linking the region (near Mount Sabalon) to the ark's final resting place.

Known as the Royal Horse of Iran, the Caspian is depicted in a wealth of ancient Persian artifacts, on the walls of the ancient palace of Persepolis, and in rock reliefs portraying the horses as the treasured property of Persian royals. The Seal of King Darius, who reigned in 600 B.C., shows his golden chariot being pulled by the small horse during a sporting event with lions. Further investigation revealed that more than ten thousand bones, found at an osteological site near Hamadan, Iran, included specimens of the early Caspian horse, hard proof that the horse lived more than five thousand years ago. This ancient time line, and the location of the breed's origins, closely parallel that of Noah and the great flood.

Discovered by Louise Firouz, this ancient horse was believed to have been extinct for the past thirteen hundred years. Extensive DNA testing of the Caspian by the University of Kentucky, however, headed by Dr. Gus Cothran, yielded compelling evidence that the breed is, in fact, the great, great ancestor of most modern-day breeds. Les Stevens, a director of the board of BASE Institute, and his wife, Anne, import, breed, and train Caspians at Texana Farms outside of Houston, Texas. Stevens says the Caspian's dramatic survival has been nothing less than miraculous. Numbering only six hundred in the world, they have survived more than five thousand years—thirteen hundred years in the wild—and managed to survive the tumultuous Iranian Revolution in the 1970s.

"We call these exquisite animals 'God's little horses,'" says Stevens. "Little did I know, when they imported the first herd of U.S. Caspians to Texas in 1994, that they were quite possibly a rare and living, five-thousand-year-old bridge to Noah and the ark."[2]

couldn't help imagining the roiling, bygone currents and breaking waves of a great flood lapping and breaking among the yawning, seemingly bottomless bowls and ridges. If the ark landed in the "mountains" of Ararat, then these towering massifs certainly qualified. To warring ancients they would have formed an impenetrable fortress—rugged mountains of the first order, immense and visually spellbinding.

We passed a chain of pleasing farm villages, where laughing, chattering groups of men sat on the shaded porches of stucco cafes. In the slanting, orange-yellow light of midday, they sipped tea and seemed not to have a care in the world. Further on we passed an occasional thatch-roofed shanty, supported by knobby poles lashed loosely together. Beneath them, teenage boys, happily shielded from the afternoon rays, sold succulent fruits and vegetables. Throughout these hills and glens I watched as small children frolicked in the soft glades and shady fields of the summer orchards, hiding among the hidden forts and magic kingdoms. Life here—in *Iran* of all places—seemed sweet and tranquil, simple and childlike, largely free of the stresses westerners know too well.

I envy them their carefree lifestyle, I thought lazily.

At one such village our driver pulled over, and we ordered orange Fanta sodas and Zam Zam Cola (from my experience the only brand of soft drinks sold in Iran) from a local shopkeeper. At once the excited natives descended, shaking our hands and asking us questions in tongues we couldn't understand. Larry thrives in such moments and takes great delight in gathering everyone about him like a favorite uncle, charming young and old alike with his boyish antics and loopy magic tricks. When his act finally ended amid much laughter and cheers, we all hopped back in the van and convened our upward course toward Sulfur City.

Sulfur City sits at the bottom of a confluence of steep canyons riding up the shin of Sabalon's spiny foothills. Its real name is Ghotor Suee, a Farsi term meaning "water that cures the wound," but we'd nicknamed it Sulfur City because of the overpowering, rotten egg smell. In ancient times, Ali explained, nomads brought their enfeebled camels to these therapeutic springs for prompt healing.

A lively, primitive-looking town, Ghotor Suee seemed an Iranian outback version of a Colorado mountain getaway; it could have served as an adobe and mud set piece from *Raiders of the Lost Ark*. The afternoon we arrived, its wood-plank storefronts bustled with visitors from across Iranian Azerbaijan—nomads, climbers, mountain folk, farmers, and shepherds—who had to come to revel in the town's semi-lively ambiance and soak in the famous hot springs.

The government recently raised a crude concrete privacy wall around the springs, allowing men and women to take turns occupying the sand-bottomed pool's tepid brown waters. At river's edge a shepherd slaughtered, then skinned, a woolly sheep, idly tossing the fat, blood, and entrails into the stream. Within minutes a hungry crowd on a crude stone patio feasted on flame-seared kebabs and nibbled on the poor beast's organs, now twisted and sizzling on a stick. And no matter where we went, the pungent smell of rotten eggs singed our nostrils.

"Do you think these were the springs Davis spoke of?" Houston asked.

153

"Well," I shrugged, "The *smell* fits."

We parked the van next to the stream and began canvassing the village. With Ali's help I sought an audience with the village elders, and, after several minutes of animated dialogue with a group of men sitting on a stone-cobbled porch, he ushered me up a flight of stairs to a second-floor bungalow overlooking the creek. Larry, Houston, and I went in and sat down on the mat-covered floor, while Trahern stayed outside, mingling with the crowds. A gaggle of onlookers gathered in the doorway as we sipped tea, Ali explaining our mission to the village patriarch, a gray-haired, sunken-eyed gentleman of about eighty, who, despite the hot weather, wore a heavy, Persian-print wool sweater. When the formalities ended, Ali translated as I asked the old man a series of questions.

"First," I began, "are there any caves nearby?" (Davis had described caves containing ancient artifacts, some supposedly from the ark, outside Badi's village).

When he calmly said, "Yes!" I continued, encouraged.

"Are there any etchings, or old paintings, of animals in these caves—such as lions?" (Davis's traveling party camped in caves on the mountain, some adorned with etchings of animals).

The old man nodded—"Yes!" My pulse quickened; and then—"Have you, or any of the other men in this village, seen or heard of Noah's ark on Mount Sabalon?"

Silence. No response.

Ali rubbed a sweaty hand over his mouth; the elders shifted nervously on their mats, glancing about the room at each other, clearly ill at ease. After a long pause the old man finally nodded—"Yes." I glanced over at Larry, standing straight-faced in the doorway, rubbing his chin. Ali put a finger to his lips; the old patriarch had something more to say.

"This man says that his grandfather and great-grandfather knew where it was."

"Where *what* was?" I asked.

"Noah's ark."

"Did they *see* it?"

"Yes," said Ali. "He says they have seen it."

With that the old patriarch began to fidget noticeably; the room now rippled with tension. Larry folded his arms, trying to look nonchalant. Then I asked, "Does *he* know where it is?" Ali slowly repeated my question. The old man sat stone-faced for nearly a minute, then slowly nodded.

"Yes," Ali said, somber faced. "He knows . . . but . . ."

"But *what?*" I asked impatiently.

"The elder says he knows about the ark . . . but . . ." he paused to ask the elder something, then continued, "He says he wants us to know that he still believes in the *Koran*."

I shrugged, confused.

"The author of the Koran," Ali softly explained: "was Islam's founder, Mohammad. The Koran has its own story of the flood and of Noah and the boat." He paused, nodding politely toward the patriarch—"but its tradition does *not* include Mount Sabalon."

I began to understand. Ali further explained that, according to the Koran, "The ark came to rest on a mountain called Jabal Judi."

I knew of Jabal Judi. Koran scholars place it vaguely in any of a dozen locations from Syria to Saudi Arabia. At one time or another throughout the Near East, perhaps a dozen peaks have been named Jabal Judi. But for this elderly gentleman, the point had graver implications. For even to hint that the ark rested on Mount Sabalon rather than Jabal Judi was at best to call Mohammad mistaken and at worst, a liar. It could get him thrown in jail for religious heresy, or worse. Anyone caught suggesting the holy prophet had erred could be tried for treason.

"I understand," I said with a concerned nod, tiptoeing into my next question. "But what does *he* know of the location of the ark?"

The old man stared me in the eyes for several moments and seemed about to speak when four young men burst into the room, shoved Larry aside, and angrily halted the proceedings. One walked over to Houston and put a hand over the lens of his video camera; another started shouting at the old man. Ali leapt to his feet and held them at bay with both arms. After a few moments of heated dialogue, during which the young men kept shouting and waving their hands at us to go, Ali turned to me.

"We must leave," he said, matter-of-factly. "They are not happy with our presence. We must leave quickly."

I could tell from Ali's stern manner he meant *now!* I stood and quickly thanked the old man, then walked outside through the angry snarl of young Muslims. Out in the sunlight Ali herded us into the van; we had to pull Trahern away from a group of children begging to handle his GPS unit. We'd gotten so close.

As the van pulled away, I could still hear my heart pounding in my ears. *What was that old man about to tell us? Would we ever have a chance to talk to him again?* I could taste the disappointment welling in my chest.

Rumbling back down the road to Ardabil, my mind racing with thoughts of this strange countryside, I settled back and took a quick mental inventory. The striking similarities between these hills and the mysterious mountain Davis painstakingly detailed kept mounting. I'd just smelled, at Ghotor Suee, the rotten egg odor he'd described; I'd seen, not just one, but *many* streams coming off the mountain, just as he'd described. And then Sabalon itself—the tallest mountain north of Qasvin—still boasted a heavy crown of snow and ice, much like Davis described. Its lowlands brimmed with agriculture, farms, orchards, and *vineyards*; and just minutes before, I'd spoken with an old man who confirmed odd etchings of animals in nearby caves. He finally confirmed he had personal knowledge of the ark.

I turned to Larry, lost in his own reverie, and asked, "What do you think of all this?"

He shrugged and took out a pad and pen. "It's pretty interesting stuff," he murmured, scribbling some notes, careful, as always, to keep his emotions in check.

Looking out the window at this rugged, yet uncommonly fertile terrain, I found it hard to contain my own excitement. Even on cursory inspection Sabalon appeared to be hitting one hundred percent in the Ed Davis sweepstakes. If nothing else, it had to be regarded, if not a sure bet for the final resting place of the ark, then as a strong candidate for where Ed Davis said he saw it. To my startled eyes almost everything we'd seen so far fit his descriptions to a tee.

Lying in bed that night, sleepless from jet lag and edgy from the stench wafting from my drafty one-holer, I felt an urgent, almost unbearable, suspense for what tomorrow's search might yield.

Twenty

IRANIAN ARREST

We set off the following morning on a reconnaissance of the villages to the south side of the mountain. Each received us with great fanfare, children and adults flocking around with delighted enthusiasm, plying us with the same ceremonial hospitality served up by Muslims throughout the eastern hemisphere. At each stop, before a constructive word was spoken about Noah's ark, the village patriarch typically ushered us into his domed tent or mud hutch for a steaming pot of bitter tea, sweetened with small rocks of sugar clenched between the teeth.

I thoroughly enjoyed these affairs, filled as they were with warm smiles and laughter, Ali translating our hearty thanks for the rich hospitality. Yet, here on the south side of the mountain, our questions about the ark inspired nothing but silence and blank stares. No one, it seemed, had any knowledge or oral traditions to share, in stark contrast to those on the *north* side, which seemed to nurture lively histories of Noah's boat.

Ali explained that villages to Sabalon's south rarely fellowship with those on the north, sharply reducing cross-pollination of such tales. After our near miss the day before at Sulfur City, these villages seemed dull and unfruitful by comparison. I did take notice that some featured the same multiple-terraced, stacked-adobe appearance of a photo I'd once seen of the village where Ed Davis said he saw the old vineyard and ark artifacts. Yet no one we talked to had heard of a Lor named Badi, or Abas.

Arriving mid-morning at our third village—a dusty mud-thatch settlement higher up the south-facing foothills—we accepted the expected invitation by the village patriarch to sit in his stucco bungalow for tea. Trahern remained out-side to check his GPS coordinates. The next hour of idle conversation passed amiably, with questions about America, our families, the reasons behind our visit to Iran. With Ali mediating, it came as no great surprise when the elder shook his head "no!" when asked about the ark. We rose to leave, when we heard a sudden commotion outside the hut: a green, four-wheel-drive Land Rover roared through the village gate and stopped a few feet from the elder's door. Three men in gray polyester suits and closely cropped beards stepped out and began barking questions at the villagers, who pointed them in our direction.

I smelled trouble and turned to Ali, whose face had grown cold and waxen. That's when I knew—our long-awaited encounter with the Iranian secret police had arrived. Glancing about, I noticed Trahern standing next to the van, looking tense and uncomfortable. I walked over and asked, "What's going on?"

He shrugged. "I don't know," he said. "Who *are* those guys?"

Ali hurried over and pulled me aside. "These villagers say Mr. Trahern told them he was a pilot."

"A *pilot?*" I shot back. I knew Iranians associate pilots and planes with the military, with *espionage*. I'd discussed this very issue with the team beforehand—"Don't even *hint* at anything that has to do with guns, war, or the military"—but when I confronted Trahern, he denied it. Moments later another team member confirmed Trahern had, indeed, been running his mouth that he was a pilot.

I couldn't fathom his stubborn refusal (or blind inability) to compre-hend our sensitive predicament. Now it looked like one of his idle boasts might sabotage our mission. His careless actions kept blowing up in our faces. Earlier that day, someone at a village near the Russian border handed Trahern a can of Russian vodka as a souvenir. He stuck it absently in his pack and didn't mention it until later. When he told me he'd put a can of vodka in our van, I nearly choked, and immediately ordered the driver to stop.

"Throw it out, before we hit the next police checkpoint!" I ordered Trahern. "You want to get us thrown in jail?"

He instinctively started to resist, when Ali jumped in.

"Mohammad strictly forbade gambling and alcohol in our country," he scolded Trahern. "In Iran, possessing alcohol is worse than getting caught with a pound of *opium*. If they catch you with that, they'll flog you and put you in jail."

It seemed we might be headed there anyway.

Trahern had retreated to the van, slipping his GPS unit back in his pants' pouch as the police grilled Ali. After many emphatic gestures and pleas, Ali struggling to explain our reasons for being in northwest Iran, he returned stiffly to the van, mumbling under his breath, "Oh my God! Oh my God!"

"Ali, what do they want?" I asked.

"They have ordered us to follow them back into Nir for questioning," he said. "Someone in this village called the police. We must go. *Now!*"

I glanced at Trahern, now conspicuously avoiding my gaze, and gathered the team together.

"Stay calm, men," I said. "Looks like we're about to see an Iranian police station up close."

We followed the Land Rover five miles out of the village, along a dusty jeep trail into Nir, a small desert town that welcomed visitors with a billboard that said, "Allah is great! Down with the United States." Driving through Nir earlier that morning, the sign embarrassed Ali, who tried to explain: "The *people* here like Americans. It is the *government* who puts up these signs."

"Remind me not to leave my business card at the Nir Chamber of Commerce," Williams quipped from the back of the van.

The heavily guarded, cement and barbed-wire police compound sat at the center of town. By the time the police Land Rover turned into the gate, we'd all managed to hide our video equipment, cameras, and Trahern's GPS unit, under seats, behind luggage and inside our packs. A stout, bearded fellow we took to be the camp commander watched us from the guardhouse steps. He wore a rumpled military uniform with medals on the lapels and gravy stains on his chest pockets. When Ali, head hanging like a scolded pup, stepped from the van, the scowling commander ordered him into the station. *Poor Ali*, I thought, *living out his worst nightmare over our clumsy indiscretions*. We waited in the van.

Every twenty minutes or so, Ali—fussing and fretting, waving his hands up and down and yelping, "Oh my God! We are in big trouble"—returned to the van with an update. "We don't have permission to be in this area," he said over and over, and then, for good measure—"This puts my wife and my children in grave danger."

In the front of the van, our Turkish driver, his head buried in his hands, whimpered similarly, "They are going to kill my family." I couldn't decide if this was meant to make me feel guilty, or if they really feared for their lives.

"Ali, calm down," I said. "Just tell them *I* made you do it."

"Oh my God!" he said, walking back to the station with his hands on his head. "Oh my God!"

For two more hours we waited inside the sweltering van, pondering our fate. In a backseat, Larry sat tinkering with his satellite cell phone, trying to place a call to the States. Trahern stared out his window, griping about how we could've avoided this whole mess by heading straight for the Iraqi border. I endeavored to record a short, clandestine cutaway for my video and sat in the front seat as Houston, hiding a small, handheld digital video camera behind his hat, recorded my whispered dispatch.

"*It appears,*" I began, in my softest whisper, "*that, in our search for Noah's ark, we've been placed under arrest outside an Iranian jail in Nir. We're not sure what the charges are, but our options appear to be . . .*"

159

Λ

". . . two to five years," Williams broke in with perfect timing, cracking us all up.

Larry was a master at keeping things loose, even in the face of real danger. No matter how dire our case, he always melted the tension with a joke or wisecrack. Since our adventures together in Saudi Arabia, we'd remained close friends. Always ready to flee the pressures of high finance with a new adventure, he'd casually ask—whenever I called to invite him on another escapade—"So . . . what ancient treasures are we *not* going to find this year?"

Times like these reminded me why I so enjoyed his company, and though he'd never really taken Christianity seriously, our mutual love for travel and adventure had strengthened and deepened our friendship. People ask me why I go on trips with an unbeliever, and my pat response is, "Because I *like* him." Larry laughs at that, saying his friends ask *him*, "Why do you hang out with a *Christian?*"

The truth is, I love Larry like a brother, and in his way, he displays more compassion and good will than many believers I've met. Almost as important, in my line of work, he keeps his head in tight spots and never panics. In moments like these, there's no one I'd rather be arrested with than Larry Williams.

Though we hadn't been charged with a crime, being held against one's will in a foreign country meant we could rightfully consider ourselves under arrest. It meant we had to act fast, because, in Iran, things could turn sour quickly.

Brad Houston asked Larry for his satellite cell phone. "I've got an idea," he said. "I could call NBC, or *Dateline*, back in the States, and tell my contacts we have a hostage situation here, that Americans are being held against their will. It may be our only chance."

Not a bad plan, I thought, and said, "Give it a try!" But repeated attempts to connect failed; Larry's cell phone couldn't pick up a signal inside the van. We tried several times to stick his phone outside the window and dial the number, but guards kept walking by, and he could never complete the call. I finally tried to divert the guard's attention by pretending to stretch my legs outside the bus, but we never had enough time and finally gave up.

Bored to death, sick of sitting and waiting, Larry reached in his bag for a deck of cards and challenged me to a game of hearts. "Deal me in," I said. We'd played a few hands when Ali suddenly reemerged from the jail, the commander following close behind him, holding a silver, snub-nosed revolver.

What's he going to do with that? I wondered, watching as he took out a single, chrome-plated bullet and tenderly loaded it in the chamber, like Barney Fife. Ali leaned in the van and saw us playing cards.

"Oh my God," he blurted. "*Quickly! Hide them. It is illegal and forbidden to play cards.*"

Without hesitating, we swiped them off the tray and tossed them over our shoulders, sending cards flying just as the commander poked his head in the van. Larry stepped on cards lying on the floor; I had cards stuffed down my shirt; Houston and Trahern sat on cards; cards were crammed under our seats and scattered in the aisle next to the cooler. We all held our breaths as the commander looked us over, then turned to Ali with another scolding. He rattled off a few angry sentences, frowned, looked us over once more, then shook a final, angry finger in our direction.

Ali turned, a shell-shocked expression on his face, and said, "We are free to go."

While it seemed inappropriate to cheer, we felt instant and profound relief. Ali barked at the driver to "get us out of here!" and as we left the compound, we all shared an unspoken sense of having received a conditional reprieve.

As our van sped past the outskirts of Nir toward Ardabil, Ali pulled me aside. "They think you are CIA," he said, "or archaeologists here to steal our ancient treasures." Noting my puzzled expression, he explained, "Foreigners come to this region to dig for many ancient landmarks. They think you are here either to spy or to excavate the graves and altars at the top of Sabalon. I could not convince them they were wrong. I said, 'You are crazy!'"

"Is that why they arrested us in the first place?" I asked.

"No," he said, nodding toward Trahern. "The way Mr. Trahern walked around with his knife and maps at the last stop and talked about flying planes, the villagers there feared he was up to something. Thinking he might be a soldier, they contacted the police."

"Perfect," I said, disgusted. "So what does that mean for our trip?"

Ali sighed. "It means they will follow us from now on."

With that, our bad times in northwest Iran began. We returned to Ardabil, where word of our arrest had spread. Having been detained by the secret police, we would now be treated as pariahs, personas non grata, scorned intruders. From the favored ranks of welcomed guests, we had passed, in a matter of hours, into the realm of hated untouchables.

Ali knew the routine, and we learned soon enough: Wherever we went now, whether in the hotel lobby or ordering meals at a restaurant, agents in dark polyester suits stopped and interrogated us. Out in the streets we couldn't walk fifty feet without being halted by some young desk sergeant and ordered to present our passports and visas. Even the desk manager at the Sabalon Hotel, kind and helpful the day before, turned surly whenever we showed up in his lobby; and the porters either scowled or ignored us as we walked by. We never knew when we'd be stopped and browbeaten by police; and I knew the longer we hung around, the worse it would get, until we'd either end up in jail or simply flee the country for relief.

The way things now stood, our chances of ever setting foot on Mount Sabalon looked poor indeed. At best, I figured, we had one more day to finish our business and get out of town. I called the team together.

"We've run out of time, men. We've got to get to Sabalon." Then I turned to Ali. "We want to climb the mountain. Take us there."

Wincing, he said, "We do not have permission."
"I understand. But we *must* climb the mountain. It is compulsory."
Ffwaap!
"Oh my God!"

SABALON RETREAT

We set out early the next morning, hired two young Kurdish drivers, and instructed them to take us as high up Mount Sabalon as the roads would go. They agreed and drove us in their battered, 1960s model Land Rover back through Sulfur City along a narrow, meandering dirt road up the west saddle of Sabalon. And then, for another two hours, we rocked and tilted along washed-out, rutted cart paths, our team trying to ignore the sharp drop-offs on either side.

We finally reached a little stone hostel sporting two tall, medieval-looking brick spires built atop ruddy, mud walls. Chiseled handsomely into the side of a cliff at about twelve thousand feet, it seemed an adequately remote, inaccessible hideout, offering temporary shelter from prying eyes. Originally constructed as a monastery during World War II, Ali said it now serves primarily as a Muslim meditation retreat, with ten stuffy, windowless rooms locked behind heavy iron doors.

"We will be safe here for a time," Ali assured. "There are no phones and no villagers, and, if you wish, you can climb the mountain from here."

Up so high we could feel the late September weather changing from fall to winter. Strolling about the grounds, a frosty tundra crunching beneath my feet, I could see my breath and feel the icy nip of Caspian humidity stinging my fingertips. Twenty yards from the hostel sat a popular trailhead frequented by local hikers, and the occasional nomad, leading up a high, spiraling ridge to the summit.

Mount Sabalon consists of six hundred square miles of rugged foothills, serpentine ravines, and plunging gorges, any one of which might harbor a weather-beaten ship. From a certain vantage the mountain appears as a huge, solitary summit among smaller, rugged peaks; but scanning it from other angles, it spreads out and stretches into a range all its own, with no less than four, similarly sized summits lined up in a row. *If Ed Davis climbed one of these peaks*, I thought, *the ark could be practically anywhere*.

We knew only that Badi and his brothers had taken Davis up a very hard, possibly forbidden route, through hidden caves and extreme, rocky terrain to reach a ledge overlooking a massive gorge. By all accounts that gorge lay hidden from view and received little, if any, foot traffic. I had no illusions that this handy footpath—no more than a quick, tourist's trail to the top—would yield much information on Davis's route. I wanted to climb it nonetheless, hoping that by doing so I'd at least gain a feel for the peak's vast, undulating topography.

Everyone in our group, of course, wanted to make the climb. But only Stuplich and I, fresh from Ararat's slopes, came prepared with proper snow gear and climbing boots. I certainly hadn't expected to climb a mountain of this enormity in Iran. We'd intended it as strictly a research trip, so the other members of the team had packed only light hiking gear. From the trail head at twelve thousand feet, it would take us eight hours to reach the sixteen-thousand-foot summit and return, a grueling stretch by any standard. To quiet any grumbling, Stuplich pointed to a towering, five-hundred-foot rock face overlooking the trail.

"To reach the top from here," he said, "we'd each have to climb the equivalent of eighteen of those."

They stared up at the cliff, a graphic picture of the effort and fortitude required to climb four thousand near-vertical feet at high altitude. Coupled with the plunging temperature, it would make for a punishing climb, even properly outfitted. The sight of the cliff cooled the others to an ascent. So less than a week after scaling Ararat, Stuplich and I stared up at another staggering peak, silently wondering what hardships *it* held for us. We returned to the hostel for a quick dinner and turned in early.

163

THE SUMMIT

Stuplich and I rose at 5 A.M., strapped on our headlamps, put on gloves and warm clothes, tightened our boots, and hit the trail with our two Kurdish guides, who set a blistering pace to begin. Having grown up in the local villages, they knew every little curve and turn in the rock, and practically galloped up the trail like mountain goats.

Stuplich and I, on the other hand, still nursing bone-deep aches and muscle fatigue from Turkey, quickly realized we were in for another punishing workout. I took several deep breaths and told Stuplich, "Don't worry about me, Bob. I'll make it." He nodded, and we set off in breathless pursuit of the wiry Kurds.

The Sabalon trail rose nearly straight up a narrow, stair-step terrace of rocky switchbacks—the polar antithesis of Mount Ararat's marathoner's grade—and shot us directly into a dense cloud bank. Over the next four, lung-searing hours, we rose four thousand feet on the surprisingly well-groomed trail, which finally emptied out into a tight, windswept plateau framed by granite cliffs and cleavered glaciers. Here we stood a mere fifty yards below the summit, yet, climbing so fast and so high without rest, my heart hammered heavy and irregular—unlike anything I'd ever felt. And even after resting several minutes, trying to relax, letting my pulse settle down, I couldn't catch my breath. *Had I pushed it too far?* I wondered. *After all these years and hard ascents, was my old ticker now about to blow a gasket?* In time the locomotive heartbeat quieted, but my breath never fully recovered while we stayed on the summit.

We stood beside a beautiful, aquamarine lake, set gently into the plateau like a milky opal. Its pristine waters would have served us well four days earlier, descending Ararat, and I was surprised to see it up so high; terrible chunks of ice had slivered down off the glacier and sat half-submerged at water's edge. I recognized the scene immediately from countless photos and paintings we'd seen of this popular local landmark, memorialized on the walls of shops and diners throughout Ardabil.

The temperature had dropped to well below freezing. The sky above swirled wild and turbulent; dense patches of purple-black clouds whipped directly overhead, wetting our faces and bathing the summit in stark, strobelike splashes of brilliant light. Ice crystals formed on our unshaven faces, and when I took out my video camera, its batteries had frozen. Stuplich turned and tried to snap a picture, but the shutter of his Nikon had iced shut. With stiff, numb fingers, I fumbled in my pack to retrieve another set of batteries, managing, at great length, to replace the frozen ones. My video camera whirred to life, allowing me to record the bitter, arctic tableau.

The summit sat just above us, but the exhausted Kurds, quaking from the cold and dressed only in thin nylon jackets, lightweight gloves, khaki pants, and tennis shoes, motioned for us to go on. I feared they might freeze or suffer frostbite, though they seemed not to be overly concerned. As Stuplich and I climbed on ahead, treading past a wintry Stonehenge of towering, heavily icicled boulders, I turned to see the Kurds curled next to one another beneath a small ledge, warming themselves like cats beside a fire.

"We've got to hurry," I shouted at Stuplich, fighting to stand in the teeth of a fierce, freezing wind. "Bad weather is coming in."

Within minutes we'd scaled the final ice-glazed pinnacle, hoping for better visibility, but the clouds grew too thick and blustery to see anything of the range below. We could barely see our *feet*.

Beside us the wind had cut the ice into horizontal spikes on the rock, like shark's teeth stuck in granite. Turning to Stuplich, I shouted, "That's our cue to leave. We won't survive long up here."

But before leaving, I took a moment to stare into the intensifying whiteout, trying to imagine the curvature and shape of the lower bowls and ravines, wanting to project myself into that wet, sleety canyon of 1943, where Ed Davis and Badi may have passed. I could not; the mountain would not allow it—this time. We could barely stand on the ice-blasted summit.

"Let's head down!" Stuplich yelled through howling gusts, and I knew we had to go.

It took us three hours to scramble back down the trail to the hostel, where hot tea and rice warmed our half-frozen limbs. Little did I know it at the time, but another year of dreams and clues would pass before I had the privilege of standing again on this awesome peak.

Part Five

IRAN, FINAL ROUND

Twenty-One

THE MAP, THE SEAL, AND THE "OBJECT"

Returning to the States, I had no burning desire ever to return to Turkey or Iran to look for the ark. Those mean slopes left me beat up and exhausted. In eight short days I'd endured more mental strain and physical danger than most people do in three lifetimes. I'd nearly broken my neck and died of thirst descending Mount Ararat in pitch darkness, then, fleeing blind across an open plain, barely dodged arrest by the Turkish military. Then came Iran, where the secret police harassed and detained us and where I nearly blew an aorta in a freezing, wet ice storm, cruising to the top of Mount Sabalon and down again in a brutal ten-hour climb. It still ranks as the toughest two weeks of my life, and I have no problem saying it would have dropped the stoutest man to his knees.

I made it home to my family in one piece, thank God. But what about next time? We'd had some brutally close calls and never knew for sure if we'd make it home alive. Maybe next time I *wouldn't* come back. Did I really need another near-death experience under my belt to prove my manhood? Could I possibly live out my days in peace *without* going back to Iran and getting arrested again, or perhaps stepping on a loose rock on Sabalon and getting buried in a rock slide? I kept thinking, *I have a wife and two young children at home; I'm nearing fifty. Maybe I'm getting too old for this.* I still felt strongly we'd found the right mountain, but I didn't want to die proving it. I'd endured enough punishment to keep me satisfied for a while and started to think: *Maybe it just isn't worth it.*

Weeks passed. I rested, spent time with my family. Both my bruised psyche and body slowly healed, and the revulsion I felt at the thought of returning to the Middle East began to blur and fade. I've learned that time has an odd way of bringing out the best in our memories—the excitement, the adventure, the exotic travel, and the rich fellowship—and strangely softens the heartache and misery. Yet even with time's mellowing influence, I wouldn't have thought seriously of picking up the chase again so soon if it weren't for two seemingly unrelated events converging directly in my path.

The first came on a chance visit from my friend Mary Irwin, the wife of my old partner Jim Irwin. She stopped by my office one afternoon, shortly after I returned from Iran, to drop off a box full of old files, pictures, letters, and charts from Jim's extensive archives. Plopping the box on the floor, she snatched out an old piece of paper and said, "You might be interested in this."

"What is it?" I asked.

"It's a map that Ed Davis drew with Elfred Lee," she said, handing it to me.

Sure enough, it was a rough, hand-sketched map of the route Davis took up the mountain to see the ark. Though crude, I found it a surprisingly detailed, black-and-white sketch of both his route up the north side of the peak and a number of topographical and geological features he remembered from the mountain. I'd never seen it before; I didn't even know it existed.

"Lee apparently drew it during one of his interview sessions with Davis," Irwin said.

Elfred Lee had been intimately involved in the ark search since the 1960s. An accomplished artist and illustrator, he'd interviewed each of the three living, self-professed eyewitnesses to the ark—Fernand Navarra, George Hagopian, and Ed Davis—and captured their memories of its appearance and the look of the surrounding terrain on canvas. He drew the map in June 1986, more than forty years after Davis said he saw the ark, so I realized it reflected the memory of an eighty-year-old man. As such, I had serious reservations about its accuracy—until I remembered that, as a sergeant with the Army Corps of Engineers, Davis's job included reading and making maps. He'd been trained to draft detailed renderings of obscure construction sites after only a brief visual inspection.

This map, while something less than the work of a skilled cartographer, nonetheless looked intricately crafted. It illustrated a cluster of prominent landmarks, such as Jacob's Well, Doomsday Rock, a handful of distinct rock formations, unusual canyon contours, and even some curious nips and hooks in the trail. Moreover, the saddleback ridge above and the gorge below—in which Davis drew the ark, broken in two pieces, a third of a mile apart—had been rendered to the exact dimensions he'd described in *our* interview. Davis's unwavering consistency shone through even in death: the map pinpointed the lake and the streambed, a current of water flowing under the ark, even a trio of rock spires looking down from a ridge.

Setting the map aside on my desk, I thanked Mary for this unexpected prize yet still didn't see how it might one day support or detract from my theory.

THE SEAL

The second incident happened soon thereafter, arriving in the form of retired Navy SEAL Dan Toth, from San Diego. He called one day, out of the blue, to say he'd seen my Mount Sinai video and wanted to volunteer his services to BASE. He said he planned to move to Colorado to start a personal fitness business and wanted to come see me in Colorado Springs to talk about my explorations.

Throughout our brief initial conversation, Toth repeatedly expressed a profound eagerness to help me with my research, which didn't exactly surprise me. I get lots of phone calls from people wanting to help. But Toth's call seemed unusual in one respect: I found his background intriguing. What would a former SEAL—whose proficiency, I assumed, lay in *water* reconnaissance—have to offer me, an inveterate climber of mountains? When I snidely quipped, "To my knowledge, Dan, the ark landed in *mountains*; but if I ever hear it came to rest at the bottom of the ocean, I'll give you a call," he wasn't amused.

169

"SEAL means 'by sea, air, and *land*,'" he said, "and trains its people in a *broad* range of aptitudes."

He said that in his twenty-five-year career, he'd supported countless clandestine military operations as a map maker and navigator, in the area of satellite intelligence, demolitions, and missions planning—and that didn't include his expertise in mountaineering, skydiving, and scuba diving. He spoke of "fingerprinting" aerial photos, or taking rough sketches of enemy terrain and "matching" them to high-resolution aerial and topographical maps. He described his extensive training in the art of inspecting satellite images to detect heavily camouflaged enemy munitions and encampments in remote mountain, desert, and jungle terrain. In other words, he could take a rough, hand-drawn map—like that which sat on my desk—and fingerprint it to a specific topographical schematic. Or he could look at an aerial image and distinguish highly camouflaged man-made objects from their natural surroundings.

I could use skills like that. I glanced at the Ed Davis sketch sitting on my desk. On the phone I had a guy who might be able to tell me if it fit the profile of Mount Sabalon. I found the timing uncanny—an ex-Navy SEAL, who'd spent his career matching virtual maps to physical terrain, calling to offer his services. Unfortunately, I didn't know anything about the guy (Who *are* you, Dan Toth?), so I took my time finding out.

In the coming weeks we kept up a spirited dialogue, sharing bits and pieces of our backgrounds and careers. Once he moved to Colorado, we met a few times and gradually got to know each other. I gained a surface understanding of his personality and motives. He truly believed God had trained and gifted him with a unique set of skills, and he saw my ministry as a natural fit for his strengths. I finally decided to share some of my research and theories about Mount Sabalon. Then, just to hear his opinion, I showed him the Davis sketch.

"What do you think?" I asked.

He looked it over carefully and said, "I might be able to help."

We had some more conversations, prayed together, and, when I'd finally determined I could trust him with my life's work, handed him a copy of the map with instructions simply to "do your thing." I had zero expectations, but I figured it couldn't hurt to give an ex-SEAL a tough assignment and see what happened.

I honestly didn't know when I'd hear from Toth again. People often lose interest once the arduous work of research begins, so it came as a stunning surprise when, less than a week later, he called to say he'd made a match.

"You *what?*" I asked.

"Yeah," he said, "I hit the bull's-eye."

"What does *that* mean?" I persisted.

"It means I bought a generic map of Mount Sabalon from the Boulder Map Gallery and ran a match of some prominent features from the Davis sketch," he said. "Then I did a topographical overlay of the mountain to isolate specific vectors." He paused for effect. "Bob," he continued, "I believe, based on these findings, that Ed Davis was *on* Mount Sabalon. If I'm seeing this right, it's an exact match."

I didn't know how to respond, so I invited him to "come on over and show me what you've got."

We hooked up a few days later to scan the two-square-mile enlargement he'd procured of a Sabalon hillside. From appearances it seemed to resemble parts of Davis's sketch, but the way Toth explained it, the contours, textures, and features accounted for an uncanny fit: the trail curving and hooking toward the top as it approached Doomsday Point, the location of a possible lake in the belly of the gorge, the warp and woof of the ravine itself, evidence of stream flow or a riverbed. Toth even pointed out a feature he interpreted as Jacob's Well, tucked up in the northern quadrant of the graph.

"And here," he said, pointing at three distinct, tiny circles in a line, "these three rock spires sit up on the ridge, just as they do in the Davis sketch. And this saddle-down, or horseshoe-shaped gorge—*that's* where Davis said he saw the ark."

Shocked by the thoroughness of his survey, I asked, "How did you *find* all this?"

Toth's eyes grew narrow and intense; his voice turned even softer and grainier than normal. Then he stared at me with the cocky half-grin of someone indoctrinated into thinking SEALs are the brightest, toughest, most resourceful dudes on the planet.

"Bob," he grinned, "we used to do this in the military *all the time*. I simply picked out the prominent terrain features from Davis's sketch, then divided the topo map into two-by-two grids, eliminated one grid after another until I finally narrowed it down to a two-kilometer area." He paused, watching my eyes, then continued: "I started putting features together: first the gorge, then these two ridge lines that look like a camel's back, then found the trail in the topography that came to a hook precisely at the hill shown in the sketch." He traced the contour with a pencil. "It matches the place Davis said he turned back, past the three tall rock formations and back up to Doomsday Point." He tapped his finger on the map. "*This* is the ledge where Davis sat and looked down into the gorge." Then he traced his finger along a long, contoured trough. "*That's* where he saw the ark."

I had to confess: it looked good. But to be honest, I would have never interpreted, or detected, any of those features to match the Davis sketch. So when he stared me in the eye and told me he'd found the exact crosshairs of the gorge memorialized as "Davis Canyon," I couldn't help but be skeptical. It seemed an outrageous claim, even from an ex-SEAL trained as a special forces navigator. So we dissected the map again and again, me peppering him with questions, Toth patiently explaining, helping me to see what he saw. Finally, I cautiously allowed that, yes, it *appeared* to be a match.

"Now what?" I asked.

"We need to confirm the site with satellite photography," he said. "If we can get some good images of this vector," he circled the area with his finger, "it should give us the confirmation we need to go over there and take a look."

THE OBJECT

Go over? Take a look? Goose bumps formed on my arms. I hadn't really considered it a remote possibility until now. But the adrenaline buzz, dormant for months, had returned.

Still I needed to move slowly. Recalling the hardship and harassment of my last trip, I told Toth, "Give me a few days to think about it."

I still wasn't convinced I wanted to proceed, when I recalled a story my Grandpa once told me about the trials of growing up in old Russia, back when people got their water from hand-pumped cisterns. "Those old pumps didn't always work right," Grandpa said, "and a lot of folks didn't like how long it took. Sometimes they'd get tired and just stop pumping, not knowing they were only a couple of pumps away from bringing up the water. Just a couple of pumps more, and they'd hit water." Grandpa's lesson in perseverance spoke to me in my moment of doubt. Having come this far, I didn't want to stop a couple pumps short of striking water. I stared at the topographical map, then compared it again with Davis's map. If what Toth said was right, acquiring satellite imagery seemed a logical next step.

I contacted an aerial image broker in Denver, Image Links, and ordered some expensive one- and five-meter data of Mount Sabalon, taken by U.S. and Russian spy satellites back in the eighties. When the photos arrived, Toth and I spread them out on my office floor and scoured them pixel by pixel. The one-meter image gave us the best definition and detail—each pixel representing one square meter of actual terrain—but both images provided revealing, trace outlines of massive troughs and valleys, rugged peaks and ridges, on Sabalon's north-facing slope.

I found it to be laborious, exhausting work, fingerprinting images that looked like little more than random lines on a page. We scheduled long meetings, painstakingly scanning each section of mountain with a magnifying glass, orienting the satellite images to both the topo graph and the Davis sketch. Toth stood on familiar ground, seemingly able to distinguish every little blotch and blur in the images.

Finally I said, "I'm only slowing you down. Just take the prints home. Spend some time. See what you find, and keep me informed of your progress."

He nodded, gathered up the maps and photos and took them home, where he kept working on the analysis, calling me daily, updating me on even trivial developments. This continued for a month with no real breakthrough, until one week he didn't call at all. I naturally assumed that he'd hit a wall and prepared myself for bad news. A few more days passed, and then one afternoon Toth called, edgy and breathless, practically shouting into the phone:

"I found it!"

"Found *what?*" I asked.

"The *ark!*" he said. *"We've got a match."*

"Slow down, slow down, Dan," I said, unsure what he meant by a "match." "Tell me *slowly*." But he could barely contain himself.

"I didn't want to call you until I was sure," he continued, "but the satellite data lines up almost perfectly with the topo map and the Davis sketch."

"Yeah," I said, "and . . ."

"And—there's an *object*," he replied.

An object? I thought. "What *kind* of object?"

"A *huge*, rectangular object at the bottom of the gorge. It's covered with two tongues of talus and scree, just as Davis described."

Now *my* heart started beating.

"Bob, this *has* to be the Ed Davis Canyon," he added, then unexpectedly blurted out, "We've found the ark; I *know* it."

He might as well have raised a big, red flag. I couldn't count how many times I'd heard those exact words.

"Hold it, Dan," I cautioned him sternly. "I've been looking for this thing for fifteen years. *Believe* me; *no* one's 100 percent certain. Try to keep a level head."

Toth didn't flinch.

"Bob," he said, pressing his case, "based on what I see in the satellite data, we have more than seventy-five facets of matching terrain, geologic features, and hydrological features that correlate *precisely* with what Davis described in his sketch."

That sounded impressive.

"Go on," I said, listening carefully as he explained how "the fundamental premise of deciphering these images is to remember that every square foot of mountain, prairie, or desert has its own unique fingerprint."

A subtle curve in a ravine, he explained, in relation to a hooked rock outcropping or a saddleback gorge—like we identified in these images—could only be found, in that particular configuration, on one place on the planet: *"Here!"* he said, "on Mount Sabalon! To have so many corresponding similarities in such an isolated area is next to impossible."

It sounded good. But I couldn't decide; should I get excited, or had Toth, in his military zeal, overstated the facts?

We met the next day, and he walked me through the new images, pixel by pixel, pinpointing a raft of features: "The runoff, the fork, and the stream, the talus and scree covering the object. It all jives. Besides, according to the Davis map, the object sits exactly where it's supposed to be."

To me, the rectangular object he cited looked like little more than a vague outline of some elongated, square-shaped *something* in a field of rock and scree. It didn't look like a boat but had more the flat, one-dimensional cast of a giant football field.

Dan explained: "We're looking at a sort of optical illusion caused by the pitch of a slope that has been battered by heavy water runoff and erosion. The object lies half-buried on one side, which has formed a dam where, it appears, tons of rock and scree have accumulated." He traced the rectangle with his finger, insisting, "You never find perpendicular or parallel lines like this in nature." Then he spread his arms wide and said, "You're looking at a *huge,* man-made object."

The more I looked at the object, the more compelling it appeared. From its vague, gray background, it seemed to emerge, like a hologram, into an object with depth and substance. *Noah's ark?*

Still I didn't see enough there to send me scampering off on another expedition to Iran. I needed more input, *expert* input. So I sent the images and Toth's findings to Edmond W. Holroyd III, a Ph.D. professor of atmospheric science and physical research for the Remote Sensing and Geographic Information Group of the U.S. Bureau of Reclamation. Holroyd teaches courses in remote sensing and image processing for the University of Denver and has the skills and equipment needed to dissect theories and give us an objective judgment. We also sent copies to Jeff

173

Λ

Sloan, a cartographer with the U.S. Geological Survey's National Mapping Division.

I needed them to give us the straight scoop and instructed them both to be brutally frank. Was this "object" worth pursuing?

Looking back, I think I subconsciously hoped to spare myself the emotional pain and expense of mounting another campaign to the far side of the planet; I secretly wanted them to tear Toth's theory to shreds. That's why I had such mixed feelings when I received back a wholly unexpected, yet altogether supportive report. In a series of correspondences between April and August 2000, both Holroyd and Sloan, using all the expertise and technology at their disposal, presented me with a startling appraisal.

Holroyd began his dispatches with a disclaimer on the nature of the rectangular object: "Bob and Dan, I was not thrilled with any of the previous objects. They looked like they could be natural objects and optical illusions." But then he added, "On Saturday morning, however, as I was using the Indian and Russian satellite images in stereo and seeing the shape of the terrain much better, I noticed a small rectangular object east of Ed Davis's observation point. It was in the middle of a debris flow channel, as he described, and of a good orientation for viewing. Soon afterwards I saw another rectangular object, of twice the length and of the same width, uphill from the first and at the lateral edge of the debris flow. It is likely that Ed Davis could not see the larger object because of a rocky outcrop just in front of it. *Together these two objects strongly appear to be what we are looking for.*"

He went on to observe: "The sum of these two objects, end to end, approximately matches the NIV interpretation of the cubit for the length of the historical object (Noah's ark). The width, though hard to see, seems to match the height of the historical object."

And finally: "Ed Davis said that his object was in the same direction as these objects and at a distance of one-third mile. The small object is just over three-tenths miles from the observation point, which is in excellent agreement with Davis's estimate. Many rock objects in the area that could provide optical illusions. These two rectangular objects could still be fooling us. However, I am presently about 75 percent certain that this pair of objects is what we are looking for. That number might change with further analysis of the pictures."

Seventy-five percent sure? That seemed unrealistically optimistic. In another correspondence, Holroyd noted the exceptional clarity of the five-meter data: "Now I more clearly see a set of parallel lines that cross the drainages. The southeast object is totally covered by rock debris (talus). The parallel lines strongly suggest that there is something under the talus that disturbs the surface distribution of the rocks. It is still possible that we are only looking at a part of buried rock strata ledges that happen to be fractured in straight parallel lines. It will take a *careful, on-site examination* to identify what is causing the features seen in the satellite images."

174
Λ

Summing up his findings on April 25, Holroyd wrote: "I am even more confident that we have found the site visited by Ed in the 1940s. All of the features match the records."

Jeff Sloan of the U.S. Geological Survey offered this opinion: "A preliminary analysis of the 5- and 1.5-meter imagery indicated features that correspond quite well with the sketch and artist rendition of the area of interest. The sketch, in its surprising detail, appears to align very well with the area outlined by Dan Toth. This is especially evident in the trails leading to the area, the geologic features (specifically the rock outcroppings and peaks), and hydrological features. The detail to which the witness describes is quite amazing and could very well be the area to which Dan is referring."

I found these reports unnerving, forcing me into another major decision. What do you do when experts with elite pedigrees and scientists with scholarly degrees quote a 75 to 100 percent likelihood that you've stumbled upon Noah's ark? It sent me scurrying back to my police training, where, as a criminal investigator, I *had* to rely on the expertise of others: specialists in blood or urine analysis, examiners of the microscopic variances of bullet striations and trajectories, expert fingerprint analysts. To win a case in court, I had to trust the experts. How could *this* be any different?

To determine my next course of action, I finally decided I had to trust the retired Navy SEAL with map-reading and navigational expertise; I had to trust the analyses of scientists trained in interpreting satellite imagery. Even though I still couldn't see it, they had to know what they were talking about. These professionals said the evidence suggested, with a high degree of probability, we'd found a real-life match of the Ed Davis sketch.

And we'd found it on Mount Sabalon.

Two months earlier I felt little enthusiasm for ever returning to Iran. Beaten and bruised, weary and disappointed, I'd cooled to the idea of following up on a growing list of evidence that seemed to point to Mount Sabalon as the resting place of the ark. Yet it seemed the mountain would not let me alone.

Back in the police force I'd been trained to keep working a case, searching out new leads and gathering evidence, until I hit a dead end. Then, unless someone came forward with fresh information or some new evidence dropped in my lap, the case often came to a frustrating halt. I knew when to abandon a case: when the trail grew *cold*.

But this trail to Mount Sabalon just kept getting hotter. Instead of stop signs and roadblocks, green lights kept popping up all over the place. I had people calling to encourage me: Mary Irwin phoned to say, "Bob, you're on the right track. Go over there and *find* it." Even Larry Williams, fresh from Iranian detention and naturally skeptical, called to say, "I have a feeling about Iran, Bob. Don't give up."

It set me to wondering: with all this new satellite data, maybe we *had* found it. If the experts were right, the ark might, in fact, lay on this remote

Iranian peak. "Lord," I prayed, "am I supposed to go back and, maybe, this time find it?"

Toth and I combed some new maps and identified a road on the south side of Sabalon—no doubt a ratty cart path—that nonetheless ascended to within a mile or two of the target site on the peak's northwest slope. For an area I had earlier judged to be remote and largely inaccessible, I found it incredible to find a road running from Sabalon's milder south side to a point of convergence high up its north-facing slope, joining at a point that appeared to curl tantalizingly close to the gorge Toth had now boldly christened "Davis Canyon." This road, where no road should rightfully be, might spare us a risky ascent up the sheer cliffs and slick glaciers I'd grown so weary of climbing. It meant we might simply drive four-wheel-drive Land Rovers to within a few miles of the target zone. Suddenly the prospect of returning to Sabalon seemed much safer and far more appealing.

I tried to keep my foot on the brake of this runaway train, but the quest now seemed to take on a life all its own. What do you do when all of the experts and all the signs seem to be calling you back? The answer is simple: you go over and take a look. Based on this new flurry of scientific opinion, I felt I had no choice but to prepare myself for another expedition to northwest Iran.

I set a rough departure date of early July, when the mountain should be relatively free of snow and ice. Starting so early, I figured, we might actually win government approval to climb the mountain.

And, with surprising ease, everything quickly fell into place: our visas, fund-raising, the selection of a team. On June 20, 2000, two weeks before our departure date, Ed Holroyd E-mailed me a final transmission. He said he'd completed a final, detailed "georegistry" of the target zone and wrote to say, "I do not see anything that should call off the expedition. The Corona pictures are obviously not as good as the Russian picture but still show the two objects as raised and linear. They could still be rock, but we will not know without much better pictures (close-up aerial photography), or the planned site visit *(best)*."

Holroyd's E-mail succinctly expressed the only practical course of action. To know for certain the precise nature of this beguiling "object," we had to go over and see it for ourselves. I'd taken my time, prayed long and hard, and now felt confident we'd given ourselves the best chance to date of proving my theory.

Twenty-Two

TEAM IRAN

On April 20, 1999, the heart of a nation broke when two gunmen entered a Littleton, Colorado, high school and turned it into the scene of the deadliest school shootings in American history. Twelve students and one teacher lost their lives that day, with twenty-three either maimed or injured.

Living in Colorado Springs, fifty miles from where the massacre occurred, I watched the news stories, read the articles, and, in turn, learned something about the lives of those slain and wounded.

I learned, for instance, that Rachel Scott, among the first to die in a hail of bullets on the school lawn, had a broken heart for the misfits and social outcasts at her school. This beautiful seventeen-year-old was an outspoken Christian, with gifts ranging from writing poetry to acting. What I didn't know (until I met her father) is that she possessed what can only be called a prophetic sense of her imminent death. Believing her life would be cut short before her prime, she set about to touch those she saw floundering on Columbine's fringes. In the weeks before the shootings, Rachel shared her faith with both Dylan Klebold and Eric Harris, not realizing that her act of courage made her a high-priority target.

I learned that another victim, sixteen-year-old John Tomlin, also loved the Lord. John talked himself into a job at fourteen so he could save for a truck and had his eye on a career in the military. Young John also had a heart for life's outcasts and underdogs (a fact I learned only after meeting *his* father) and took up their cause at every opportunity. John Tomlin lost his life in the school library, while doing his homework.

As I've shared my adventures at churches and rallies across the country, it's been a great privilege to meet some of the parents of these precious slain. Darrell Scott and John Tomlin Sr.—the fathers of Rachel and John—have both become close friends.

I met Darrell at a World View Weekend conference in Wichita, Kansas, shortly after he left a lucrative career to launch "Chain Reaction," an evangelistic, antiviolence ministry aimed at teens. I saw in Darrell a man of serious intellect, reserved and humble, trained as a theologian, yet loving to laugh, play golf, and tell jokes.

People say John Tomlin comes across as a big, gentle, soft-spoken bear of a man—and he does—but I can still see the pain of his terrible loss lingering just below the surface. John shares Darrell's vision for reaching teens with a message of hope through Christ.

Our paths kept crossing on the conference-speaking circuit, and we'd invariably end up spending time together, having lunch or seeing a movie, sharing our lives, talking about God, his purposes. But too much talk of Columbine wearied them. They spent the better part of every day, after all, discussing the minute details of the tragedy. Our discussions inevitably turned to my travels chasing after lost arks and holy mountains. Hearing of these wild adventures, their eyes lit up, and their faces changed from somber men into those of schoolboys at a hay ride.

When I described my plans to return to Iran to look for Noah's ark, they didn't hesitate to ask me to take them along. Their enthusiasm blessed me, and I promised that I'd think about it, but, in truth, I didn't feel overly optimistic. I get so many requests—sometimes as many as ten per day—from people asking me to take them on an adventure. It seems that everyone from Fortune 500 executives bored with life, to little old ladies wanting to get out of the house, are dying to put themselves at risk.

Yet the more I pored over our maps and planned the stages of our itinerary, the more I realized this might not be quite as harsh a trip as I'd imagined. If we really could take four-wheel-drive vehicles to within a couple miles of the target, we wouldn't have to hike for days across high plain or endure endless hours of technical climbing up high cliffs and deadly boulder fields. That meant I might be able to take some friends—who needed a break but might not have the necessary skills or physical conditioning—on a once-in-a-lifetime adventure.

I finally decided, "Why not?" Whatever risks we might face couldn't possibly outweigh the fun and diversion such a trip would give John and Darrell, who had spent the past year immersed in the horror of Columbine. With that I called them both with a message: "If you still want to go, mail me your passports for the visa applications!"

THE TEAM

Now I had to settle on the rest of the team, never an easy task for the simple reason that "everyone" always wants to go. With few exceptions I've never had to go begging for team members; and as word leaked out about our recent satellite findings, the interest level soared. Who *wouldn't* want to be a part of the first team to confirm the true location of Noah's ark?

The list started out long and grew longer. And while I hate saying no to anyone, I finally limited the team to a group of eight men. The difficulty and expense of travel in Iran demanded the smaller team.

Dan Toth had certainly earned a seat on the plane, having put in countless hours studying maps and poring over satellite photos. Besides, he had the navigational skills and charting equipment we'd need to locate our target in the vast mountain range. Next I invited my brother, Paul, a member of the BASE board of directors, whose support never has waned. He'd traveled with me to Turkey, and if our new data proved true, I wanted him in Iran to share in the excitement.

I also asked David Halbrook, coauthor of this book and a Christian brother with whom I've become close friends. (Halbrook also coauthored our first book together, *In Search of the Mountain of God: The Discovery of the Real Mount Sinai*.) As the Iran trip approached and we found ourselves deep into the manuscript of this book, I felt Halbrook needed to taste, feel, and see the culture, countryside, and people of Iran through his own senses. Having spent two years interviewing me to draw out the details of my travels, he now needed to experience Iran firsthand. We both knew it would stir his senses and inspire his writing.

I met Todd Phillips on my last trip to Egypt and Ethiopia and agreed, after some initial misgivings, to take him to Iran. A youth pastor from Austin, Texas, Phillips heads a growing ministry called Metro Ministries, which targets the spiritually disenfranchised youth of Generation X. After witnessing the potent impact of my ministry on young people, Phillips yearned to learn more about biblical exploration; he told me God had "compelled" him to accompany me to Iran. How could I argue?

Finally, I gave Larry Williams a call. We'd been on so many trips together, it just seemed natural he'd want to go on this one. Always skeptical about our chances for success, Williams nonetheless rarely turned down a chance for adventure. These trips give him an excuse to run away from the high pressure world of commodities trading, to rough it for a few days with the boys. Besides, he hadn't yet heard about the Ed Davis map or the satellite data, and I knew if he thought we had even a remote chance of finding the ark, he'd want to be there. In a conference call shortly before our departure, he picked up on the optimism rippling through the team and broke in: "We've been looking for this thing for fifteen *years*. Why are you guys suddenly so bullish about finding the ark?"

"Because," I explained, "we have a definite object. Some highly cre-dentialed scientists have dissected our satellite photos and told us they're 75 to 100 percent sure we've found the real Davis Canyon. We'll be traveling to a specific spot on Mount Sabalon to locate an object that showed up on the images."

I waited a moment for his response, then asked: "Are you still in?"

He laughed. "You know me, Bob; I keep my expectations low. But if you luck out and hit a home run, I want to be there."

At the last minute I asked Dick Bright, leader of our latest, ill-fated Turkish expedition, to join us. It occurred to me, as I wrapped up the final details of our trip, that Dick had devoted thirty years of his life to finding the ark, had endured terrible hardships, and ultimately played a major role in furthering the search. I invited him out of deep respect for his rugged determination and steely fortitude; besides, he'd invited me along on *his* expedition, and I wanted to return the favor. As I described to him the nature and extent of our research, he shocked me by his humble, hearten-ing response. "Your research is impressive, Bob. Maybe we've all been wrong all these years. Maybe the ark *is* in Iran." From a man who had invested much blood and tears in his search for the ark in Turkey, I found his words deeply encouraging.

"I welcome the opportunity to join you," Bright said, "but I'll use my own contacts in Turkey to obtain my visa. I'll drive across the Turkish bor-der with Micah and meet you in Ardabil in five days."

With the team settled I turned my attention back to the laborious, always tricky visa application process. Hoping to gain permission to trek on Sabalon and visit the surrounding villages, I'd already applied for the stan-dard "tourist" visas, keeping our larger motives of searching for the ark ambiguous. Unfortunately, Iran's tourism ministers, recalling my name from previous trips and somehow alerted to our recent run-ins with the secret police, finally informed our travel agent, Nahid, that they didn't buy our story.

"They know you aren't tourists," she said, explaining why our visas had been rudely rejected, less than two weeks before our departure. "They *know* you plan to conduct research," she added, informing us that our only option would be to reapply for "research" visas and hope for the best. So close to our departure date, it seemed like a long shot and put the whole expedition in jeopardy. I reapplied nonetheless and E-mailed our former guide, Ali in Tehran, to put in a good word for us.

If our visas came through, Ali stood to earn a handsome guide's fee, for I had already requested his services. So he went to bat for us, aggressively informing customs officials that if our research on Mount Sabalon proved fruitful, it would trigger a gold rush of western tourists flooding into the cash-strapped country.

They apparently listened.

Four days before our scheduled departure—even as I explored the prospects of using Bright's contacts to get us visas into Iran via Turkey—our research visas came through, no strings attached. In an unprecedented turn of events, Iran granted a team of Americans full access to Mount Sabalon and its surrounding villages. We would be allowed to travel and climb anywhere, interview anyone, in the general vicinity of the mountain. Ali would be our official guide and handle all of our arrangements.

Suddenly finding myself in the good graces of the Iranian government, however, on the eve of a major expedition, seemed odd and unfamiliar. I didn't know quite how to feel. I can't say I was disappointed, exactly, but it seemed to steal some of the fun. A year earlier we'd gotten arrested; now we'd been given carte blanche to conduct our search unhindered.

For a fleeting moment, I thought, *It's a trick! They'll arrest me the minute we land.* But soon enough I saw this godsend for what it was: an unheard of blessing, a gift of free access in a culture of unbending constraint, enabling us at last fully to test our thesis.

Part of me remained suspicious of all this goodwill. But then I wondered: *Could it simply be God's perfect timing, smoothing the way for a crowning discovery?* As the day of our departure neared, I confess it felt good knowing we wouldn't be hassled and hounded at every turn by the secret police.

Packing my bags and video equipment on the eve of our flight, I knew only three things: in two days I would lead my third expedition into the "closed" country of Iran; we had a definite "object" in our sights; and, God willing, I'd soon have an answer to a question that had dogged my footsteps and teased my daydreams for fifteen long years.

181

Twenty-Three

PERSIAN REPRISE

Darrell Scott showed up at Chicago's O'Hare International Airport decked out in a red-, white-, and blue-striped polo shirt and Bermuda shorts. He'd missed our conference call a week earlier—in which I explained the finer points of keeping a low profile in Iran—and showed up in this comic-book violation of the Iranian dress code. I told the team to avoid loud, garish colors and prints and then added: "Don't even *pack* shorts!"

No one wears shorts in Iran, but for an American to show up flashing his knees in a pair of baggy Bermudas might incite a riot. What's worse, our bags had been checked through to Tehran, and all the clothing shops at O'Hare had closed for the night. We faced the first official crisis of our Iran expedition: if we couldn't find Scott a pair of pants before we reached Tehran, he'd be whisked away before we cleared customs.

I couldn't resist needling him: "Darrell, you might as well have worn a shirt that says, 'I'm an American Tourist!'"

And while he kept a good humor about it, we had reason for concern. We had only a brief layover in Germany in which to find and purchase a pair of pants before our flight to Iran. Fortunately, our eight-hour, trans-Atlantic flight put us into Frankfort in the early morning, just as the shops in the main terminal opened for business. Racing through customs with our carry-ons, we scouted out the first clothier on the concourse and found Scott a pair of khaki safari pants—ill fitting and grotesquely priced at $100, but pants nonetheless.

He decided to stick with his Polo shirt at those prices, trusting the customs agents wouldn't hold it against him.

Boarding our Tehran-bound flight in Frankfort was like entering a portal to Persia. The Lufthansa jetliner, filled front to back with women in full-length black chadors and scarves wound tightly around their heads, had the pungent look and feel of Iran. The women sat near the back of the plane, while their husbands and male children sat together toward the front.

It didn't take long to realize that, in a plane filled with citizens from Iran, *we* were the curiosities. As we milled about the cabin, members of our team were frequently asked their country of origin, sparking amazement among whole groups of Iranians.

"How did you get visas?" they asked, while others seemed delighted to see us, as if our presence signaled Iran's sudden emergence from a long, dark isolation. "It is a positive omen for our country that they let you in," smiled one gentleman.

With that, however, came the reality of actually landing in Iran. In the minutes before disembarking, every woman covered her head with a large, dark scarf and made proper adjustments to her makeup and wardrobe. Though the body language of many registered a sort of powerless contempt for the ritual, none chose the moment to try to buck the social code or make a feminist statement. Any woman not prepared to observe the rules in Iran, they knew—regardless of her citizenship—is guaranteed an extremely unpleasant stay. I did notice a few of the more daring, liberal-leaning ladies intentionally wrapping their heads loosely, even carelessly, leaving a large, defiant shock of hair exposed in the front.

I'd briefed the team that deplaning in Tehran can be a tense, suspense-filled ordeal. One never knows until clearing customs how well things will go. Depending on the agent, one might get passed through with a warm, smiling welcome or find himself detained for a round of frightful interrogations and inspections. Scott silently fretted that his loud shirt might draw unwanted scrutiny; and Halbrook, paranoid some official might search his briefcase and accuse him of bringing subversive literature into the country, got cold feet and ditched an entire file of news articles on Iran in an overhead bin as we walked toward the exit.

Neither should have worried, for customs proved a breeze. We passed through clean and free, with no delays or controversies of any kind—presaging an altogether different kind of trip. Even as we collected our bags—the last point at which trouble might occur inside the terminal—a cheerful customs agent nonchalantly patted down Toth's duffel bag and asked us about our business in Iran.

"We're going to climb Mount Sabalon," Todd Phillips replied honestly, eliciting laughs and smiles from the delighted agent. He shook Phillips's hand and waved us through the checkpoint, where Ali, in remarkably high spirits, waited to help us pile four carts high with our mountain of duffels and luggage.

"Welcome gentlemen, welcome," he said to members as they introduced themselves.

The clock in the waiting area said 2:30 A.M. Ali led us to a large, air-conditioned van, where we loaded up our luggage and sped off into the smoky heart of Tehran, arriving thirty minutes later at a spartan yet serviceable hotel (whose name I couldn't pronounce). We found our rooms and slept hard for six hours, rising at noon for a quick breakfast of fruit and juice in the hotel cafe. Ali showed up on schedule to lead us on a tour of Tehran and introduced us to his son, Alireza, a bright, handsome youth, impeccably mannered, fluent in English, and well-versed in American computer-speak.

"Alireza will accompany us to Ardabil," Ali announced, adding to our team what would prove to be a valuable asset.

Ali took us on the standard tour of Tehran, kicked off with lunch at the airy Persian restaurant I so enjoyed on my first trip—the one with the traditional musicians, raised platforms, and water pipes. There we feasted on a customary meal of chicken and lamb kebabs, succulent Iranian rice, fresh tomatoes, and hot tea. Our large group, moving awkwardly through the meal's various courses, had a grand time in spite of some cold, curious stares we drew from other patrons.

Yet even here, a calming, generous mood prevailed. Acknowledging our table from the stage, the band welcomed us as "esteemed American guests," then serenaded us with a spirited Iranian folk tune. Women and children nearby, sitting apart from the men, smiled and giggled, lowering their eyes as we asked permission to videotape them; the men regarded us cooly, however, reminding us how our strange presence unsettled the natives.

From there we visited a couple of museums and toured downtown Tehran's busy streets and sidewalk markets, ending up at the old American Embassy building, where the team gawked—half amused, half intimidated—at the icy collection of anti-American slogans splashed over its walls and towers. The skeletal likeness of the Statue of Liberty wrapped, bleeding, in barbed wire, provided the team its first mandatory photo opportunity.

Ali then took us to the north end of town to a beautiful, lushly vegetated range of hillsides and large homes where, I assumed, the Iranian moneyed class reside. We parked at the bottom of a tall hill and walked nearly a mile to the top to reach the former shah's opulent palace: a magnificent, tile and brick castle surrounded by thick stone walls, heavy reinforced balustrades, and steep, beautifully appointed gardens and fortified embankments. Admiring the mansion's formidable defenses from its stately, marbled terrace, Toth remarked, "The shah knew what he was doing. It would be nearly impossible to stage a successful coup against this fortress."

The palace interior, a riot of gilded glass tiles and wall-to-wall, silk brocade Persian rugs, recalled a majestic house of mirrors, every square foot inlaid with elegant panels of hand-cut crystal and gaudy, silver-and-gold-filigree wall hangings, diamond-cut glass ceilings, and Persian chandeliers. Contrasted with the drab, concrete chaos of lower Tehran, the shah's emerald-encrusted citadel stood as a painful reminder of that regime's brazen self-enrichment.

JOLTING NEWS

We strolled back down the hillside to a quaint, outdoor cafe, where we took off our shoes under thick, shady oaks and reclined on a traditional dining platform. As we sat drowsily in the humid afternoon heat and fought off a sudden wave of jet lag, a young boy brought us cold Fanta sodas. While we sipped and chatted, Ali came over and sat down next to Halbrook and me; he pulled from his briefcase a ream of loose notes and well-used writing tablets.

"Mr. Bob, I have found some news that might be of interest," he said, casually informing us that he'd been doing some research on Mount Sabalon.

I'd asked him in advance to locate a few books about the mountain but didn't expect what he'd found. Beginning with a short history lesson on Mount Sabalon, from the *Iranian* perspective, his first tidbit concerned the mountain's legacy as the birthplace of one of Iran's revered prophets, Zoroaster.

An ancient Iranian prophet and founder of one of the world's oldest religions (Zoroastrianism), Zoroaster set the tone for Persia's early spiritual temperament. Even today, much of Iranian art, architecture, and philosophy can be traced to the Zoroastrian influence. Though its social impact has been greatly diminished in the Islamic state, Zoroaster is revered locally as one of the first prophets to postulate an omnipotent, invisible god—symbolized in ancient rock reliefs by fire and still worshiped in Zoroastrian temples in the form of "eternally" burning flames.

"Yes, so what?" I asked.

In halting, delicately dictioned English, Ali politely replied: "I have found a book by a famous Iranian scholar, Professor Poordavood, who confirms that Zoroaster was born in Iranian Azerbaijan, near Mount Sabalon. Professor Poordavood cites ancient texts attesting that, during Zoroaster's lifetime, Mount Sabalon was known as Var-Jam-Kard."

"OK," I said, missing the connection. "What does Var-Jam-Kard mean?"

"I'm sorry," said an embarrassed but smiling Ali. "Var-Jam-Kard comes from the Old Persian, or ancient Zoroastrian language. Var-Jam-Kard means *Noah's Mountain*."[1]

Halbrook and I turned and stared at each other, our expressions registering astonishment.

"Mount Sabalon was once known as Noah's Mountain?" Halbrook asked. "Tell us, Ali, when did Zoroaster live?"

Ali explained that Professor Poordavood had been attempting to prove that Zoroaster lived as far back as four thousand years ago, though the best scholarly estimates tell us he lived between 638 B.C. to 551 B.C. Even so, the title "Var-Jam-Kard," conferred upon Mount Sabalon, made it, if not the oldest, then one of the oldest known references associating Noah with a specific mountain. If true, it represented another brick in a mounting wall of evidence connecting Sabalon to the final resting place of the ark.

"If what you're saying is true," Halbrook said, "it introduces a new timetable for one of the first mountains named in respect to Noah." (We later investigated all references to verify Ali's claims, and each checked out.)

This stunning revelation had far-reaching consequences, for to my knowledge no other mountain associated with either Noah or the ark could be traced back as far as Mount Sabalon.

Brightened by our enthusiasm, Ali said, "There is *more*."

The rest of the team now sat back against the rails, fighting off sleep. But Halbrook and I hovered intently over Ali and his notes.

"What is it?" I asked.

"It seems, from my research," Ali continued, "that the original capital of Urartu was also near Sabalon, below the Aras River."[2]

It took a second to register: The *first* capital of Urartu? . . . the ancient kingdom of *Ararat*? . . . near Mount *Sabalon*?

"Tell us more," Halbrook insisted. "We've always thought the original capital of Urartu was situated near Lake Van in southeastern Turkey."

Hanging on Ali's words, we knew this new wrinkle had enormous implications. We'd already determined that Urartu, at its zenith, spanned most of southeastern Turkey, northwestern Iran, and realms beyond, encompassing both Mount Ararat and Mount Sabalon. The Urartian Empire dates back to about 1400 B.C. and died out in about 600 B.C.; and, until now, it was thought by most western sources to have emerged as a loose confederation of city states from the region of Lake Van, near modern-day Mount Ararat. Ali relished his new role as our coresearcher.

"No, no," he said, wagging a finger, as if to scoff at any non-Iranian spin on his country's history. "According to a famous Iranian scholar (Dr. Abdul Hussein Zarinkub), the first capital of Urartu grew up alongside the Aras River, seventy miles due north of Sabalon, at a city called Arazshkoon."

This meant that the earliest political center of Urartu had carved its foothold in the region of Lake Urmia and Mount Sabalon, in the first millennium B.C.

Ali paused, then added: "Only *later* did the Urartian rulers move the capital west to a city near Lake Van in Turkey, called Torvashbeh."

186

Zarinkub's conclusions, Ali said, corroborated with those of another renown Iranian author, Dr. Mohammad Javad Mashkur,[3] who also identified the Sabalon region as Urartu's birthing ground.

Taken as a whole, Ali's research confirmed that the "land of Ararat" cited in Genesis had *first* arisen in northwest Iran, in and around Mount Sabalon. It lent incredible strength to our thesis, asserting in the strongest terms that the Urartian/Ararat empire didn't, in fact, spring from the region about Lake Van in Turkey (as widely suggested in western literature) and only later broaden its imperial reach to include Mount Sabalon and Lake Urmia (see map, pg. 110).

Barring some unseen Iranian prejudice skewing the bounds of Urartu's ancient borders, Ali helped us resolve a troubling scriptural dilemma: for if the Urartian political center had, indeed, grown up around Lake Van in Turkey, then the region described in Scripture as "Ararat" might not have yet grown to include northwest Iran (or Sabalon) at the time Moses penned Genesis. That scenario had always troubled me because it seemed to cast doubt on northwest Iran as the hub for the "mountains of Ararat."

187

Λ

With this latest revelation, however, that fear seemed to wane on the authority of a top Iranian scholar, commentating on the early roots of his homeland. Professor Zarinkub resoundingly declared Urartu a first millennium outgrowth of a region closely encircling Mount Sabalon. (We later ran across another reference by esteemed British historian, David M. Rohl, who agreed with Zarinkub that "the later kingdom of Urartu [Ararat] was also originally located here [east of Lake Urmia] in its early days, before shifting its heartland to the area around Lake Van."[4])

How heartening, on the eve of our journey to Sabalon! A completely unsolicited, highly credentialed declaration that, from its earliest origins, Mount Sabalon lay at the heart of Urartu; that, from its earliest origins, the Sabalon range formed the backbone of the "mountains of Ararat"; that, beginning with Genesis, Old Testament writers referring to the land of Ararat had, in all likelihood, intended to identify the region immediately surrounding Mount Sabalon in northwest Iran. What's more, it wasn't *our* theory, but that of top Iranian scholars who best understood the region's history.

Few things could have excited us more as we prepared to return to Ardabil—another priceless nugget from antiquity pointing us to Sabalon.

Together with news of Zoroaster's birth in the vicinity of Var-Jam-Kard/Sabalon, centuries before any other mountain in the Near East had been linked to Noah, this new data on Urartu represented a major breakthrough in the search for Noah's ark. Pondering these events, sipping my soda, I casually mentioned to Ali that, back in 30 B.C., Nicholas of Damascus wrote of the ark coming to rest on a mountain "above the Minyas in Armenia."

"The Minyas?" Ali echoed, well versed in that region's ethnic origin. "Minyas corresponds to the Minni tribes, who lived in the region south and east of Lake Urmia in northwest Iran. So . . . what mountain did Mr. Nicholas mean?"

"Well," I said, "the tallest mountain in a mountainous region above the Minyas is Mount Sabalon."

"Ah," he said, thumbing through his notes. "Everything seems to be pointing to Mount Sabalon." He looked up and said, "That is good, *no?*"

I looked over at Halbrook, now wildly scribbling notes on his legal pad. I knew exactly what he was thinking. With all of our other findings, the focus of the world's search for the ark looked about to shift from southeastern Turkey to northwest Iran, from Mount Ararat to Mount Sabalon. Anyone with an open mind—even the staunchest proponents of Mount Ararat in Turkey—would now have to give strong consideration to this new information.

"Ahem," Ali interrupted, holding up a small scrap of paper. "I must share with you one more piece of related news."

By this time the rest of the team, refreshed by the cold sodas and revived in the shade, listened attentively as Ali noted an ancient passage he'd uncovered pertaining to Ardabil, the holy city located in the plain ringing Mount Sabalon. Thumbing through a book by another noted Iranian historian, Iraj Afshar Sisany, Ali said he ran across an obscure reference to an early Persian writer named *Ardebil*.

"This writer, Ardebil," he said, "claimed in some of his ancient writings that the original buildings and towns near Ardabil, by Mount Sabalon, were built by the prophet Noah."[5]

"And . . . ?" I asked, expecting some deeper analysis.

"Who was this Ardebil fellow?" Halbrook wondered. "When did he live?"

"It was just a short notation," Ali replied. "I don't know the author's sources."

We waited for more, but Ali had finished. He had nothing else to declare on the subject. We simply marked it in our notebooks as yet another clue, teasing us on.

"I'd say it's been a fruitful day," I said, as we all rose to leave. "In the morning we fly to Ardabil."

Besides Halbrook and me, the others didn't seem overly excited with all these staggering revelations. They'd gleaned enough hard facts through our discussions to know we hadn't flown halfway across the world to chase shadows; they trusted me. What they craved was the smell of mountains and the promise of adventure.

Darrell Scott rubbed his hands nervously as we climbed in the van, more animated than I'd ever seen him. "Let's get on with it," he said. "Let's go find that ark!"

John Tomlin, normally soft-spoken and self-contained, walked up behind me and slapped my back. "I'm ready!" he said. "This is *great!*"

No matter the outcome of our journey, it did my heart good to see their infectious smiles. We hadn't even seen a mountain yet, and they seemed to be having the time of their lives.

Little did they know that tomorrow the *real* fun would begin.

189
Λ

Twenty-Four

WILDERNESS ROAD

Dan Toth struggled to find the road. On day two of our reconnaissance of Mount Sabalon, we'd done little more than drive around in circles, trying to find the right rutted dirt path to the summit. Dan had his GPS unit and maps out on the hood of the Land Rover, and we could all see it clear as day—a squiggly line representing the road we had to find, tracking alongside a serpentine river that seemed to coil down from a high ridge, finally emptying out near the craggy gorge Toth believed to be Davis Canyon. But finding it in this enormous, inscrutable mountain range had become a backbreaking chore.

The morning had digressed into an endless series of starts and stops, false reads and blind alleys; we'd turn down a road that seemed headed in the right direction, but after a mile or two we would come to an unexpected fork or dead end. We'd stop, turn back, and ask the locals where we went wrong or which way we needed to go. They'd send us scurrying off on some new path, and the maddening cycle would repeat itself.

Through it all, we usually remained in full view of the humpback ridge we'd targeted near the summit, but it loomed forever in the distance; we could never seem to stay on course. Just when it seemed we might span a rise and come face-to-face with our prize, the road would end and leave us stranded on another dead-end plateau.

Through it all, Ali and Dan seemed like Siamese Twins. You never saw one without the other, wrestling with maps and arguing with our drivers over routes that didn't exist. At every stop they'd huddle together, entering into harried dialogues with a nameless succession of nomads, village chieftains, and ruddy young shepherd boys. None had much help to offer in understanding the meanderings of these back country byways. So off we'd drive, up the next ragged goat path spiraling into the next towering succession of lethal switchbacks, until, once again, the road simply ended or vanished into a field of clover, leaving us back where we started.

So it went, on and on. Toth and Ali would hustle out the maps while the rest of us stretched our legs, staging impromptu rock-throwing contests, snapping a few photos of the rugged hills, the odd goat or grazing camel, or simply admiring the majestic sweep of Sabalon's roller-coaster lowlands. Then Toth would shout, "Let's go!" and we'd pile back in the cramped, dusty Land Rovers and backtrack down the road, grinding overheated gears up some new sheep path. It went on like this through the cool of the morning into the stifling heat of midday.

The problem boiled down to this: Dan had purchased ten-year-old Russian maps of the plain of Sabalon at a reputable map store in Colorado. But in the Middle East, the smartest-looking maps often have little in common with the actual terrain. I'd seen it before. Our maps illustrated roads that had either fallen into misuse or might never have existed at all. Looking at the actual terrain, I found it a stretch to think *any* of these miserable, narrow camel trails had found their way onto an actual map. Little more than wispy tire tracks breaking dirt through stands of tumbleweeds, most appeared freshly graded and destined for a short life.

I've compared it to driving to the foot of Pike's Peak or Mount McKinley here in the States. But instead of taking one's pick of any of America's modern highways, imagine four-wheeling it up a rugged maze of scrubby foothills and high-flowing streams, pitching and bouncing over ill-maintained, half-eroded bike trails and tractor ruts that keep spinning off in unpredictable directions. Under these conditions, it would take days, possibly even weeks, to reach the most obvious destination. The best map in the *world* wouldn't help.

Likewise, we'd do our best to choose a road that seemed right, based on all the maps and available data . . . and still end up farther off course than we'd started.

RETURN TO SABALON

We had arrived in Ardabil a day earlier, checked into the charming Hotel Sabalon (they gave me the same aromatic room as before), and promptly disembarked to Sulfur City, hard by Sabalon's fertile north slope. I needed to videotape the area and could think of no better way to acclimate the team to the Persian outback than to drop them in the middle of this set piece from a Stephen Spielberg movie.

The town hadn't changed and greeted us with the same semi-rowdy, holiday crowd as before. Any hard feelings from our last visit seemed to have been forgotten. The townsfolk met us with open arms and much fanfare, mobbing each member of the team in a crush of goodwill.

Paul, ever the daring gourmand, quickly accepted one group's invitation to a sizzling feast of fresh-grilled kebabs; Larry wandered about, charming everyone with his magic tricks; John and Darrell must have shaken a hundred hands and had their pictures taken with dozens of children; and even Dan Toth, normally standoffish, granted himself a few moments of frivolity. Shortly into our stay, we accepted what seemed to be an invitation by the entire community to sample the hot springs and entered the gray-walled compound, shed our clothes, and found ourselves instantly, raucously, embraced by a throng of bedazzled bathers. Men and boys flocked about, peppering us with questions and greetings, receiving our presence as an act of fellowship, one nation to another. An old man waded near and whispered in strained English, "Welcome you to our country. We are glad you are here."

The only tense moment occurred when a young, rifle-bearing soldier marched down the hill and ordered Paul to stop videotaping. This young stripling, barely into his twenties, approached our team with rifle in hand and demanded we pack our cameras. My body stiffened. We'd been harassed and persecuted a year earlier, but this time we had official *permission*. We'd flown halfway around the world to film this town; I knew if I backed down now, the restrictions and intrusions might never cease.

"Alireza!" I called to Ali's son, who had been watching sheepishly nearby. "Come over here and tell this soldier that I have *permission* to be here; we have permission to take pictures anywhere we want on this mountain."

Alireza looked stunned.

"But he is a soldier," he sputtered. "He has authority in the village."

"But we have permission," I repeated, pointing to Paul's video camera. I walked over and stood eye to eye with the soldier. I knew his game; he intended to make a big show for the village and demonstrate his clout; but I stood my ground. I looked him in the eye, nudged the barrel of his gun, and told Alireza, "Now tell him, we *will* film, and he will *not* stop us."

Alireza swallowed hard, reluctant to be the bearer of such bad news, but he finally spit it out. The soldier reared back, looking aghast. We stared at one another for a moment; he pulled his rifle close to his chest. Then, red-faced and bewildered, he retreated. I could feel my heart pounding in my fingertips.

"Paul," I said, "start filming those kids over there."

Before we left Sulfur City, Halbrook and I found an old man, well into his eighties, on the outskirts of town. Seated in the front seat of a battered, 1950s model Peugeot, his face had the heavily whiskered, sun-burnished look of a Kurdish nomad. He sat cheerfully smoking a cigarette, surrounded by a cloud of children and grandchildren. With his granddaughters giggling uncontrollably at the sight of us—big, odd-looking Americans—and with Ali translating, we asked the old man if he knew anything about Noah's ark on Mount Sabalon. He nodded.

"Yes," said Ali, "he says he knows about the ark from his father and grandfather."

But when I asked him where, he simply smiled and gazed back toward the summit. Recalling the sudden meltdown of our last visit, I knew not to press him and simply said good-bye, consoled that traditions of the ark do flourish among Ghotor Suee's dwindling elder population.

As we returned to the van, the young soldier suddenly reappeared, causing the hair on my neck to bristle. But his rigid manner had softened; his disciplined countenance slowly melted into a smile, and he addressed me with a series of shy, rapid-fire sentences. Alireza, standing nearby, said, "He asks forgiveness, Mr. Bob, for being so rude before. He says he feels sorry."

193

I looked at Alireza, then the soldier—*Forgive him for being rude?* I had never imagined such a thing: a military policeman *apologizing*—to me, an American. What other wonders awaited us on this trip?

It had been this way since we set down in Ardabil. Wherever we went, the locals treated us uncharacteristically well, with genuine warmth and respect. Out on the streets, the teeming crowds regarded our group with startled looks, as if to say, "Are those men really *Americans?*" But everyone remained unfailingly polite. And back at the Hotel Sabalon, the porters and wait staff, surly and brusque a year earlier, had undergone a dramatic transformation. They seemed chipper and gracious this time around, attending promptly to our multiple needs. *What a difference it makes,* I thought, *to have the proper visas and permission.*

Something else felt different, too. With all the activity I didn't immediately identify it, but once I stopped to take a breath, I realized . . . *I'm having a great time.* For the first time in memory, I didn't feel the strain of a typical Middle Eastern expedition. I wasn't looking over my shoulder at every turn, wondering when the next disaster might strike. Traveling with this special group of friends—all of them in fun-loving, high spirits—I felt completely at peace. Our every movement seemed blessed and protected; the favor of the people rested upon us—a point hammered home when we returned to Nir (of the infamous "Down with USA" billboard) to hire drivers to take us up the mountain.

Milling outside the van while Ali handled the negotiations, I glanced across the street and saw the constable who had detained us on our last trip. Watching him march down the sidewalk on the opposite side of the street, I turned my head lest he see us, but I was too late. He walked straight over to Larry and me, stern faced as ever, the lapels on his coat still stained with gravy. I expected him to give us a good tongue-lashing for returning to his town, but instead he raised his hands in greetings, smiled warmly, and, in clipped English, said, "So . . . you decided to come back. We have *missed* you!"

I nearly choked on my trail mix.

We have *missed* you? Oh, that was good. I looked at Larry, and we both laughed. I slapped the constable on the back as if we were old friends; we all shook hands and, for a few silly moments, made light of our former incarceration. As the constable took his leave, Larry called out mischievously, "Did you keep our *cell* warm for us?"

The police chief turned and stared at us with the same steely expression that had, a year earlier, struck terror in Ali's heart—then let out a loud belly laugh and marched off, grinning.

"What's going on here?" I asked Larry. "Is this the same Iran we visited last year?"

By now the others had begun to roll their eyes at my sordid tales of abuse and arrest at the hands of the evil Iranian police. Darrell Scott even joked, "OK, so what *does* a person have to do to get arrested around here?"

Though it seemed to be turning into one of the milder adventures on record, I didn't complain. Things were going so well, in fact, it shouldn't have surprised me when we ran into navigation problems on Sabalon.

RETREAT AND REGROUP

Another wrong turn. The vanishing road ended abruptly at a small Turkish shepherd's camp at ten thousand feet, the humpback knoll of our desire still squarely in our sights, still eight miles off, according to Dan's GPS. Still too far to walk.

In the early afternoon heat, little children from the camp eyed us from behind their fathers' coattails; women baking flat bread on a makeshift stone hearth barely glanced our way. Toth and Ali struck up a dialogue with a young Turkish shepherd; our drivers tended to their overheated radiators. With nothing else to do, the rest of us accepted an unsolicited invitation by the village patron to share a cup of tea inside his domed, Mongol-style tent. This aging shepherd, deeply tanned and heavily whiskered, smoking a cigarette and wearing a dark, rumpled pinstripe suit (the apparel of choice in these high hills), reminded me of a mildly undernourished, slightly weathered Anthony Quinn.

We took off our shoes, ducked inside the dome, and sat on a floor carpeted with beautiful, ornately woven red, gray, and white Persian rugs. A shaft of light slanted in from an opening in the wood-ribbed ceiling; the shadowed interior remained amazingly cool and accommodating. After five hours bouncing around in the back of a Land Rover, it felt good to stretch back against the sturdy Persian pillows and sip strong, hot tea.

Our host had never seen a westerner before and sat grinning at us, complaining to Ali that "we cannot speak each other's language. All we can do is sit and stare at each other." We asked him about the ark, but this south-slope nomad had no knowledge of it. Instead, he insisted we stay on and help ourselves to a tray of warm flat bread, peeled thin and steaming from the baking stones. It tasted wonderful, and I would've gladly stayed longer, but Toth poked his head inside with news of another route up the mountain.

For the third time that day, we backtracked four miles down the mountainside to another obscure turnoff. The Turks said it might take us where we wanted to go, but they couldn't be sure. The maps we showed them drew blank stares, so we threw caution to the wind and sped up the slope to nearly twelve thousand feet, landing precariously atop a teeth-rattling washboard of steep cliffs and breathtaking valleys. Here we embarked on the most dangerous part of the trip. The road pitched violently down one washed-out set of switchbacks after another, and our poorly suspended Land Rovers leaned around blind shoulders and rumbled over fragile narrows barely wide enough to support our vehicles. On either side of us gaped fatal drop-offs, and, as we crept along, our tires kicked loose dirt and rocks into the abyss.

Halbrook asked Alireza kindly to inquire of our driver: "Do these steep roads make you *nervous?*" I thought it a silly question.

"These guys drive these roads all the time," I snapped back.

Yet the young Kurd nodded grimly. "Yes," Alireza said, turning to show us his own ashen countenance. "He says he is *very* nervous right now."

That made *me* nervous. One mistake on these unstable switchbacks and we'd disappear over the ledge. Suddenly gripped with vertigo, I turned to the driver and said, "Get us down off this cliff!"

We finally reached the valley floor but found ourselves badly off course once again; the summit had now vanished behind the cliffs, and the road fizzled out at a dry creek bed. We'd been rambling aimlessly around these mountains for five hours and still hadn't come close to our target. After talking it over, we decided to return to Ardabil and regroup while we still had some daylight.

"Let's get a good night's sleep and start over tomorrow," I told the team.

Dan needed a break from the relentless pressure of navigating these twisting roads. He'd been pressing and overselling our position all day, insisting he knew "exactly where we need to be," and telling us, "We'll be there any minute." Whenever anyone dared ask him a question, he'd snap back, "I've got it under control."

I could sense the mounting frustration; we'd been bouncing around the mountain all day with no results. It raised a very real concern: Would tomorrow be any different? Did the road we saw on the map even *exist?* Would we *ever* find it in this rugged maze of mountains?

The five-day window we had to find the object already had shrunk to three. And Dan had begun to concern me, sealing himself off from the group, reverting to SEAL tactics.

195
Λ

"I'm just wired differently from you guys," he said. "I'm not used to working with civilians."

The rest of the team just wanted some action, wanted to get out of the Land Rover and hike or climb. But the fact remained, we had cast our fate with maps and roads that no westerner had ever seen, much less driven. I needed to get Dan off the mountain, let him gather his wits.

"C'mon Dan," I reminded him, "You're part of a team. We're all in this together."

Beyond the creek bed sat a wide, well-traveled gravel road leading back to Ardabil.

"It is a shortcut," Ali said. "It will enable us to avoid driving back up those dangerous passes."

"Let's do it," I said, and within two hours we had made it back to the hotel. Dan skipped dinner, choosing instead to spend the evening going over his maps and re-calibrating his GPS.

"Tomorrow I'll *nail* it," he said. "I'll take GPS readings every few hundred yards to make sure we're on course. If we get off on a wrong road, we'll know it immediately. You wait, Bob," he kept repeating, "we'll find the ark tomorrow, and everyone's jaw will be hanging down around their feet."

At this late stage I had no choice but to trust his expertise. But his overconfidence troubled me. I wanted to tell him neither he, nor anyone, had a prayer of finding anything—much less Noah's ark—if God didn't will it. With Sabalon we faced a huge system of gnarly hills and plunging valleys, accessible by roads that could only be described as a mess. I now understood how the Urartian kings so successfully warded off Assyria's repeated attacks three thousand years ago. These mountains, as Esarhaddon once wrote, indeed loomed vast and impenetrable; they constituted a forbidding netherworld.

I slept fitfully that night, worried about the creeping sense of confusion that plagued the day's efforts. I had to ask myself: "Lord, are we being glib or flippant? Are we too overconfident, arrogant, or self-reliant?"

Sure, our team had prayed each day for God's blessing; but had we truly thrown ourselves at his feet, depending on his guidance alone? I had no doubt that God would shut this expedition down in a heartbeat if we forgot, or took for granted, the sacred nature of our task. A group of men on a mountain can digress into a coarse affair. Of that we might be forgiven, but God would never reward a lack of humility. The mission demanded a sense of holiness, reverence, and awe. I suddenly feared we had let our guard down.

Early the next morning, as the others stuffed their packs, Halbrook came into my room with identical concerns. We knelt down and prayed, pleading for God's hand to settle our hearts and guide us afresh into the day.

Twenty-Five

TARGET ZONE FOUND

Day three of our quest began early. We had to reach the target zone this day or, in all likelihood, concede defeat.

As he'd promised, Dan pinpointed the road off the main highway needed to take us up the mountain. He led us west, thirty miles past Nir, to a little wisp of a trail pointing off into a dusty stretch of lowland rising toward Sabalon. We pulled off, switched our packs from the van to the Land Rovers, and headed north. True to his word, Dan knew it the moment we began to stray off course.

The first time the road failed us, we didn't waste time debating; we backtracked to the nearest village and asked directions. But when that course quickly brought us to another dead end, I made an executive decision. I could now see that Dan's GPS coordinates and Russian charts would take us only so far. I told Ali to return to the last village and hire as guides two of the men we'd consulted. Dan didn't argue. We knew they wouldn't cost much, but they knew the area, and Ali assured us they'd keep us on the right trail.

When Ali returned with our new team members, I sat back in the third Land Rover and, keeping my thoughts to myself, tried to enjoy the ride. The morning began with a quick flurry of false starts, but I stayed calm, knowing it was par for the course, typical of the most well-planned expedition in this part of the world. I felt confident that hiring guides who knew the roads to work with Dan and his coordinates would pan out.

We drew some spirit from the day's date: July 17, 2000—the "seventeenth day of the seventh month" (Gen. 8:4), the same day the Bible says the ark came to rest on the mountains of Ararat. We hadn't planned it that way. In fact, it hadn't crossed anyone's mind until we woke up that morning and looked at our watches. Though July doesn't correspond to the seventh month of the Jewish calendar, upon which the Old Testament date is based, it certainly added energy to the day's quest. I knew that some privately wondered if God intended to reveal the ark to us on this promising "anniversary."

Dick Bright had joined our team. He showed up at 6 A.M. at the Hotel Sabalon, having crossed the Turkish-Iranian border in the middle of the night. He'd already finished breakfast when I entered the restaurant. He sat complaining to Ali about the trouble he had clearing customs—even with the visas he'd secured from Micah and using all his contacts in Erzurum, "They still wanted to know what business I had in Iran," he said. "I told them, 'I'm *going to climb Mount Sabalon!* I'm meeting *Americans* there!'" Two hours later they let him through; he showed up road weary and famished at our breakfast table, devouring a large plate of fried eggs, hot tea, heavy sweet bread and honey before most of us had showered.

It felt good to have him along. Driving these dusty foothills, we needed an old, steady hand like Bright; he brought a seasoned perspective to the team. He'd begun to see the evidence stacking up for Mount Sabalon, and I noted the keen interest in his eye. But I didn't delude myself into thinking he'd be wildly enthusiastic about our theory: he had invested far too much time, money, and energy searching for the ark on Mount Ararat. Still, as a good friend and fellow explorer, he supported our efforts.

Given the tension and strain the coming hours would impose on Toth and Ali, I found a seat in the last Land Rover, bringing up the rear. On a day like today I thought it better to lead from behind. With our new guides on board, I tried to relax and take in the scenery.

Halbrook, Tomlin, Alireza, and I shared the same cab and passed the hours in lively conversation. The topics touched all aspects of our lives. We talked to Alireza, for instance, about his Muslim beliefs, and it turned out religion had little impact on his everyday life and dreams. He found talking about computers and his girlfriend—or griping about Iran's stagnant, dead-end economy—far more interesting than spiritual matters. A brilliant student, I gathered, Alireza said that no matter how far he might advance in college, he would still end up working at a restaurant or selling shoes at a bazaar.

"The economy is so bad," he complained, "that Iran's brightest Ph.D.'s feel lucky to get jobs selling radios and tape players in the street corner shops. It is why so many want to come to the United States. There is no opportunity in Iran."

During one lull the topic turned to Columbine High School. Halbrook asked Alireza, a high-schooler himself, if he'd heard of the massacre.

"Only the name," he said. "I think the government has kept it from us."

Tomlin never shied away from the topic and was surprisingly forthcoming on the subject of his son's death. In a tone both measured and calm, he told us what he'd learned about the shooters, then described the grisly aftermath of the shootings in the library. Halbrook asked if his son had ever said anything prior to the shootings that might have hinted of problems at the school, but Tomlin said no. Then his voice got quiet, as he recalled an eerie, recent conversation he had with his twelve-year-old daughter Ashley.

Looking Halbrook in the eye, he said, "Ashley recently told me that the night before the shootings—as she hugged John goodnight in his bedroom, as she did every night—she had an overwhelming urge to turn back and simply *look* at him. She told me she felt she would never see him again. But then she shrugged it off as something silly and saw him again in the morning before he went off to school."

John covered his eyes; tears began to flow. We all sat there with lumps in our throats as this big, gentle man fought to regain control. When his eyes cleared, he looked up and said: "It took Ashley six months to find a way to tell us. It hurt her so bad to keep it to herself, but she wanted to protect *us*."

No one spoke for a long time after that.

ANOTHER FORK IN THE ROAD

We bounced around for another hour in the back of the Rover until our driver braked to a sudden stop. Up ahead, the lead Rover, with Toth and Ali navigating in tandem with our new guides, had stopped at a nomad's camp. We'd come to another baffling fork in the road, and our Kurdish guides didn't seem familiar with the terrain.

Dan and Ali walked up the slope to a nomad's domed tent, trussed up beside an old, green Jeep. We finally managed to gain some elevation and the crown of the camelback ridge stood tall to the west, squarely in our sights—but . . . we'd stopped again.

"Do you know where we are?" I shouted to Toth, but he barely acknowledged me.

That's when I began to wonder: from what I could see of the terrain, these never-ending shepherd's camps ran all along the lower portion of the mountain, from the lowlands to its upper flanks. At some point, I realized, we'd have to reach an elevation beyond the reach of these camps and flocks, for as long as we crossed foothills so busy and populated, we would find no ark.

Toth and Ali sauntered down the hill with a new list of instructions, but I'd had enough. More of these delays would cost us another entire day. The time had come to toss out the GPS and maps and throw in our lot with the native sons. I didn't want to insult Toth, but the mission looked to be in jeopardy. I'd given him every chance; now we needed to take advantage of the people who grew up in this area, and let them take us the rest of the way.

As Toth stood by the Land Rover, taking another set of GPS readings, someone joked: "We could probably hike from here."

Toth jumped down his throat: "We're not walking, I told you! We're *driving!*"

The time had come.

"Dan," I said, "Go back up to the camp and hire that guy who owns the Jeep. Pay him what he wants. He's going to lead us the rest of the way in."

Toth stared at me, map in hand, but didn't protest. While clearly stunned by my decision, he walked back up and offered the shepherd $20 to get us to within hiking distance of Doomsday Rock. The young fellow held out for $25. Done deal! At this stage, $200 would have seemed a bargain.

The young shepherd piled into the Jeep with a crowd of kids, cousins, and assorted relatives and led us five miles back down the slope, down the same route we'd come up. Then he switched back, slanting up a facing hillside and intersecting a road running parallel to a fast-rushing river. We'd driven a couple of miles when it hit me: *The road by the river!* We'd found the road on Toth's map, the road running parallel to the river. Thanks to our new guide, we had gotten ourselves back on track.

Immediately we began to gain elevation. Humming along in his rugged Jeep, the newcomer led us straight up the slope to the ten-thousand-foot mark, then the eleven-thousand-foot level. Only once did we stop, when our Land Rover got stuck up to its axles crossing a stream. Our delay caused each succeeding Rover to lose momentum and get stuck in turn. It took us the better part of an hour to push them all out; but surprisingly, our road-weary crew turned it into a fun, slapstick exercise, slipping around in the mud, racing up the hill to push the creaking Rovers until their bald tires spun a foothold in the mud-slick slope and reached dry gravel.

NO FOOD FOR THE HUNGRY

We'd just passed twelve thousand feet and crossed a small stream high above the valley, when another crisis hit. Our drivers had stopped alongside the stream to fill up their radiators when I realized our two-day supply of food had mysteriously dwindled. Checking our provisions, I found only a few bottles of water, a loaf and a half of bread, and a couple of cans of tuna to feed nine men, not including Ali and Alireza. Somehow, all our food had disappeared.

"How did *that* happen?" I asked the team, bewildered. We'd hardly eaten all day, nibbling instead on one another's personal stashes of Power Bars, nuts, and trail mix. I turned to Ali, who wore a doleful expression. "Ali, do *you* know?" I asked.

Wringing his hands, he said, "Oh my God! I am sorry, Mr. Bob," and confessed that he'd overestimated our provisions and had given our food to a growing family of guides and drivers at each stop.

I pulled him aside so as not to embarrass him. "Why did you give away our *food?*" I asked, my hands in the air.

Slapping his forehead, he tried to explain: "They were very hungry. They had nothing else to eat."

"But now *we* don't have enough to eat," I replied.

The food I'd bought to last us through the night and the following day had been almost entirely consumed. We couldn't turn back now to buy more. We'd driven five hours into the foothills and finally had the target zone squarely in our sights. We felt too close. No, I decided, there would be no turning back tonight.

At first I wanted to scold Ali but quickly recognized he had acted out of compassion. So I steered the conversation elsewhere. We still hadn't climbed above sheep country. Wherever we turned, we passed another shepherd's camp, with grazing flocks nearby. It gave me an idea.

"Ali," I said, "What about these nomad camps? Can we buy food from one of them? Do you think they would sell us a *sheep?*"

It seemed a rational request, given our circumstances: simply buy a sheep and pay them whatever they asked to cook it for us. Certainly, someone up here would sell us a sheep.

Ali pondered it a moment, then said with a clap of his hands, "You have money? No problem. We can buy food."

I called the team together—by now, quite a sight: hot and gamey, tired and hungry, ready to throw down a sleeping bag, build a campfire, and spend a night on the mountain. They'd been bouncing in the back of Jeeps so long their kidneys ached.

"We're not going back down tonight, men," I said. "Tonight, we live off the fat of the land."

TARGET FOUND

In the waning light of dusk, we crested the final high ridge of a peak just west of Sabalon's towering summit and parked our caravan. We all tumbled out on the green tundra and stretched our legs on a mildly sloping plateau near an abandoned shepherd's camp. To the west, we could see an oblique, deep blue tract of snow-spattered mountains and sinewy ravines.

Dan walked over to the ridgeline, took out his GPS, and stared into the first rays of a brooding sunset. Two miles off stood a giant, dome-shaped knuckle of granite, hunkered, clawlike, over a range of high mountain meadows. If our estimates were right, this tangle of granite overlooked the deep, yawning gorge that could only be . . .

"*Doomsday Rock!*" Dan shouted from the hilltop. He pointed toward the huge cleft of fractured granite, turned, and cried, "That's it! We're here!"

We'd made it, but at an hour so late that I felt more relief than joy. The gorge sat two, maybe three, miles away, an easy hike with backpacks. But it would have to wait until morning. Hungry, tired, and thirsty, we had to secure our accommodations for the night. Driving up the pass, I'd noticed a mile below us a small shepherd's encampment tucked into a beautiful, bowl-shaped meadow; a large flock of sheep grazed peacefully on the ridge above.

"Let's go eat!" I said, as we all climbed back in the Land Rovers and coasted back into the valley, praying we might find food and a place to pitch our tents for the night. If all went well, in the morning we'd complete our journey, climb the mile or two up and over a towering hogsback butte, and stare down into Davis Canyon. Our moment of truth had come.

Now, I wondered, *how well would our unexpecting hosts below receive this gamey crew of hungry Americans?*

LOW ON THE MOUNTAIN

The young boy raised his rifle and fired into the air—a signal to his father, still tending flocks on the mountainside, to hurry down. *We have visitors!*

We stormed into their camp with all the subtlety of a traveling circus—three dirty, overheated Land Rovers piled with packs and large, unshaven strangers. From their perspective I doubted our entrance had made a great impression, but Ali went straight to work, tendering our proposal: he represented a team of American explorers searching for a valuable artifact from history; we had government approval to be on the mountain; we were hungry, and, if they agreed, we would buy a sheep from them, price no object; and for an additional fee (if they agreed, of course), they would slaughter and cook our meal; then, at the going rate, we'd pitch our tents just outside their camp for the night; in the morning we would climb the mountain, attend to our business, break camp, and be gone by evening.

From the looks on their faces, it struck them as a most unusual request. Halbrook had an interesting take on it all: "Imagine," he said, "coming home at the end of a long day to a group of pushy, unwashed Iranians standing in your driveway. They ask to spend the night in your backyard, and, by the way, they are hungry and would like to eat one of your dogs, which they will pay you to kill and cook for their dinner. Price is no object!"

In such a light it indeed seemed a crude and preposterous proposal. We laughed at the absurdity of it, but after several minutes of lively negotiations, Ali struck a deal with the young shepherd. Since his father hadn't yet returned, he and his brothers selected for us a fine, healthy-looking sheep. They brought it to us, and we all took turns holding the beast—smelly, kicking, and bleating—in our arms, trying to determine its weight. I had no idea what a pound of sheep went for on Mount Sabalon, but Ali finally negotiated a price of $35 for the whole animal, minus the pelt.

The boys ran off to build a fire. We unloaded the trucks and chose our tent sites amid a building sense of excitement. With our accommodations secured, thoughts returned to the mission at hand. Our camp sat in the shadow of a towering ridge cresting over the lip of a canyon, below which, Dan assured us, sat a dreadful gorge known as Davis Canyon.

"Bob and I will have to rappel down with ropes and pitons," he said, implying that the rest of the team would watch from above. From there, he said, we would see, jutting from the gorge, the ark, broken in two, partially concealed under two prongs of talus and scree. "It's right over that rise," he insisted to anyone within earshot, heedless of my caution to temper his remarks. "I've never been more confident of *anything* in my life."

I rolled my eyes but didn't say anything. I now doubted we would find the ark.

Judging from our position on the mountain, it didn't seem logical. I had frankly lost confidence in man's ability to find *anything* if God didn't guide the search step-by-step, and our lead navigator had taken the position that we couldn't fail. I didn't understand such overconfidence, especially since, with all the maps, scientists, satellites, computer imaging, and global positioning technology at our disposal, it took two hungry Iranian villagers to lead us to this high valley.

I turned east: Mount Sabalon's angry purple tips stared down at me. Its row of spines towered above us. The Bible said the ark came to rest on the mountains of Ararat, and as the waters began to recede, the tops of the surrounding peaks became visible (Gen. 8:5). I looked up at those awesome spires and knew we had indeed landed in the mountains of Ararat. We'd found the lost mountain of Noah!

But as I inspected our campsite, far below those imposing crags, I thought: *The ark is up there! This camp of ours rests in a high meadow, not high on the summit. It's just not high enough. Flocks and children scamper carefree among the hills. Sheep encampments dominate these glades. If the ark sits just over the ridge, as even now Dan insists it does, these people would know about it. But Ali already asked them, and no one here has ever seen or heard of the boat that inspired Ed Davis to gush, "You won't believe how big it is!"*

I recalled Davis talking about steep canyons and dangerous gorges, about sheer, dangling trails and ropes they'd used to tie themselves together, of having to claw up desperate, craggy cliffs and intense, ice-covered ledges.

Dangerous cliffs? Ice-capped ledges? I saw nothing of the kind in the scenery all around us. Oh, the cliffs and glaciers Davis spoke of were near enough, I speculated, less than five miles across the valley, towering overhead on Sabalon's true summit. Judging from Scripture, our camp probably lay on one of the peaks Noah saw from his soaring perch, slowly rising from beneath the waves as the flood waters receded.

A creeping disappointment began to set in. I'd trusted the experts, been swayed by their opinions about our so-called "object." I'd visited other mountains where experts said they were "100 percent sure!" I kept thinking, *Not again!*

In hindsight—and in all fairness to the experts—I realized these satellite images are a lot like looking at the top of someone's head; you don't know what the person really looks like until you get down to eye level. Each of the facets Toth pointed out, corresponding to Davis's map, remained deeply compelling, even spellbinding. But here, at eye level, our target left much to be desired. Had I known the satellite images represented *this* spot on the mountain . . . well, no need to second-guess now. The evidence and scholarly opinions had left us no choice but to come and see it in person. The good news was, we'd taken a tight target zone and narrowed it even further. It bode well for future expeditions.

I looked over at Halbrook, busily pitching our tent, energized, expectant. Larry, Dick, and I had been on enough of these trips to know the frightful odds of hitting a home run, but Toth's over-the-top commentary had gotten everyone's hopes up *way* too high. They believed we had a decent chance of climbing over the ridge and seeing the ark. I wanted to tell them, as gently as I could, "Don't get your hopes up too high," and direct their gaze toward Sabalon's jagged peaks. I'd say, "Chances are, men, if the ark came to rest on the highest peak in the region, that's *it!* Up *there*."

Truth be known, it may have already occurred to them, but I could see it in their eyes—no one wanted to concede anything until we had a good look at that ridge. To them, the adventure had just reached its climax.

While I suspected that technology and experts had failed us again, it did me no good to worry about it. The window had closed; our visas expired in two days. Even a team of experienced mountaineers would need a week to climb high enough to explore one of Sabalon's high clefts. That expedition would have to wait.

I tried to stay optimistic, but at that moment my heart said our target zone sat too low on the mountain.

Twenty-Six

THE BLOOD OF THE LAMB

The temperature dropped dramatically as the sun ducked below the mountains, and the chilling breeze sent us to our packs for jackets and sweaters. The shepherd boys called us over to a tripod of lashed logs, where they'd stacked wood for a fire and tethered the sheep we'd purchased for our dinner. Its front legs had been hobbled with leather straps, so that it knelt involuntarily on its knees—as if in prayer—head bowed to one side.

It might have been my imagination, but its eyes had a strangely sad cast to them, as if it knew what was coming. It knelt before us, the picture of meekness, not struggling, not making a sound, seeming in that moment the most timid creature I'd ever seen.

The sight of this poor animal hobbled before us quelled the fun and frivolity of our camp-out and turned the mood into something more somber. Todd Phillips and Darrell Scott stood over the sheep, running cold hands through its dense wool, intending, perhaps, to comfort it. Up until that moment, we hadn't given it a second thought; but the sight of an animal awaiting slaughter sobered and unsettled us. What had we expected? Dinner to be served to us on a silver tray, dressed and sizzling, as in a restaurant? To our hosts this ritual was a daily routine, more common than commonplace. But to us, presiding over the live slaughter of a living creature so that *we* could eat was a foreign experience. None of us knew quite how to feel.

We stood together in a quiet circle as the lad walked over, put an arm around the sheep's head, and calmly lay a blade to its neck. Before he could make the fatal slash, I shouted, "Wait!" Startled, he stopped and looked around, confused.

"Give us a minute, please," Dick Bright chimed in. "We must pray first."

Bright cupped his hands under his chin to help the lad understand. We'd already decided to formalize our prayer for this momentous meal. We'd been extremely fortunate to find the target zone amid these baffling hills and roads and blessed to make the acquaintance of these hospitable nomads. We wanted to consecrate the meal to the Lord and offer it up, after the manner of the Israelites, as a burnt offering of thanksgiving.

As the boy pulled back and shuffled to the outskirts of our circle, we joined hands around the prone sheep. Bright led us.

"Lord," he began, "we thank you for this wonderful adventure, for these gracious nomads, and for these great brothers. More than that, we thank you for loving us even when we didn't love you, and for dying in our stead. We thank you, Father, for this gentle, fettered lamb, who, like your Son, has laid down its life so that we might live. As it says in Isaiah, Jesus was oppressed and afflicted, yet he did not open his mouth; he was led like a lamb to the slaughter, and as a sheep before its shearers is silent, so he did not open his mouth.

"So Lord, we give you honor and praise, and present to you this gentle animal as a burnt offering, that you might receive it as a sweet fragrance of our love. And we receive it back from you—as we have your Son in our hearts—to give us strength and sustenance for our trials ahead. In thanksgiving and praise to your holy name, we pray. Amen."

Bright's stirring prayer, delivered with a depth of emotion I hadn't expected—so befitting of the drama playing out before us—captured beautifully the kaleidoscope of emotions coursing through me. Hobbled before us lay perhaps the truest picture of Jesus I'd ever encountered: a gentle lamb, a living sacrifice, bound on an altar, silent before its executioner. The gravity of the moment stole my breath.

I looked around at the others: everyone stood motionless, glassy-eyed and speechless. The boy walked back over, reached down and, in one smooth motion, made a deep slit across the sheep's throat. A violent spurt of blood shot ten feet across the meadow. The animal dropped to its stomach, supported by the boys' steadying hands. Halbrook and my brother, Paul, turned away and walked up the slope to the tents, unable to watch. The rest of us remained, jaws clenched, watching a life bleed out before our eyes.

"It's the nomad way . . . how they live and survive," I kept telling myself, thinking that by making the ritual seem as normal as possible, it might lessen the sting. Killing a sheep this way seems as normal for them as it does for us, back in the States, to buy cellophane-wrapped hamburger at the grocery.

Then why did it *move* me so?

I'd seen the same ritual acted out time and time again in my travels but always, I recalled, as an observer on the sidelines, studying someone else's exotic customs, never as a needy, hungry recipient having to slaughter a lamb for survival. Yet here we stood, hungry, out of our element, by any measure in need. And there it lay, heaving its last, quivering breaths. Intellectually, it couldn't have been a more pragmatic transaction: for thirty-five bucks we'd bought ourselves a sheep, and we would soon eat. Yet the reality of watching the cut, seeing the sheep slump, then slowly fade away, left us shaken, uncomfortable, wrestling with an image that would not soon be erased. Surprisingly, Toth spoke first.

"A lamb is the only animal that doesn't cry out when it's dying," he said, matter-of-factly. He pulled on his gloves, for the temperature continued to drop.

I hadn't thought about it, but it was true: the animal had neither whimpered nor fussed, even as the knife did its work. Again, my thoughts drifted back to Jesus, how he had stood silent before his jury, quietly enduring his beatings, refusing to defend himself, and ultimately suffering an agonizing death on a cross. I glanced about the circle; did the others catch this piercing allegory?

The sheep's body lay slack, its breathing ended. It had indeed died silently, but the agony and desperation of its final swoon had been painfully real, just as the agony of Jesus erupted in a final, desperate cry: "My God, why have you forsaken me?"

As a last step, the boys cut off the animal's head, then began massaging the carcass to drain the rest of the blood; then, not five feet from that red, spreading pool, they skinned and butchered it as if they were peeling a potato.

The silence among our group cut deep; no one spoke; some walked away; others hesitated, wanting, it seemed, to pay homage to the dignity of a moment they couldn't quite wrap their minds around. It reminded me of the disciples after Jesus' death, fraught with confusion, wracked by indecision. Darrell Scott and John Tomlin stood side by side, transfixed by the rustic passion play. One could only imagine what thoughts now consumed them.

One thing I knew: our team would not go hungry tonight. We would have our meat for dinner.

FEAST OF THE LAMB

The elder shepherd, trailing two huge Kongal dogs with spiked collars, finally returned to camp, and, apprised by his sons of the nature of our visit, began cheerfully to supervise the cooking chores. Through it all, I watched Ali maintaining a close vigil, dog tired and dirty—his face unshaven, his eyes at half-mast—looking completely frazzled and strung out. It made me feel guilty, for we'd run him ragged.

As Americans in Iran, we were the equivalent of babes in the forest, unable to speak the native language, ill equipped to manage our own affairs. As our *de facto* baby-sitter, Ali translated every question, negotiated every transaction, changed our money, bought our groceries, saw to it that our laundry had been properly washed, ran every errand, made every phone call—all this and much more, for eight grown men. These past two days Ali had mediated every turn and pass up the slope, trying to make sense of the maps and roads, dealing minute by minute with Toth and a rotating cast of guides. I knew he hadn't slept more than a few hours since he picked us up at the Tehran airport four days earlier. Yet he never complained, never even raised an eyebrow as we pressed him on all sides. He just kept on grinning his punchy, overtired grin, doing his best to make our every wish his urgent command.

Now, at a point in the trip when no one would have noticed or blamed him for ducking into a Land Rover and catching a quick nap, he dutifully managed the butchering and cooking chores, barking soft orders, and sticking his nose in the thick of things. With finicky care he supervised the cleaning and cubing of the meat, skewering it himself, even instructing the shepherd boys how to stir the coals so it didn't scorch the kebabs. He made sure everything was properly prepared and grilled to perfection.

From my last trip to Iran, I knew Ali to be an energetic, competent servant, but I hadn't realized, until this remarkable display, what a thoroughly undeserved gift we'd been given in this small, humble man. When the elder shepherd tried to scoop the sizzling meat into a cold metal basin, Ali stopped him. "No, no, no!" he scolded. "It will get *cold*. Bring me a basket of hot flat bread." The boys sprinted off across the field and returned minutes later with a steaming platter of fresh-baked, paper-thin, flat bread. With great care Ali wrapped the pieces of meat, like a blanket, inside several layers of bread, then covered the whole affair in a clean white linen. This steaming bundle he carried himself, nuzzling it in his arms like a baby, up the hill to our campsite, and laid it tenderly at our feet on a large blanket. By now ravenous we watched Ali unwrap the linen cloth and unfold the bread, releasing a cloud of savory steam, filling the air with a spit-roasted aroma. Then we stood staring—ready to pounce, mouths watering—at our sumptuous feast: easily seven pounds of sizzling, flame-seared, prime cuts.

Children arrived minutes later with fresh goat cheese and homemade yogurt in silver serving bowls, then brought up a steaming pot of tea. With rumbling stomachs we each took turns handpicking our cuts, wrapping the lightly charred chunks in sheets of flat bread, like a giant burrito, and ladling on the goat cheese and yogurt. For the next forty minutes we stood there, laughing and eating, scarcely making a dent in the delectable, deeply satisfying meal.

A lovely sweetness had drifted back into our midst. From the evening's heaviness came a spirit of revelry and companionship. Camping out above timberline in mountains few westerners had seen, enjoying the company of a rare collection of men, and relishing each bite of a precious, priceless meal had unexpectedly ushered in a depth of fellowship and raw feeling few of us knew back home in our busy lives.

Still the weight of the day's events pressed down hard upon us. In frosty darkness we strolled down to the fire pit and lingered about a blazing campfire. Firewood seemed scarce up so high, but our generous hosts tossed what looked to be their last logs on the fire, just for our pleasure. The mountain air kept getting colder by the minute, so we huddled close about the blaze, sipping hot tea from dainty cups among the grinning, chattering nomads, squeezing the marrow from a moment we knew would never be repeated.

In the quiet Todd Phillips cleared his throat as if to speak. He seemed perfectly at home among these cheery nomads. Within an hour of our arrival, he'd made quick friends with the youngsters, gathering them about like nieces and nephews, teaching them martial arts tricks, even riding one of their horses bareback up the ridge. His face shone bright in the firelight as he addressed us with a quiet smile.

"I just want to thank you all for letting me tag along," he began, his subtle Texas twang barely noticeable. "I've been thinking about the ark. But I know that, whether we find it or not, this night alone has made the trip worth it for me. The trip has taught me something about myself: for the very act of stepping on a plane in the United States and flying halfway around the world to search for Noah's ark—believing in my heart that it really, *truly* exists, based simply on what God said in his Word—has become one of the most significant actions of my life."

He paused, raising a finger to dab an eye, then added: "What does that *mean*? It means that the very fact I'm standing here around this fire with all you guys allows me to go back home and minister God's Word in a fresh new way to a lost, and . . ." He caught himself, checked the quaver in his voice, then proceeded. "It allows me to go back and minister to a lost and *incredibly* damaged and pessimistic section of our youth in a way that's going to change their hearts." He glanced my way, "And as far as I'm concerned, regardless of what we do or don't find over that ridge tomorrow, the entirety of this trip has already been an absolute success. It has become my rejuvenation. I can't fully explain it, but just finding this meadow has energized me like no other time in my life."

Everyone smiled—even some of the nomads—and nodded softly in agreement. The fire had burned down to embers. No one wanted to leave. With the last dying sparks spiraling into the air, we all talked quietly, stretching the moment out as long as possible. Nomad children stood close by, serving us piping hot tea with rocks of sugar—simply, it seemed, to be near. While they didn't understand it, our presence seemed to give them a vague cause for celebration.

209

As the biting chill drove us one by one to our tents, I stayed for a minute longer, staring up at the stars in the vast, ebony expanse. And that's when it hit me. My flash of revelation.

Scanning the heavens, replaying each stage of the trip in my mind, I suddenly knew why I'd spent almost two weeks riding in planes and vans and Jeeps, cramped and uncomfortable, bouncing across a rugged wilderness in suffocating heat, to reach this half-acre of paradise. Certainly, we'd found undeniable evidence to support our theses about the ark; I now believed, beyond a doubt, that we'd found the lost mountains of Ararat and now camped at the foot of a peak where Noah's ark most likely came to rest. And while the consequences of that alone exceeded anything I could fathom, I had stumbled unwittingly upon treasure of a deeper kind. Something about *this* moment, *these* guys, and *this* experience had opened my heart to a discovery far more subtle yet far greater than I could ever have hoped for.

To my left Darrell Scott spoke in thoughtful whispers to Larry Williams about life, its purpose, forgiveness, the love it took for God to send his only Son, an innocent Lamb, to die for us. Larry listened carefully, nodding in agreement, asking questions. We'd come here as a team, and, as a team, it seemed, our thoughts had shifted from the physical to the spiritual, from raw adventure to something truly miraculous.

Until that moment I hadn't fully seen it. I hadn't understood, or fully grasped, what I'd lost, traveling the world, giving it my all, trying my best to point others to the Savior. Hurrying along on my ministry treadmill, I had stayed sharply disciplined, focused on who Jesus *was*, why he lived and died. I knew well the details of Christ's birth, death, and resurrection. Amid the clamor of "Jesus talk," I could talk with the best.

But I'd lost something slowly, steadily. I'd visited so many churches that looked alike and heard so many messages that sounded alike that the raw message of Christ had become blurred and diluted. Somewhere along the line the Bible got wrapped in cellophane, the church packaged in Styrofoam.

Somewhere out there on the road, through endless repetition, through the business and chaos of life—through my own globe-trotting wanderlust, searching for emblems that should have kept my heart fixed and fervent—the pain, the anguish, the miracle, and the ecstasy of the gospel had become a Sunday school lesson, a dry curriculum. It had lost its immediacy, its power. But here, on a chilly, windswept mountain in northwest Iran, I'd watched the blade make its cut; I'd seen and smelled the blood, and it was harsh—a harsh remedy for our needy condition.

My thoughts flashed to the harshness of sin in our lives and to the extreme remedy that had been required: an innocent Lamb, butchered in my place, saving me, transforming me, giving me strength and sustenance to go on. On a night in which even the bracing breeze seemed to speak to these matters, God restored to me the joy of my salvation. Surrounded by friends, confronted by the meekness of a dying lamb, he reintroduced me to his Son.

Such a spiritual awakening could have happened nowhere else. I'd come looking for an ark, with its decayed footings and wooden timbers; but on a bristly cold, pristine night on Mount Sabalon, God chose to reveal his Son.

GOOD NIGHT, SABALON

Sabalon loomed above us, a stoic, black pyramid framed in the light of a full moon. Behind us stood the tall, slender ridge we would climb in the morning, to find . . . ? I had no idea.

I stared up at the brooding, reddish moon hanging high in the south and heard Halbrook talking to Bright by our tent. I could hear the excitement in his voice as he wrestled to put words to his own clarified insights.

211
Λ

"To have the opportunity to experience a night like this," he whispered, "and still to have even a remote expectation of walking over that ridge in the morning and, just *possibly*, seeing the remains of Noah's ark. It just seems so . . ."

"Blessed?" Bright replied, completing the sentence. "Yes, I would agree, we are blessed. And whatever happens tomorrow, we can rest assured that God led us to this mountain for a purpose."

By now suspecting that he had led me here, at least in part, to hear those very words, I strolled back toward our tent. Darrell Scott walked up from the campfire to join me. I could tell from the intense look in his eyes he had something important to say, but his voice rang out so soft and distant I asked him to speak up.

He smiled and said, "I just wanted to tell you that I've named this valley 'Rachel's Valley,' in memory of my daughter. You might not know that Rachel's name *means* 'God's little lamb.'"

I listened, quietly amazed, as he proceeded to describe how the sacrifice of the lamb had dialed up such a profound sadness that, for a few agonizing moments, he didn't know if he could bear it. But strangely enough, he emerged from his grief to a new strength and resolve. Glancing back at the ruby patch of blood-stained hillside, still shiny in the moonlight, he continued: "I can't fully explain the symbolic impact of that moment, but . . . a few weeks before the shootings, Rachel had performed for the Columbine talent show a pantomime titled 'Watch the Lamb.' In it she acted out the passion and crucifixion of Christ."

His eyes seemed distant, fixed on a faraway memory. "Watching that sheep die today," he said, "reminded me of something I read in Rachel's journal shortly after she was killed." He took a deep breath and said, "She'd begun to share her faith boldly at school. She'd even recently witnessed to Eric Harris and Dylan Klebold but, in the process, had begun to feel rejected by her friends. I read in her diary an entry that said: 'Now that I've begun to walk the talk, I've lost friends at school. But I will not hide the life God has put in me. If I have to sacrifice everything, I will. If my friends have to become enemies in order to keep my *best* Friend, Jesus, so be it.'"

Then, very softly, he said, "Rachel felt God had showed her that she was going to reach her generation for Christ, but . . . she knew it had to be soon. She wrote that she didn't believe she'd live long enough even to get married."

Scott looked at me with sad eyes, yet smiled. "Tonight brought a lot of that into focus for the first time. Thanks for a wonderful trip."

Watching him walk down the slope to his tent, I marveled that a nameless meadow on an obscure, Iranian ridge could hold such rich meaning for a bunch of Americans. I walked up the meadow to the tent entrance, where Halbrook knelt organizing his gear.

"Feel it?" he asked. "It's raining."

A soft, gentle rain had indeed begun to fall. But when we looked up, we saw nothing but stars.

"It must've blown over from some of those clouds over the summit," said Bright, listening from the shadows a few feet away. He'd decided to sleep out in the open and set his sleeping bag on the dewy grass so he could fall asleep watching the stars.

Zipping up our tent, the campsite grew very still. We listened to the soft, mournful wail of the Kongal pups whining in the shepherd's camp and heard the collar chains of adult dogs jostling down by the fire pit. Then it got completely quiet and peaceful.

Suddenly Bright's husky voice shattered the cool mountain quiet.

"I can't believe I'm in Iran!" he shouted. And with that I rolled over and fell asleep, scarcely believing it myself.

Twenty-Seven

FINAL ASCENT

Our energy level had peaked. Well-rested, well-fed, tingling with suspense, we woke at first light, gobbled down a quick breakfast of hot tea, flat bread, goat cheese, and yogurt, donned sweaters and gloves, and strapped on our packs. Warming my hands by the fire pit in the minutes before we left, my eyes drifted toward the patch of grass where yesterday's blood had spilled. It had disappeared, or somehow been wiped clean. I remember thinking the rain must have washed it away.

Dan Toth, more eager than any of us to see what lay over the ridge, broke out in front, endlessly checking his compass and GPS, occasionally swerving around to bark critiques of our climbing technique: "Walk slowly, lock your knees between steps—quit dancing around like a bunch of mountains goats." His drill sergeant's intensity incited some grumbling, but we all just kept slogging up the ridge like earnest mountaineers turned loose, puzzling over what sights awaited us five hundred feet above.

The children provided the final tip-off. Climbing up the steep ridge toward Doomsday Rock, a gaggle of shepherd boys in off-brand tennis shoes and short sleeves skipped merrily beside us, as carefree as a day at the beach. While we all sweated profusely, sucking air, trying to pace ourselves at twelve thousand feet, *they* trotted up the slope without a sign of strain. Playful Kongal pups licked at our heels, sniffing and yipping among the rocks. The boys cast inquisitive glances our way, as if to ask, "What is it, again, that you expect to *find* up here?"

Flocks grazed nearby, too, and could be seen grazing on slopes across the valley, appearing as distant, dishwater tufts of wool stuck to the opposing mountainside. I'd held out hope that, by some strange happenstance, our shepherd hosts had never ventured this high over the ridge; but these frisky kids scampering about like mountain goats killed that fantasy. Even the slim chance that we'd found the real Davis Canyon had vanished, for if children and sheep roamed this high ridge with such ease and vigor, I doubted their fathers had overlooked something so obvious as an *ark*. Clearly our target zone sat too low on the mountain, and the harsh truth tasted bitter in my mouth.

I looked east, out across the wide, yawning valley and up the slow, ascending face of Sabalon's jagged summit, thawing in the morning sun. Its ice-capped pinnacles towered above us. No doubt about it, my instincts a day earlier had been correct: we should be searching up *there*.

I didn't say anything yet. We were all having far too good a time.

DOOMSDAY ROCK

From base camp, traversing diagonally along the slope, it took us two hours to reach the saddle. With each breathless step, I could feel the excitement level growing. The look in Todd's wide eyes said: "I'm about to reach that ridgeline, look down into the gorge, and *see* it."

Toth arrived first at the swayback plateau beside the huge, granite knob we'd dubbed Doomsday Rock. From fifty yards back, I saw him staring intently into the ravine, charts in hand. As each of us arrived, one by one, to stand with him at the cusp, we peered expectantly over the lip and into the brink. But where we hoped to see a plunging abyss, we beheld only a gentle, descending basin falling away into a mild succession of valleys. Instead of the yawning gorge we all knew as Davis Canyon, we saw a deep, rolling meadow, hollowed out like a bowl beneath an arching rim of granite-laced foothills.

I looked at Toth and asked, "Where's the deep, ugly gorge you've been telling us about?" He didn't answer but just kept staring down at the basin.

All of us began feverishly to scan the valley floor. But where we should have seen an ark, we saw instead a patchwork quilt of mossy, snow-fed meadows, rugged moraine fields, and—quite surprisingly—a number of large, rectangular corrals built by the local shepherds to partition their flocks. Carved into the landscape like lunar craters, these rugged corrals were hand-built of loose, jagged rock, each piece appearing about to topple but fitting together like bricks in a wall. We'd seen them scattered throughout the hills, as common as the domed tents on the outskirts of every shepherd's camps. But seeing them from this vantage—in this light and from this distance—they appeared oddly . . . *ark* shaped. While each looked far too small to be the huge, rectangular outline we'd seen in the satellite image, they served as more evidence (if any more we needed) that our target site amounted to little more than a well-traveled pasture, *anything* but remote and inaccessible. We could see man's fingerprints everywhere. On the far side of the basin, a shepherd tended his flock; Kongal dogs prowled a nearby meadow.

Still we stood, staring into the vale, craning our necks and scanning every possible crack and contour for some clue or hint of a boat. Higher up the caldera-shaped ridge, thick patches of snow and ice filled furrows and trenches, forming drifts in the clefts between hillocks. We kept staring down and around, straining our eyes, sweeping the plain with binoculars, hoping to see *something*—something hidden or disguised—which might emerge into a man-made structure, a decomposing hull, perhaps, or even a rotting pile of timber.

But we saw nothing, no ark, a tune I knew too well. While I'd privately expected nothing less, actually seeing the empty basin made my heart ache. I'd held out a thread of hope until the last moment; I'd even prayed I was wrong. For long, unbearable moments, no one said anything. But after several minutes reality began to set in.

Toth remained quiet, aloof, staring blankly at his charts, his eyes flitting up and down, endlessly scanning the basin, trying to align every facet, feature, and landmark that now seemed to have vanished. What had looked so compelling on the maps, and in satellite comparisons of Davis's sketch, at ground level appeared as little more than random wrinkles, folds, and outcroppings carved from wind, rain, and winter runoff. The huge rectangle that Toth incessantly assured me *had* to be the ark—and which our friends at the United States Geological Service conditionally endorsed—never materialized. Its subtle lines had either dissolved into the elements or looked so different at ground level that we couldn't distinguish it from other rubble. The satellite image, Toth reminded me, had been taken more than ten years ago.

"Whatever that shape *was* might have simply washed away during runoff, or gotten buried by rock slides," he said, noting, "There was an earthquake up here a few years back, so anything's possible."

Hearing those words now struck a bitter chord. Suddenly I'm told that hazy outline could've been practically *anything*.

"Show me the object, Dan," I said, trying to modulate my voice. But his eyes seemed frozen, glaring dumbstruck at his chart. He brushed me off.

"Just a *minute*," he said, followed by several tense moments of silence; then, "I don't know"; then, "This doesn't make sense." Then, finally, "It's *got* to be here."

I turned to see the disappointment fall across the face of every team member. Halbrook looked at me with a shrug and a sigh, then pointed up toward Sabalon's summit. "It's got to be up there somewhere, don't you think?" he asked. "That looks like the stuff Davis described."

It didn't surprise me he'd noticed it, too. We'd both gone over Davis's testimony so many times, and these mild, rolling inclines just didn't fit. Tomlin patted me sympathetically on the shoulder, while Scott just kept sweeping the lower bowl with his video camera. Todd Phillips stared into the precipice, wanting so badly to see what he'd come for. Larry Williams walked over and stood by Dan, helping him adjust his charts and photos.

Dick Bright and my brother, Paul, took off up the slope; Halbrook, John, and I followed close behind. We wanted to climb the upper section of the ridge and drop back down, opposite the saddle, to gain a better view of the foot of the cliff. The rest of the team stayed behind on the saddle, transfixed, still in denial, unwilling to abandon their perch.

"We'll holler at you from the other side of the ridge," I called down to Larry, who replied, "Or else, we'll meet you at the bottom."

Already Bright had scrambled out of sight, off on his own reconnaissance. An old mountain goat at heart, he intended to canvass the area alone, liberated from the team's slower pace. We lagged behind, hiking slowly to the top, then cautiously crunched and hacked our way back down an unstable ridge to a broad gully, pitching low to face the saddleback. Halbrook juked down to the lip of the cliff and stared into the ravine, then turned and yelled, "Nothing there!" I waved to the others, who still watched us from a half-mile away: "We'll meet you at the bottom!" I shouted. Ali waved back. But even at that distance, I saw Toth standing apart. "Dan!" I yelled, "meet you at the bottom." He didn't look up and offered no response.

We scrambled down to the valley floor, using our boots as skis to slide down a loose moraine field. Tomlin stayed at the top, canvassing the snow line and skittering down the far rim of the bowl. At the bottom, after an exhilarating descent, we found the basin spreading out into a beautiful patchwork of rolling cliffs melting into marshy green meadows. No one talked much; we all cut our own path, methodically searching every nook and shadow, wanting to be sure that we'd carefully inspected the whole area before we abandoned the quest.

Following Halbrook down the crumbling moraine to a wet, spongy heath, my mind wandered, and I saw how easy it could be to read too much into satellite imagery. I saw how each of the facets and geological features Toth used to argue his case might well have matched a host of other features on this, or *any*, mountain. Up on the cliff face a hook-shaped rock; out across the valley floor, an odd curl in the streambed. Viewed with a little creative license, they line up perfectly with the Davis map.

I'd seen it many times before, under different circumstances: a malady known as "ark fever." Intelligent, grounded men, wanting to see something so badly, they conjured it up, whole cloth, from rock and ice. Larry calls it the "Rorschach" effect, the tendency to see distinct objects in random splotches of ink. Dan Toth wanted badly to see the ark in those photos. And while I couldn't read satellite images, I *wanted* it to be there just as much as Dan said he "saw" it. Maybe we all wanted to see it too badly.

Dick Bright sauntered across the grassland and joined us at the bottom of the ridge where we stood on a huge shoulder of granite, looking down at a descending series of ledges leading to a meadow. I could tell Bright felt relieved, if not altogether vindicated, that we hadn't found the ark on this trip.

"Compared with Mount Ararat," he said in a bit of a huff, "this climb was a piece of cake." Then he pointed up to Sabalon's dark purple, beetling crags, and privately confided: "Bob, if it's anywhere, it's somewhere up in that mess." He looked me in the eye, flashing that mischievous, bulldog expression, and said, in all earnestness, "So, Bob, are you ready to go? How about let's climb up there and have a look."

I knew he would do it, in a second. And for a moment I sincerely considered it. Then I turned and saw John Tomlin soft-footing it down the crumbling slope; he looked like a big kid, out for a hike, looking for Noah's ark. Red-faced, panting, yet sporting a huge smile, he walked over and said, "Man, this is great." Then, taking in a huge gulp of mountain air, he looked up and said, "That's a big mountain up there, Bob. Do you think . . . ?"

"Yeah," I said, "if the ark is anywhere, it's up there."

I looked south and saw Darrell Scott, Todd Phillips, Ali, and Alireza practically jogging down the ridge to join us on the ledge. Scott seemed upbeat and breathless, the fair skin on his forehead sunburned, already beginning to peel. I smiled and asked, "Are you disappointed?" He shrugged, then squatted down to catch his breath. "No," he said, gulping in air, "I'm not disappointed. But I'm sort of surprised it wasn't here." Then, as Tomlin had five minutes before, Scott gazed past me toward Sabalon's summit. "The more I've been thinking about it," he said, "it just makes sense it probably has to be up higher."

From the advantage of hindsight, we'd all come to realize the same thing. It didn't take a genius to see it; I just wished I'd seen it *sooner*. Toth slowly appeared from behind a stand of rocks, making his way laconically toward us, seeming dazed and disquieted. I knew he felt humiliated, thinking he'd let everybody down, especially by sounding so cocksure. He walked up, and I put a hand on his shoulder.

"Don't worry about it, Dan," I said. "You did your best. We gave it a good try." The others chimed in with kind condolences:

"Thanks for your hard work, Dan. We had to give it a look."

"No one here blames you."

Dan nodded, apparently surprised by the warm response, but still avoided eye contact.

"I can't figure it out," he said. "You just don't *see* that many similarities on one mountain. It all *jived*."

I picked up my pack and told the team, "Let's head back to camp."

As the others walked down, I pulled Bright aside. "I can't go with you to the top on this trip," I said. "Our visas have run out; we don't have any supplies; and these guys are tired."

I knew that to start poking around on Sabalon's uncharted peaks at this stage of the journey would exceed the physical limits of the team. Though most would undoubtedly jump at the chance, Sabalon remained a behemoth of a mountain, and I couldn't in good conscience subject them to such a risk.

"Not this trip, Dick," I said. "We found our target. It just wasn't the right place. Maybe next time."

Bright remained as sanguine as ever. He put a hand on my shoulder and said, "You know it wasn't a failure, Bob, because we can now eliminate this portion of the mountain." Then he looked skyward again, winked, and said, "That's where you need to be. I'll climb it with you next time."

A CALL TO ARMS

Walking back to camp, everyone lost in thought, we all struggled to sort out our emotions. To start out with such high hopes, based on such seemingly strong evidence, and then to find *nothing*—well, it broke our spirits. It would take time for all of us to come down off that cloud. We made it back to the shepherd's village shortly after noon and began to break camp.

Gathering up my equipment, I took a moment to survey our fine meadow once more. Paul stood down by the fire pit, next to the Land Rover, loading his pack on the roof. At that moment I felt a fondness for my brother I'd never known; our relationship had grown these past weeks to a different level, and for that I would be forever grateful. On the other side of the streambed, I could hear Darrell Scott and John Tomlin busily recounting their spin on the day's events. Only time would tell how this adventure ministered to them, but I found it a comfort to think they'd left Columbine behind for a few days.

Todd Phillips lingered near the shepherd's tent, exchanging gifts with the nomad children. I sensed his time in Iran would one day touch the alienated generation he'd been called to pastor.

David Halbrook sat, boots off, on a rock by our tent, furiously scribbling notes into his tablet. This trip would put flesh to thoughts, sights, and feelings he'd never encountered and enrich his writing for years to come.

I watched Larry Williams stuffing gear in his pack across the meadow. He looked up and saw me staring at him. He smiled, and I smiled back. We'd been through so much together. He'd come along for the fun, for the adventure, but I'd come to sense something else stirring his heart. He startled me earlier that morning by walking up, placing a reassuring hand on my shoulder, and telling me, "I prayed for you last night, friend; I prayed that you'd find the ark." In the fifteen years I'd known Larry, he had *never* said he'd prayed for anything. With those words he gave me the ultimate gift.

I looked for Dan and saw him sitting alone in the front seat of a Land Rover. I walked down and asked him to sit with me on the way back to Ardabil. He needed to be restored, and we needed to be reconciled.

"Dan," I noted, "we've all learned important lessons on this trip. What did you learn?"

With his head drooping halfway to his knees, he said simply, "Maybe I should be a little more humble."

I smiled. "That's true for all of us," I replied, yet knowing in my heart that for Dan—an ex-SEAL trained to control every word, mood, and facial tick—that signified a greater discovery than if we had found Noah's ark. I considered it a testament to the power of the mountain.

As for myself, I felt peace. I sensed God smiling on our team, not necessarily for our brute determination to climb a mountain and find a boat, but for our willingness to discover something new within ourselves. My initial disappointments had disappeared. Once I realized the full scope of what had been accomplished, it became, in all respects, the best trip I'd ever experienced.

I felt God's peaceful, sheltering presence about us the whole way, guiding us, molding us. On our last night on the mountain, he launched me on a new adventure of the soul and revealed the depth of his Son's sacrifice. At a time I needed most to see it, he gave me a glimpse of Golgotha. I'd been privileged to participate in the essential truth of Jesus' death, and the experience burned his love afresh into my heart.

And even as we stared down into the valley this morning and saw nothing, I felt optimistic. I'd been obedient to my call. I'd done my part. God led me to Mount Sabalon in Iran for a purpose, if only, perhaps, to point the way for others. I counted it an undeserved honor to have played any role at all.

Was it the end of a journey for me? I doubted it. I'd return home, gather my wits, spend time with my family, and probably return one day to search those angry crags. That seemed to be my nature; I always returned.

But even if I never returned to Iran, I believed this journey would serve as a beginning for someone else. Though I knew how hard old traditions die, I had proposed a new theory. People have been looking for the ark on Mount Ararat for two centuries. Literally hundreds of expeditions have explored its shadowy cliffs, and they are *still* looking. This counted as only our second serious trip to Mount Sabalon. *How long, I wondered, would it take before these peaks came to the world's attention?* Larry and I had discovered what many now believe to be the real Mount Sinai in Saudi Arabia. Yet it took ten years for top scholars to begin to accept our evidence and the leading Bible publishers to place the new site on their maps. I had little doubt that Mount Sabalon would one day be cited by those same scholars and appear on those same maps, as the most likely landing site for Noah's ark.

If I never came back to this mysterious netherworld, I would leave Iran more certain than when I arrived that we'd found the lost mountains of Ararat. As such, I felt released and, in a certain sense, reborn. Though I figured to return, I would gladly hand off the baton to someone younger, perhaps more anointed to the task, knowing that whoever takes up the search faces a severe challenge. For who can conquer such a vast region? Certainly the kings of Assyria couldn't, back in the days of Urartu. And there remains the problem of Sabalon itself. Unless one of the tight-lipped elders from Ghotor Suee, or in any of the other north-slope villages, comes forth with a mind to share the mountain's sacred secrets with an outsider, each one of Sabalon's spiny peaks will have to be explored. It will require money, time, and untold patience to search its harrowing heights.

As our Land Rovers pulled out of camp, I turned and looked once more at the crest of Mount Sabalon, its frigid peak obscured under a thick mantle of haze. Rumbling out of the village, it seemed as if voices from the past—Ed Davis, Josephus, Nicholas, the old man at Ghotor Suee—still called out: "This is it! This is it!"

In publishing this account, I am issuing an official call to arms. Even if I never again step foot on Sabalon, I know that one day (I believe it in my heart) another ark searcher *will*. Perhaps they will find themselves standing on a ledge in the middle of a sleet storm, overlooking one of Mount Sabalon's cavernous gorges. As the fog clears, they'll look down—and there it will sit, half protruding from ice and water, one section lying low in the canyon. And on that momentous day, how I would love to be there to hear them say:

"I can't believe how big it is!"

Notes

Introduction: Noah's Mystery

1. Quoted by Rex Geissler, "Preface," in B. J. Corbin (compiler), *The Explorers of Ararat* (Long Beach, Calif.: Great Commission Illustrated Books, 1999).

2. Charles Berlitz, *The Lost Ship of Noah* (New York: Balantine Books, 1987), 3–4.

Chapter 4: Far From Home

1. A year later Aaron himself committed a similar error of mistaken identity. He and a fellow named Bob Garbe flew over Ararat in September 1989 and spotted some shadow or structure encased in ice at 14,500 feet on a sheer cliff on the peak's west side—apparently ark-shaped and protruding from the wall at an angle. Photos of the object incited TV and newspapers world-wide to proclaim: "Noah's Ark Found!" But on closer inspection by a ground team—and later, by Aaron himself—it turned out to be nothing but rock.

Chapter 5: The Mountains of Ararat

1. James Bryce, *Transcaucasia and Ararat* (London: Macmillian, 1877), 232.

2. Bill Crouse, "Noah's Ark Sources and Alleged Sightings," in B. J. Corbin (compiler), *The Explorers of Ararat* (Long Beach, Calif.: Great Commission Illustrated Books, 1999), 49.

Cʜᴀᴘᴛᴇʀ 6: Wʜᴇʀᴇ Wᴀs Eᴅ Dᴀᴠɪs?

1. Bill Crouse, "Noah's Ark Sources and Alleged Sightings," in B. J. Corbin (compiler), *The Explorers of Ararat* (Long Beach, Calif.: Great Commission Illustrated Books, 1999), 49.

2. Ibid.

3. Ibid., 47.

4. David St. Vincent, *Iran, a Travel Survival Kit* (Hawthorn, Victoria, Australia: Lonely Planet Publications, 1992), 23.

Cʜᴀᴘᴛᴇʀ 7: Tʜᴇ Mᴏᴜɴᴛᴀɪɴs ᴏꜰ Nᴏᴀʜ

1. Some Bibles translate "from the east" differently, to read "journeyed in the east" or, as in the NIV, "moved eastward," making it unclear from which direction Flood survivors traveled. Dr. Roy Knuteson, Ph.D. in New Testament Greek, writes, "The Septuagint translation of the Hebrew Bible into Greek in 250 B.C., reads: 'from the east,' significant since the Greek-speaking Hebrews knew the exact equivalent of the Hebrew into the Greek, and chose a preposition *(apo)*, which means 'from'—not 'in,' or 'towards,' or 'eastward.'" The KJV translation "from the east," therefore, is correct, putting the mountain of the ark east of Babylon.

2. Lloyd R. Bailey, *Noah, The Person and the Story and History and Tradition* (Columbia, S.C.: University of South Carolina Press, 1989), 15–16.

3. Ibid., 12–15.

4. Lloyd R. Bailey, *Where Is Noah's Ark?* (Nashville: Abingdon Press, 1978), 24.

5. Nicholas served as Herod the Great's biographer, the author of a universal history, a scholar renowned for his accuracy, who had access to the great libraries of the time.

6. Bill Crouse, *"Noah's Ark Sources and Alleged* Sightings," in B. J. Corbin (compiler), *The Explorers of Ararat* (Long Beach, Calif.: Great Commission Illustrated Books), 272–73.

7. Lloyd Bailey, *Where Is Noah's Ark?*, 24.

8. John Warwick Montgomery, *The Quest for Noah's Ark* (Minneapolis, Minn.: Bethany Fellowship, 1972), 62.

9. Crouse, "Noah's Ark Sources and Alleged Sightings," 271.

10. Lloyd Bailey, *Where Is Noah's Ark?*, 26.

11. Crouse, "Noah's Ark Sources and Alleged Sightings," 275.

12. Lloyd Bailey, *Where Is Noah's Ark?*, 29.

13. Crouse, "Noah's Ark Sources and Alleged Sightings," 279.

14. Ibid.

15. Ibid., 280.

CHAPTER 8: EAST OF SHINAR

1. It should be noted that in Isaiah 46:11 Cyrus is described as "a bird of prey" summoned from the east, "a far-off land," to fulfill God's purposes. The capital of Cyrus's Median kingdom was the region of Hamadan in Iran. This same phrase, "from the east," is used in Genesis 11:2 to describe the land from which Noah's descendants hailed.

CHAPTER 9: INTO PERSIA

1. Roman Ghirshman, *Persia: The Immortal Kingdom* (Greenwich, Conn., New York Graphic Society: 1971), 20.
2. W. B. Fisher, ed., *The Cambridge History of Iran*, vol. 1 (London: Cambridge University Press, 1968), 294.
3. Ibid., 309–23, 372.

CHAPTER 12: THE MOUNTAINS OF ARMENIA

1. *The Cambridge History of Iran*, vol. 2 (London: Cambridge University Press, 1985), 72.
2. John Warwick Montgomery, *The Quest for Noah's Ark* (Minneapolis, Minn.: Bethany Fellowship Inc.), 62–63.
3. Lloyd R. Bailey, *Where Is Noah's Ark?* (Nashville: Abingdon, 1978), 18.
4. Lloyd R. Bailey, *Noah, The Person and the Story and History and Tradition* (Columbia, S.C.: University of South Carolina Press, 1989), 59.
5. Ibid., 59–60.
6. Bill Crouse, "Noah's Ark Sources and Alleged Sightings," in B. J. Corbin (compiler), *The Explorers of Ararat* (Long Beach, Calif.: Great Commission Illustrated Books, 1999), 270.
7. Roman Ghirshman, *Iran: From the Earliest Times to the Islamic Conquest* (Baltimore: Penguin Books, 1954), 75.
8. Lloyd Bailey, *Where Is Noah's Ark?*, 14.

CHAPTER 13: DISCOVERING URARTU

1. Lloyd Seton, *The Archaeology of Mesopotamia*, rev. ed. (London: Thames and Hudson, 1984), 188.
2. Paul E. Zimansky, *The Kingdom of Urartu in Eastern Anatolia*, in *Civilizations of Ancient Near East*, vol. 2., editor J. M. Sasson (New York: Scribners, 1995), 1135.
3. *The Assyrian Empire*, vol. 3, *The Cambridge Ancient History* (London: Macmillian, 1925), 65–66.
4. Ibid., 175–76.
5. Ilya Gershevitch, ed., *The Cambridge History of Iran*, vol. 2 (London: Cambridge University Press, 1985), 85.

6. Roman Ghirshman, *Iran: From the Earliest Times to the Islamic Conquet* (Baltimore: Penguin Books, 1954), 96–97.

7. Paul E. Zimansky, "The Kingdom of Urartu in Eastern Anatolia," in *Civilizations of the Ancient New East,* edited by J. M. Sasson (New York, Scribners, 1995), 2:1140.

8. Georges Roux, *Ancient Iraq* (London: Penguin Books, 1966), 313.

CHAPTER 18: TRACKIПG ED DAVIS

1. Phil Trahern is the fictitious name of a real-life character on the expedition.

CHAPTER 19: UGLY AⅢERICAПS

1. "The World's Oldest Wine Jar," University of Pennsylvania Museum of Archaeology and Anthropology Web site (www.upenn.edu/museum/News/wine.html), 5 July 2000.

2. For more information on the history of Caspian horses, see www.caspianhorse.com.

CHAPTER 23: PERSIAП REPRISE

1. *Yassna,* Poordavood, (To Worship) (Tehran: Ibn-nesina, 1960), 43.

2. Abdol Hussein Zarinkub, *Iranian History Before Islam* (Tehran: Amir Kabir Publication, 1988), 74.

3. Mohammad Javad Mashkur, "The Discovery of Urartu Inscription in Iranian Azarbaijan," *Iranian Art and Culture Society* 1 (1957): 1, 23.

4. David M. Rohl, *Legend: The Genesis of Civilization, A Test of Time,* vol. 2 (London: Arrow Books, Random House, 1998), 104.

5. Iraj Afshar Sisany, *Research in Iranian Cities* (Tehran: Iyla Publication, 1998), 72.